Joyce among the Jesuits

Joyce DISCARDED

among the Jesuits

BY KEVIN SULLIVAN

> ℟ You allude to me as a Catholic . . .
> now you ought to allude to me,
> for the sake of precision
> and to get the correct contour on me,
> you ought to allude to me as a Jesuit.
>
> —JAMES JOYCE

New York and London

COLUMBIA UNIVERSITY PRESS

For Ann Geoghegan

1927–1952

Contents

Joyce among the Jesuits

Throughout this book references to James Joyce's works will be abbreviated as follows: FW, *Finnegans Wake* (New York, The Viking Press, 1939); P, *A Portrait of the Artist as a Young Man* (New York, The Viking Press, 1916); SH, *Stephen Hero* (New York, New Directions, 1944); U, *Ulysses* (New York, Random House, 1946).

Introduction

Every honest to goodness man in the land of the space of today knows
that his back life will not stand being written about in black and
white. Putting truth and untruth together a shot may be made at
what this hybrid actually was like to look at.   [FW 169]

To concentrate solely on the literal sense or even the psychological
content of any document to the sore neglect of the enveloping facts
themselves circumstantiating it is just as hurtful to sound sense
(and let it be added to the truest taste).   .   [FW 109]

THIS STUDY of Joyce's Jesuit schooling was originally projected
along lines far more ambitious than those that now circumscribe
it. Critics of Joyce, kind and unkind, and commentators, informed
or misinformed, seem generally agreed that, however various or
significant the influences that converge in his work, the earliest,
most nearly central, and most pervasive was the Catholicism of
his youth. Whether inspiration or infection, Joyce's Catholicism,
they agree, was at the root of both his qualities and his defects.
Accepting it, Joyce inherited a past, a tradition, and a world-
memory; rejecting it, he sought a future and found, in perilous
balance over the void of an intensely doubtful soul, a world-view.
Consequently, his Catholicism is as essential to an understanding
of Joyce as it is to an understanding of Dante, Cervantes, or Augustine. It does not, of course, afford a complete or final explanation of the man or his work, but no final and complete explanation

is possible which fails to take it into account. Yet no Joyce critic or commentator, to my knowledge, has yet made a thorough, systematic study of Joyce and Catholicism.[1] Such a study, therefore, seemed to me both necessary and desirable.

Further reflection convinced me that Joyce's Catholicism was of a special kind, so special that it would allow, and might even demand, specialized treatment. Let me say at once that by "special" I do not mean simply "Irish," though such a brand of belief is, God knows, special enough. For Irish Catholicism, in order to hold its own in a land dominated by an English Protestant culture, had developed many of the characteristics of English sectarianism: defensive, insular, parochial, puritanical, the Irish had become more self-consciously Catholic than their coreligionists on the Continent or in the Americas. But Joyce's Catholicism, though Irish, was special in still another and more significant way. As a small boy he had been placed in the care of the Jesuits, and he remained in their charge until almost his twenty-first year. Understanding—*experto crede*—that Jesuitism is a concentrate of certain basic elements of Roman Catholicism, I thought I saw in that large and obvious fact a right and just approach to Joyce's love-hatred of Catholicism. "You allude to me as a Catholic," Joyce had once remarked; "you ought to allude to me as a Jesuit."[2] Who could ignore so obvious a hint? The paradox suggested a fresh *point d'appui* for a study of Joyce.

The first step in such a project was, of course, to assemble certain basic facts about his education, and this I proceeded to do.

[1] For a systematic but less than thorough treatment, see Hynes, "The Catholicism of James Joyce," *The Commonweal*, LV (February 22, 1952), 487–89. Perceptive but less systematic valuations of Joyce's Catholicism may be found *passim* in Strong, *The Sacred River*, and in Ussher, *Three Great Irishmen: Shaw, Yeats, Joyce*.

[2] "Portrait of James Joyce," edited by W. R. Rodgers, produced by Maurice Brown, broadcast by the British Broadcasting Commission, Third Program, February 13, 17, and March 22, 1950.

But in doing so I soon discovered that my first step was a journey in itself, a journey that no other Joycean had yet undertaken. The literature on Joyce is mountainous, much of it impressive, often awesome; but in all that cloud-topped, critical landscape I found few certain landmarks, rooted in plain, indisputable fact, which could be entirely trusted. It was a landscape, too, haunted by the Joyce myth, an amorphous shadow with a distressing tendency to materialize as Stephen Dedalus and sounding, from a distance, very like Herbert Gorman. I determined then that, if I was going to get anywhere, I must skirt the heights of criticism and follow the humbler road of pedestrian fact. Along the way I discovered that there is nothing indeed more interesting than a fact.

All this is a roundabout way of saying that the present study of Joyce is not concerned with "influences" of any kind, or with tracing those influences through Joyce's work. It is neither an assessment of Joyce's Catholicism nor an analysis of his Jesuitism, though it may provide others with a standard for their own analyses and valuations. My work is primarily one of definition— a definition, hitherto lacking, of Joyce's actual relationship with the Jesuits. It is, therefore, factual and biographical rather than critical or theoretical. It is based very largely on primary sources and original research; when I have made use of secondary materials, it is as often as not to correct or amend them by the factual evidence turned up in the course of my own research. The method is sufficiently clear, I believe, in the text and notes of the work itself.

The results of such a study are of value to both biography and criticism. For a long time the Joyce critic read the *Portrait* as more or less straightforward autobiography. The consequences of this were, to say the least, curious: not only was Stephen Dedalus a surrogate of James Joyce, but—and this is not quite the same— James Joyce *was* Stephen Dedalus. In the first full-length critical

study of Joyce to appear, Louis Golding, disregarding Valery
Larbaud's informed observation that the *Portrait* should be read
as "l'histoire de la jeunesse de l'artiste en général, c'est à dire de
tout homme doué du temperament artiste," confidently asserted
that the artist of the *Portrait* was "the only artist we can conceive
capable of producing *Ulysses*." [3] Some years later Herbert Gorman
apotheosized the Joyce-Dedalus union.[4] To Gorman this was more
than hypostatic: Joyce and Dedalus not only shared the same
nature, they were one and the same person. He arrived at the
same astonishing conclusion as Golding: Stephen Dedalus wrote
Ulysses and, presumably, was already at work on *Finnegans Wake*.
This conclusion was too perversely logical to satisfy the critics
for very long, and they have gradually corrected their perspective
on Joyce and the *Portrait*. But in some instances there has been a
tendency, noticeably on the part of critics like Hugh Kenner, to
overcorrect and to see the *Portrait* as a complex study in objective
irony.[5] It may be that (I believe it is), but it is not merely that.
The tendency of this sort of criticism is to out-Joyce Joyce, and
the presumption of this sort of critic, a dogmatic fellow usually,
is to insist that what is real or phantasmal for him could not
have been otherwise for Joyce. This study should provide the
advocates of objective irony with grounds more relative than
their presumptions or their dogmas. It should also show that

[3] Golding, *James Joyce*, p. 36.
[4] Gorman, *James Joyce*. Commenting on the *Portrait*, Gorman states un-
equivocally: "It was a book in which he had pictured his youth with an un-
comprising fidelity to facts and an implicit indictment of the civilization that
had attempted to mould him into an image of itself." (2d ed., p. 220). Joyce, it
may be said, in his correspondence (see *Letters of James Joyce*, ed. by Stuart
Gilbert, *passim*) makes frequent reference to Gorman's biography, but his interest is clearly in its publicity value rather than its factual accuracy. In an unpublished letter to Helen Joyce he expresses satisfaction that the circumstances
of his marriage to Nora Barnacle have been happily glossed over—an indication,
perhaps, of his interest in Gorman's "facts."
[5] Kenner, *Dublin's Joyce*, pp. 109–33.

Joyce's irony can at times be quite as personal—even private—as it was objective. But, above all, this study should lay the ghost of Stephen Dedalus and preclude any further reading of *Stephen Hero* or the *Portrait* as either actual or "spiritual" autobigraphy.

This conclusion, that Dedalus is not Joyce, is nothing new in the history of Joyce criticism. More than twenty years ago William Troy cautioned readers of the *Portrait* against a too-ready identification of the mature artist Joyce with "the morbid-minded aesthete and embryo philosopher" Stephen.[6] Later, William York Tindall, in refutation of Rebecca West's charge that Joyce is sentimental, accurately pinpoints that lady's error as "a confusion of Joyce with Stephen."[7] Again, in the introduction to his edition of *Chamber Music,* Tindall, commenting on the autobiographical basis of Joyce's art, stresses the "aesthetic distance" that separates the artist from his surrogate Dedalus, who, Tindall reminds us, is only one of many such surrogates: Leopold Bloom, H. C. Earwicker, Richard Rowan, Gabriel Conroy, James Duffy, and the like.[8] I share with these critics the same rather obvious conclusion, but I have arrived at it by a somewhat different method of approach. Records of Joyce's Jesuit schooling, hitherto unknown or unavailable, support the critical analyses of these earlier critics in revealing a young man very different indeed from the Dedalus of the *Portrait*.[9]

[6] "Stephen Dedalus and James Joyce," *The Nation,* CXXXVIII (February 14, 1934), 187–88.
[7] *James Joyce: His Way of Interpreting the Modern World,* p. 16.
[8] James Joyce, *Chamber Music,* ed. by Tindall, pp. 49–51.
[9] Mention should be made here of one source of material which, though known, is still unavailable. According to Father Roland Burke Savage, superior of the Jesuit residence on Lower Leeson Street, Dublin, many of the records of Joyce's old university were transferred, on the Jesuits' removal from the college in 1908, to the Leeson Street residence. Unfortunately, however, they are there stored among the private archives of the Jesuit Order, and Father Burke Savage, though in every way courteous and accommodating, was not free to give me access to these files.

But though Joyce was not writing autobiography, he was, as everyone knows, constantly exploiting autobiographical material. I have been concerned to show how and to what extent Joyce actually did exploit such materials; consequently, I have found frequent occasion to juxtapose Joyce's fiction with the facts in so far as I have been able to uncover them. At times fiction and fact will seem almost to coincide, as in my discussion of Joyce's prefecture at Belvedere. At other times the disparity between the two —for example, in connection with the general course of Joyce's career at the university—will be clear from the simple act of juxtaposition. The reader may at first be confused by this constant shuttling back and forth between fact and fiction, and an unwary reader might even suppose that I am supporting one by the other; but in each instance—and explicitly in these introductory remarks —I believe I have indicated my method with sufficient clarity to obviate any real difficulty.

A study based on fresh factual material is only incidentally concerned with matters of interpretation. This does not mean, however, that any and all explication of Joyce's text is thereby excluded. New facts frequently suggest new questions that may be asked about that text (why, for example, are Gleeson and Conmee identified by name while Dolan and Arnall are aliases? or, why is Brother Michael said to be "different" from other Jesuits?), and the answers to these questions may involve fresh interpretations of Joyce's text. But such interpretations are not of course to be taken as substitutions for facts; rather they follow as a natural consequence of them. The study is not after all a mere accumulation of statistics; the beginning of knowledge may be with a fact, but its end is the discovery of significance. That too has been one of my objectives.

Inevitably, it seems, a work of this kind will also turn up, almost accidentally, new sources of Joyce's material. It is more curious perhaps than significant that as a small boy at Clongowes Joyce should come upon (and remember?) a character in a play called Jacob Earwig. But it is not at all curious that a prayer book, *The Sodality Manual,* which he used as a somewhat older boy at Belvedere should be a primary source for the famous sermon on hell and other passages in the *Portrait.* And it must come as a surprise to those who believed, like Stanislaus Joyce, that Joyce and the Jesuits afterwards shared only mutual suspicion and distrust, to discover that it was a Jesuit's cordial assistance that enabled Joyce to correct the first draft of an episode in *Ulysses.* The debt Joyce owed to the Jesuits he generously acknowledged, and on their part the Irish Jesuits even today admit that he treated them "more than fairly." [10] They have certainly had more bitter critics, and they have perhaps suffered more from the adulation of their admirers than from the prejudices and slanders of their enemies. Joyce never slandered them, and the bias of his mind was, if anything, a Jesuit bias.

Canonically, the age of reason is assumed to begin about the end of the seventh year. Joyce, then, came under the influence of the Jesuits while he was still, canonically, an infant. He was to remain under their tutelage, though not always their guidance, till the end of his twentieth year. Consequently, he received the whole of his *formal* education from the Jesuits. Only once during these fourteen years was his study with them interrupted, and during this period—from the beginning of the year 1892 to April, 1893—he seems not to have attended any school whatever. In so far, then, as formal schooling may account for Joyce as man and artist, the Jesuits are responsible. If there is blame, they must assume it, and if there is praise, they must not be denied it.

[10] I am quoting the exact words of an Irish Jesuit with whom I spent a pleasant day in the summer of 1954 at Clongowes Wood. There were exceptions, but for the most part other Jesuits at Belvedere and University College, Dublin, shared this opinion.

The Irish Jesuits left on Joyce a psychological, moral, religious, intellectual, and even social impress which, in so far as it explains the kind of person he at any time was, helps to an understanding of the kind of work he later produced. They had his mind and spirit too long in charge for this to be otherwise. He was for many of those years a submissive obedient charge, and even his rebellion was an acknowledgment of their power and influence over him, a reluctant homage which disobedience must always pay to authority. But this study deals with Joyce before the time of his overt rebellion. One must not, as Herbert Gorman admits he does, read history backwards; for if you read Joyce's history backwards, you can never go back so far as to get out from under the long shadow that his genius casts over the whole of his past life. But to come to know Joyce, and eventually to come to a full appreciation of his achievement, you must forget for a while the genius and begin to remember the boy.

At Clongowes Wood the child was immersed in a deeply religious atmosphere, almost monastic in its intensity. These years between September, 1888, and December, 1891, were, in a sense, the period of his first exile. At an age when most small boys have the comfort and authority of home and parents, young Joyce was under the discipline of Jesuit Fathers and the special care and protection of Mother Church. The psychological impact of his spiritual orientation during these early years was never wholly lost on him, even after faith itself was lost. The discipline, the orthodoxy (in Eliot's sense of orthodoxy), and the traditionalism of the mature writer had their root in the classrooms and cubicles, in the fields and forests of Clongowes. The artist's sense of an ideal "other world" set against the too solid reality of "this world" was again the inheritance of his childhood. Others, friends and relatives, have attributed his dedication and artistic integrity, his personal fortitude and professional perseverance, directly to the moral and religious training begun by the Jesuits at Clongowes Wood. The rightness of their judgment may be shown by the thoroughness of that training, which the present study has also attempted to demonstrate and document.

The religious predilection of Joyce's childhood, fostered by the Jesuits at Clongowes, became at Belvedere a preoccupation which the Jesuits continued to encourage, possibly in the belief, or hope, that the boy was planning to enter the order. My discussion of Joyce's vocation could not of course be documented, and I do not claim for it the same factual certitude that may be claimed for other conclusions reached elsewhere. Even so, I believe that the conclusions I have reached do enjoy a high degree of probability. These are, first, that Joyce thought longer and more seriously about becoming a Jesuit than is generally supposed or admitted; secondly, that Stephen's spiritual crisis in the *Portrait* is neither a factual nor a psychological reenactment of a similar crisis in Joyce's own adolescence; and thirdly, that Joyce's refusal of a vocation is quite distinct from his later rejection of Catholicism, though in the *Portrait* Stephen's refusal and rejection are made to appear simultaneous. It would also seem that what has been called Joyce's "sacerdotalism" had its origin in this same adolescent experience, that the religion of art which he celebrated in his works was a substitute for the art of religion from which he turned away in his youth.

Joyce was at Belvedere College for five years, between the ages of eleven and sixteen, and these were perhaps the most impressionable years of his life. One may judge from this the seriousness with which he received the moral and religious counsels of his Jesuit teachers and the deep impression these made on the boy at the time. But the Jesuits, though dedicated to the salvation of souls, were no less concerned with the training and development of the mind. It was while he was at Belvedere and, as we shall see, only while at Belvedere that Joyce's intellectual formation can be said to have been typically Jesuit. The instrument of that formation was the *Ratio Studiorum,* a plan or method of education which, like the trivium, whose pedagogical orientations it incorporated and perpetuated, was designed to achieve its most effective results on the primary level. It was here that Joyce's powers of memory, already considerable, were further strengthened by the school discipline of daily and weekly "repetitions." Here, in the discipline of the "prelection," the boy developed habits of mind which placed a premium on intellectual order and thoroughness, and on the systemization and schematization of knowledge. The schoolmaster who wrote *Finnegans Wake* was born of the schoolboy who, by way of the "emulation" prescribed in the *Ratio,* took special, silent pride in excelling his fellows. For if many of Joyce's intellectual virtues were the product of his Jesuit training, so it must be said were many of his vices—his pedantry, his perpetual seeking after first principles, his implicit sense of superiority that will not explain and cannot apologize, the sense that he leaves with even his most patient reader of being party to a secret which he will not share.

Contrary to popular belief, the influence of the Jesuits on Joyce after he left Belvedere was negligible. At University College, Dublin, where he spent the years 1898–1902, the Jesuits, as I have been at pains to point out in my final chapters, were no more than educational caretakers. The university, through no fault of the Jesuits or the Irish people (both of whom were distressingly conscious of its defects), was a second-rate institution which could provide no more than a third- or fourth-rate education. Nevertheless, Joyce managed to acquire during these four years a really first-rate education which was in part made possible by the Jesuits. The Jesuits helped in this by founding or reactivating college societies and academies in which the intellectual energies of their best students could find an outlet not otherwise provided by the university. Joyce, unlike Stephen Dedalus, took generous advantage of many of these opportunities. But this was not the only way in which he educated himself. He was fortunate in his contemporaries at University College, and he was persevering in his ambitions, for his dominating ambition—to realize himself as an artist—was fully formed early in his university career, if not indeed earlier. I have commented at some length on those contemporaries of Joyce who seem to have been most important to the life of his mind at this time and about whom little or no mention has been made in Joyce studies. Others like J. F. Byrne, whose connection with Joyce has already been defined in private memoirs, I have passed over rather more quickly, pausing only to correct certain false impressions that have been left behind by the memoir-writer. Finally, I have made no attempt to discuss what may well have been the most important element in Joyce's self-education—his private reading. Though aware of its importance, I have not discussed this subject for two reasons: first, because such reading, being private and carried out independently of Jesuit direction, is really outside the limits, as I have defined them, of the present work; second, to digress on any of the authors whom Joyce was reading at this time—Ibsen, for example, or Hauptmann, or even Mangan—would, if the treatment of them was to be at all adequate, amount to a separate and distinct study.

At the end of the work, surveying the whole of his Jesuit schooling, I cannot escape the impression (I do not claim it is more) that had Joyce's—or, more properly, his father's—fortunes taken a different turn, had the young man not seemed destined to the corrosive and contemptible milieu of Dublin's lower-middle class, there would have been no deterioration in his relations with the Jesuits, no rejection of Catholicism, no abandonment of home and

country, and possibly no *Portrait of the Artist as a Young Man*—
or, at least, a very different kind of portrait. The weakness of
such contrary-to-fact hypotheses is, of course, that to prove them
one would have to rewrite history. But Joyce's history, or that part
of it I have reconstructed here, is, like the story of Stephen
Dedalus, fixed forever in the place of the infinite possibilities it
has ousted. It cannot be relived, but it may with effort be understood. Prerequisite to any understanding of the artist or his work
is the simple truth which this study again reaffirms: life and
literature do not so interpenetrate that the story of Stephen
Dedalus may be read as the history of James Joyce.

O, you were excruciated, in honour bound to the cross of your own
     cruelfiction!   [FW 192]

1 ⚔

Clongowes Wood

Clongowes Wood was founded in 1813 [sic], in the pleasantest part of Kildare, and stands in the midst of beautiful and well-wooded grounds of 500 acres in extent. . . . The drive from town through the valley of the Liffey, occupying about two hours, is one of the most picturesque in Ireland.

CLONGOWES WOOD COLLEGE Prospectus, JULY, 1886 [1]

FROM KINGSBRIDGE STATION, Dublin, to Sallins, County Kildare, it is less than an hour by train.[2] The view along the way is less "picturesque" than that by carriage or coach through the wayward valley of the Liffey. But at Sallins there is a change. Here the traveler in the eighties would step from his compartment into a waiting car and ride through a stretch of land neither mountainy nor flat, but gently rolling under the hush of burnt-yellow farmlands, whispering hedges, and patches of thick turning wood, the few remaining miles to Clongowes. The woods deepen as one nears the castle demesne, and when the car eases from the road under a long arch of old arrogant elms, the sense—but faint before—of moving through an ancient and historic countryside now

---

[1] The text of the *Prospectus* is given in the Appendix. The original is in the office of the rector at Clongowes Wood.

[2] Pasted in an old scrapbook now in the rector's office at Clongowes is a copy of the following memo: "Christmas Holidays begin Thursday, Dec. 20th, 1888. Masters accompanying boys travelling to Dublin by train—leaving Sallins at 8:51 A.M., due at Kingsbridge 9:45 A.M. All are to return punctually on Jan. 10th. —J. S. Conmee, S.J."

also deepens. The new road under the elms is long and very straight, and in the distance where the elms and shadows end, there is just visible a great gateway and above and behind it a castle tower caught in a fret of sunlight.

James A. Joyce, accompanied by his parents, made his first journey to Clongowes Wood in the early days of September, 1888. "Due to his precocity," his brother Stanislaus reports, "he was admitted . . . when barely turned six, though the minimum age requirement was nine." [3] Actually, this minimum age was seven,[4] and young James, born February 2, 1882, was exactly six years and seven months of age when his name was first entered in the academic register.[5] As for his precocity, the memory of him around Clongowes today is of a small boy "more delicate than brilliant" who, however innately gifted, made no remarkable display of those gifts during his three and a half years at the college. One memory may be as unreliable as the other, but Stanislaus Joyce, who was not quite three years old at the time of which he writes, has perhaps an edge in unreliability. There is often the temptation, when writing about a man of genius, to envelop his early childhood in trailing clouds of one kind or another. But no such clouds appear in the Clongownian sky of Joyce's boyhood. His days at the college were to be serene and uneventful, and if the Jesuits at Clongowes have not remembered precocious performances by their pupil, one may feel sure that this is because there were no such performances to remember.

[3] Stanislaus Joyce, "James Joyce: A Memoir," *The Hudson Review*, II (Winter, 1950), 487.

[4] Clongowes Wood College *Prospectus*, July, 1886, Section VI.

[5] In a Clongowes account book marked Students' Ledger H 1886–1907, there is the following entry (folio 132):

"J. S. Joyce Esq—Collector General's office 43 Fleet Street Dublin 1 Martello Terrace, Bray

"Master James Joyce entered Sep 1888 £25 per.an. to include everything"

Father John Conmee, S.J., who welcomed the Joyces to Clongowes that September day, was himself an old Clongownian. Older masters then serving under him would have remembered him as an erect, fair, good-looking boy. They would have remembered his natural graciousness, more pronounced but no less natural in the man as in the boy, his gaiety, his quickness of mind, and above all the tenacity with which he held to his convictions and the force and felicity with which he expressed them. "He had," an acquaintance said of him later, "an amusing horror of a bore." [6] In his last year he was the Clongowes debate medalist, the most coveted distinction to which a Clongownian, the memory and example of O'Connell in mind, could aspire.[7] Conmee's talents had clearly marked him for success, and had he not decided to enter the Society of Jesus, there would have been few careers that he could not have followed to advantage. His career as a Jesuit bore this out. Beginning with his installation as rector of Clongowes, he continued to serve the Society in positions of trust and responsibility for the remainder of his life, and on August 7, 1905, he was named by Rome Provincial of the Irish Jesuits.[8]

[6] "Clongowes and Father Conmee," *The Irish Monthly*, XXXVIII (August, 1910), 424. This is an obituary of and "filial tribute" to Father Conmee and is unsigned. However, the editor of the magazine, Father Matthew Russell, S.J., has identified the author as Father Henry Fegan, S.J. The obituary is apparently a reprint from the college yearbook, *The Clongownian*, 1910.

[7] Corcoran, *Glongowes Record*, p. 149.

[8] *Catalogus Societatis Jesu Provinciae Hiberniae.* These catalogues are published yearly—*ad usum privatum*—by Browne and Nolan, Dublin. The pages are unnumbered. Each catalogue lists separately all Jesuit schools, parishes, and houses of study in Ireland, the names and status of the Jesuits assigned to each, and the number of years they have been on their current assignment. Included also is an alphabetical index of the names of all living Irish Jesuits, their date of birth, date of entrance into the Society, and the date on which they pronounced their final vows as Jesuits. The catalogue for any year is hereafter cited as *Catalogus S.J.*

He appears in *Ulysses* (U 216) not as Provincial, but simply as "the Superior." [9] As in the *Portrait* he had been cheered by the boys as "the decentest rector that was ever in Clongowes" (P 64), he is here presented as a kindly Christian humanist who would have the will of God done in all things and yet can be moved to pity that so many souls created by God should be lost (U 220). The progress of his walk out through the country lanes toward Artane is paralleled by the viceregal procession through the streets of the city. The reader shares in the interior life of Conmee's spirit, in the gentle orderly drift of the priest's reveries; he hears with him the joybells ringing in gay Malahide (U 220), feels the stubble of Clongowes field tickling his ankles (U 221), and receives the Assisian curtsies of ample-leaved cabbages as he passes by (U 220). But the reader shares nothing with the vice-regent, Lord Dudley, for there is no spirit in Dudley to be shared. His procession is no more than a show of pageantry and display of power; it is accompanied not by joybells ringing but by the blaring and drumthumping of "unseen brazen highland laddies" (U 250). It is greeted not by cabbages and schoolboys but by obsequious policemen and "the Poddle River hanging out in fealty a tongue of liquid sewage" (U 249). If this episode, in which Conmee and Lord Dudley figure most prominently, is regarded as Stuart Gilbert suggests, "as a small-scale model of *Ulysses* as a whole," [10] then these two men, priest and vice-regent, are, in addition to being obvious representatives of the spiritual and temporal powers that dominated Ireland, symbols of those metaphysical polarities between which the whole world of *Ulysses* rotates around its philosophical axis. Conmee, in minia-

[9] According to the *Catalogus S.J.* for these years, Conmee was in fact superior of the residence of St. Francis Xavier, Upper Gardiner Street, Dublin, from October 24, 1898, until June 16, 1904. The Irish Provincial at this time, also residing at St. Francis Xavier's, was Father James Murphy, S.J.

[10] *James Joyce's Ulysses*, p. 225.

ture, is form and spirit, a source of existence and life; Dudley is the surrogate of matter and progressive materialism, whose end is denial and death.

Metaphysical considerations aside, the human personality that emerges from *Ulysses* is a close likeness of the actual priest who walked the paths at Clongowes Wood "and heard the cries of the boys' lines at their play, young cries in the quiet evening. He was their rector: his reign was mild" (U 221). So one might expect from a Jesuit whose favorite saint was not the soldier Ignatius or the firebrand Xavier, but the gentle man of Assisi, who "loved best of all the towns in Europe" not dear dirty Dublin or any of the great capitals of the world, but an old Bohemian town on the River Moldau—Prague.[11] Father Conmee—"Don John Conmee" (U 220)—was a romantic, with a romantic's deep attachment to the past, especially to the medieval past, and to all things "softened and beautified by the hand of time." [12] So "his little book *Old Times in the Barony*" (U 220) is a nostalgic but unsentimental recall of an older way of life, rural and uncomplicated, around the neighborhood of Luainford; a way of life which, even in his own day, had all but vanished from the Irish scene. Conmee's duties as a Jesuit superior left him little time to write, and *Old Times* is his only published book. This is perhaps unfortunate, for his prose style is as simple, gracious, and courtly as was the man himself.

It is unlikely that Father Conmee resented the pressures of the work which made difficult or impossible the exercise of his literary gift.[13] But any resentment he might have felt was more

[11] "Clongowes and Father Conmee," p. 425.   [12] *Ibid.*

[13] Conmee also published some verse, but this has hardly the "originality and power" attributed to it by the writer of his obituary. An example of it, entitled "Lines for the Opening of the Debate," is reprinted in the same volume of *The Irish Monthly* in which his obituary appears. The title of this poem has little to do with its content, which is an account, in ballad form, of the conversion of St. Ignatius Loyola.

likely due to his being kept from the company of schoolboys, great and small, with whom he loved to mix freely in "cheerful decorum" (U 219). Readers of the *Portrait* recall the courtesy shown to young Stephen Dedalus when the latter appealed to Conmee's justice and charity. There is a story told which shows how accurately Joyce's fiction, in this instance, fits the facts of the rector's personality.

When James Joyce first entered Clongowes Wood College, there entered with him an eight-year-old boy, named Eugene Kenny, who had come all the long way from South America to attend the Irish Jesuit School. Like Joyce, he lived in the infirmary apart from the other boys, and when Joyce and the rest of the students departed Clongowes for the Christmas vacation in 1888–89, Eugene Kenny was left very much alone in the large and empty infirmary. On these lonely December evenings, Father Conmee would have the boy up to his rooms where, while the rector worked at his desk, the boy amused himself as he could in front of the rector's fire. Like many eight-year-old boys, Eugene Kenny was a talking catechism, and Father Conmee, the roles of priest and pupil now reversed, submitted aimiably to a barrage of questioning of the sort which has been known to drive less spiritual fathers to the edge of sanity. The questioning turned one evening upon St. Nicholas, and it was soon evident that young Kenny had serious misgivings about the ability of the saint to get from South America to Clongowes Wood in the span of a single night. Father Conmee was noncommital. But on Christmas Eve the boy awoke to the sound of priestly boots tip-toeing down the corridor outside his room. He rushed to the door, but just missed seeing an oddly soutaned St. Nicholas disappearing down the stairwell. On turning back into his room, any doubt of the saint's existence dissolved at the sight of the great stockings, bulging with sweets and toys, that hung over the fireplace. They were not his stockings either, but great, long, roomy things like those worn by the fellows at the top of the school.[14]

This is the kind of man Father Conmee was, and it is as this kind of person that he appears in the *Portrait* and *Ulysses*. He may have preferred to spend his life among the boys at Clongowes Wood, but the will of his superiors ordained otherwise. A simple, generous, gifted man, he had the complications of authority and responsibility thrust upon him. After his death on May 13, 1910, a fellow Jesuit summed up his career: "Indeed it may be said with truth that he hardly ever served in the ranks as a simple private." [15] This may not have been what Father Conmee would have desired for himself, but neither, as a Jesuit, would he have desired it otherwise.

Since he was thus distinguished both as student and alumnus, and was presumably more familiar than most with the history and traditions of Clongowes Wood, one is rightly surprised when reading his first prospectus to find Conmee in error about the date of the founding of the college. The actual sale of Castle Browne, as it was then known, to representatives of the Society of Jesus had been finally effected on March 4, 1814.[16] The Jesuits themselves took possession of the property a month later, and the first scholar was enrolled on May 18, 1814.[17]

[14] "Clongowes and Father Conmee," pp. 426–27.

[15] *Ibid.*, p. 422.   [16] Corcoran, *Clongowes Record*, p. 45.

[17] *Ibid.*, p. 85. The name of this first scholar was John MacLornan. He and some forty other students began their actual studies on July 3, just five weeks before the restoration of the Jesuit order by Pope Pius VII on August 7, 1814.

This business of the transfer of the estate to the Jesuits had been a delicate and difficult transaction. One remembers it now principally because it involved the names of two men—O'Connell and Parnell—who, more than all others, were to give "a shape and a destiny" to Joyce's Ireland. At the time that the sale was being negotiated, the Penal Laws were still technically in force, Catholic Emancipation some fifteen years in the future, and Father Peter Kenny, S.J., superior of the Irish Jesuits and prospective purchaser of Castle Browne, had as a priest few legal rights and as a Jesuit no legal existence. On the advice of Daniel O'Connell, Father Kenny had originally intended to gain title to the land

I

Father Peter Kenny, S.J., founder of Clongowes Wood, had great but guarded hopes for the future when in the spring of 1814 his college, under the patronage of St. Aloysius Gonzaga, welcomed its first handful of scholars. But in Ireland it is seldom possible to escape the past. It is like the turf of the country, everywhere under foot, the stuff of fire to warm old memories over at the hearth, or to lend a flame to passions that have burned out the hearts of men and cities. That past was deep and rich around Clongowes. Within Father Kenny's own lifetime, Hamilton Rowan, friend and companion to Wolfe Tone, had fled across the fields from neighboring Rathcoffey and, once within the castle, eluded pursuit by the goddamning British through a "priest's door" in the great Round Room. That door itself was a relic of an earlier, crueler time when the Penal Laws lay heavily on the land. It was a time which sent Irish soldiers to fight abroad in the service of foreign princes, and it was said that one such soldier, Marshal Anthony Browne, slain at Prague, would afterwards return to Clongowes Wood wrapped in the ghostly white folds of his marshal's cloak, and appear to servants and simple folk in the castle hall. But even before the Brownes had posses-

---

in the name of some Protestant landlord of prominence, and the name first proposed was that of Mr. William Parnell of Avondale, County Wicklow. This gentleman, author of a well-known history of the Penal Laws, had a sympathetic understanding of the Irish Catholic position—a sympathy generated, one may believe, more by the fact that it was Irish than that it was Catholic. Ultimately, however, this legal subterfuge was deemed unnecessary. Through the good offices of O'Connell and the diplomacy and bargaining skill of Father Kenny a clear title to the estate passed from Lieutenant-General Michael Browne, one of an illustrious line of Irish soldiers (who fought other peoples' wars), to the new owners for the sum of £16,000. One wonders whether Father Conmee, observing the meteoric career of Charles Parnell in the eighties, thought of him as the grandson of that William Parnell of Avondale who years before had stood ready with O'Connell to assist the Jesuits in founding a college at Clongowes Wood. See Corcoran, *Clongowes Record*, pp. 45, 47–48, 52.

sion of the castle, its walls had been pummeled by Cromwell's cannon, and long before Cromwell the once powerful Eustaces —now but a dim memory—had stood medieval guard on these *frontures des marches de guerre* that stretched miles north and east and south of *silva de Clongowes*. Beyond history, most remote memory of all, was legendary Queen Buan, asleep now in her grassy mound beside the castle walls. All this was in the past of Clongowes Wood and was with the years to become part of the lore of successive generations of young Clongownians.[18]

And yet Father Kenny, thinking of the future, was probably little concerned with the romance, legendary or actual, associated with castle and countryside. Seventy years later his successor, Father Conmee, could be so little mindful of the past that even the date of the founding of the college could slip his memory. For the Jesuits are an order more interested in creating history than in recalling it. And the Irish Jesuits, more so than most Irishmen perhaps, seemed willing to let the past bury the past. Looking to the future they hoped to come to terms with the present.

By Conmee's time many of Father Kenny's hopes had already been realized. Clongowes Wood College in the eighties was one of the most distinguished Catholic school in the British Isles, certainly the most fashionable Catholic school in Ireland. Most of the students came from comfortable rather than wealthy homes. A few were of the gentry, all a solid cut above the peasantry. Generally they were the sons of well-placed civil servants, of well-to-do merchants and businessmen, or of a new professional class which, after Catholic Emancipation, began gradually to emerge into Irish public life.[19] Many of them, on leaving Clongowes,

---

[18] *Ibid.,* pp. 39–51.
[19] In the *Portrait* (p. 3) Stephen Dedalus is quickly made aware of the class-consciousness at Clongowes:
"Nasty Roche had asked:
"—What is your father?

were themselves to find careers in the civil service or in the army, in medicine or in law. Always a representative few were destined for the priesthood, often in the Society of Jesus. They were all, as a result of their Jesuit training, prepared to be respectable members of society and obedient children of the church.

Few were anything less. One or two were a good deal more. The rascally Father Prout, alias Francis Sylvester Mahony, had taught at Clongowes for a few years before the exasperated Jesuits expelled him from the order. The Jesuits could no more fasten Mahony, wit, linguist, raconteur, in the bonds of blind obedience than they could have Joyce a half-century later. The man who translated Moore's *Irish Melodies* into Latin and Greek and issued them as "Moore's Plagiarisms" [20]—much to Moore's distress— was clearly more at home among *Blackwood's* gang than in the disciplined ranks of the Black Pope. Another of Joyce's predecessors at Clongowes Wood who hardly conformed to pattern was Thomas Francis Meagher. His career as a revolutionist was short-lived. It ended, like that of a good many Irish revolutionists, aboard a British convict ship bound for Tasmania. Escaping to America he practised law for a while and at the same time edited an Irish newspaper in New York City. When the Civil War broke out, torn between his humanitarian impulses and his revolutionary beliefs, he was finally to decide in favor of the former

---

"Stephen had answered:

"—A gentleman.

"Then Nasty Roche had asked:

"—Is he a magistrate?"

Recall also Stephen's sour recollection in *Ulysses* (p. 40): "You told the Clongowes gentry you had an uncle a judge and an uncle a general in the army. Come out of them Stephen. Beauty is not there."

[20] Hoagland, ed., *1000 Years of Irish Poetry*, p. 790. Mahony was a student at Clongowes between 1815 and 1818. He then entered the Jesuit novitiate at Rue de Sèvres, Paris, and after completing his philosophical studies at Rome returned to teach at Clongowes in 1825. Restrained mention is made of him by Corcoran in *Clongowes Record*, pp. 106, 116.

and join the Union army, in which he served, with some distinction and much disgust, as a brigadier. After the war, in recognition of his services, he was appointed secretary and later temporary governor of the Montana Territory. This career too was short-lived. It is possible that he attempted to govern the territory after the manner of his Jesuit schoolmasters at Clongowes Wood; it is certain that his autocratic rule was far from popular with American frontiersmen, who had always an expeditious way with unpopular government officials. One evening Thomas Francis Meagher simply disappeared, it is said into the wide waters of the Missouri.[21]

But Meagher and Mahony were the exceptions. Nothing in the scholastic background of a Clongownian prepared him for the role of social or political rebel. His Jesuit preceptors at Clongowes were staunchly conservative, and when they took any stand at all it was generally on the side of the reactionary elements in Irish society. Politically, according to Meagher, they were "not O'Connellites even." [22] Today, from a liberal point of view, this state of affairs must be thought unfortunate; in the view of an Irish nationalist it may still be thought unforgivable. But at the time it was at least understandable. The boys who were placed in the Jesuits' care at Clongowes Wood came mostly from conservative homes, from families that were supported by and in turn supported the status quo. The Jesuits considered it their duty to complete the training begun in the home, not to undo or reverse

[21] Athearn, *Thomas Francis Meagher*, pp. 165–66.
[22] Meagher, "Clongowes Wood," in *Meagher of the Sword*, ed. by Griffith, p. 272. "It is an odd fiction," Meagher wrote, "which represents the Irish Jesuits as conspirators against the stability of the English empire in Ireland. With two or three exceptions, they were not O'Connellites even. In that beautiful grand castle of theirs, circled by their fruitful gardens and grain-fields, walled in by their stately dense woods of birch trees, walnut, and firs, they lived and taught —so it seems to me now—rather as hostages and aliens, than freemen and citizens."

it. They were the educators of O'Connell's sons, not of O'Connell's "beggars." Again, the existence of their school and their own existence as an order depended on the complaisance of a government which tolerated rather than encouraged their activities. They could count on continued toleration and hope for future encouragement only so long as, in the view of that government, they educated young Irishmen in what were considered the ways of responsible citizenship. But one who was a responsible citizen in the view of Dublin Castle and the landed gentry would hardly be thought a responsible Irishman by the Young Irelanders or the Fenians. The Jesuits, then, willing to forget the past, could not have felt it was their duty to keep dangerously alive the memory of the 'Ninety-Eight, or Limerick, or the Yellow Ford. They were not conducting a school for young rebels, agitators, or a revolutionary breed of native patriots. Had they thought to do so, they would quickly enough have found themselves without school or students. Finally, if any of them ever reflected that in terms of the national struggle their course was less than heroic, they had the consolation of their Jesuit vows which pledged them to the salvation of souls, not to the saving of Ireland.

But to come to terms with the present is often to compromise the future. There is no way of estimating accurately what may have been lost to Ireland, and possibly to the Church, by the political and social compromise of the Jesuits at Clongowes, but any speculation about such losses must, in fairness, be measured against what was actually gained. One must assume that from the Jesuits' own view, as shepherds of souls, the principal gain was spiritual, but final knowledge of such matters is beyond the scope of human enquiry—even by Jesuits. Certainly Father Purdon's spiritual bookkeeping, a little too naive and a good deal too worldly, is quite impracticable.[23] Fortunately there were more tangible temporal gains. First among these was the very real advance in education of an articulate Irish Catholic laity; now on the secondary level, eventually, one hoped, at the university level. There was some truth in John Eglinton's remark that "it was in Irish Protestantism that Ireland, dumb through the ages, had found a voice."[24] But this was not the voice of Joyce's Ireland, nor that of the vast majority of the Irish people.

In the cruel days before Emancipation, learning had glimmered like hidden turf fires behind the hedges of the Irish countryside. There native "philomaths" sat ready to teach a ragged circle of young peasants "bookkeeping by single and double entry, geometry, trigonometry, stereometry, mensuration, navigation, gauging, surveying, dialling, astronomy, astrology, austerity and fluxions; or in the classics everything from Aesop's fables and the colloquies of Erasmus to Cornelius Agrippa and Cholera Morbus; or anything from Greek Grammar to Irish radically and a small taste of Hebrew upon the Masoretic text."[25] Sometimes this philomathic glimmer shot up into a real flash of talent as in the case of William Carleton, "the great novelist of Ireland,"[26] who came out of the hedge-schools of Tyrone. Or the Munster poet, Owen Roe O'Sullivan, who once "while still a common farm-

[23] Father Purdon, in the short story "Grace," has been identified by Stanislaus Joyce in "The Background to 'Dubliners,'" *The Listener*, LI (March 25, 1954), 526–27, as the popular English preacher Father Bernard Vaughan, S.J. For Conmee's opinion of Vaughan, see *Ulysses*, pp. 216–17.

[24] *Irish Literary Portraits*, p. 81.

[25] Kiely, *Poor Scholar*, p. 22. Kiely is here paraphrasing Carleton's amusing but lengthy catalogue of accomplishments which the philomath, Matthew Kavanagh, claims for himself in "The Hedge School." The original may be found in Carleton's *Traits and Stories of the Irish Peasantry*, I, 296.

[26] Yeats, *Stories From Carleton*, p. xvi. It should be said that Yeats thought Carleton "the great novelist of Ireland by right of the most Celtic eyes that ever gazed from under the brow of story-teller."

hand . . . amazed his master's son (just returned from a Continental college) by construing for the latter a Greek passage that had puzzled him." [27] But Carleton was seduced from the faith, and O'Sullivan's best remembered poem in English, "Rodney's Glory," is a ballad celebrating the victory of an English admiral over Ireland's friend and ally, the French.

When all that was admirable in the hedge-schools and schoolmasters—their courage, their comedy, their genuine if sometimes pathetic love of learning—has been acknowledged, it must still be said that if the lamp of knowledge is truly to illumine men's minds, it must be made to burn with a flame that is more than a flash or a glimmer. The Jesuits, realizing this, and perhaps realizing too that the political salvation of Ireland depended on a trained Catholic leadership, set as their goal the education of leaders who, when it was necessary and possible, could meet Ireland's adversaries on grounds of social and intellectual equality. Whether this was the Jesuits' intention or not, it was an effect implied in their educational activities at Clongowes Wood. One could not expect such results to be either immediate or spectacular (as they certainly were not); if they were to be achieved at all, they would require patience, time, and industry. No one doubted the Jesuits' industry, and as for time—the Jesuits had eternity. Meanwhile the Clongowes Jesuits got on with the job of patiently teaching young Ireland to speak again with a Catholic voice.[28]

If, to the patriotic ear, that voice had at times a decidedly West British accent, the reason for this was not hard to find. It was located squarely in the general social and cultural orientation of

---

[27] MacManus, *The Story of the Irish Race,* p. 462, note 16.

[28] One such voice was that of the Irish statesman John Redmond. He was at Clongowes twenty years before Joyce (1868–74) and while there was, like Conmee, the debate medalist. "To the end of his life," his biographer states, "he valued that early honour more than any other." For his fulsome acknowledgment, at the end of his career, of his debt to the Jesuits at Clongowes, see Gwynn, *The Life of John Redmond,* pp. 40–41, 323–25.

Clongowes Wood. Generations of Irish Jesuits had been educated abroad, in England or on the continent. On their return to Ireland their vision could embrace more than an Irish parish or province, and most of them generally would have a more catholic view than, for example, the native Irish clergy trained at nearby Maynooth. Consequently, to see Ireland as part of Europe meant for most of these men to see it also as part of the British Empire. And not merely as a political or economic entity within the Empire, but as a differentiating yet integral part of a larger social and cultural pattern. This may explain why at the turn of the century so many Jesuits (notably Father William Delany, rector of UCD) were as impatient as Joyce himself with the noisy propagandizing of the Gaelic League. On this one point at least Joyce and the Jesuits always saw eye to eye, and largely for the same reason. Irish was taught in Jesuit schools, but it had no preferred place in the curriculum. At Clongowes Wood the West British influence extended even to the playing fields. Cricket and rugby had been imported from England; the ancient Irish game of hurling and the more lethal forms of Irish football were far from the fashion.

What, in short, the Jesuits at Clongowes tried to do, and generally succeeded in doing, was to prepare Irish young men for that place in society which the fortunes of birth or money seemed to entitle them to. The world their students were to enter was for the most part a Protestant, commercial, self-consciously moral world. They must then be Christian, civilized, industrious, and free from those more parochial prejudices—always excepting the faith, which was "universal"—inherited from their insular Irish backgrounds. If this was snobbism, and no one will deny that it was, it was a most realistic snobbism. An Irish Fenian might spit contempt at news that Lord Churchill, accompanied by the Countess of Londonderry, had a polite and sociable tea with the

Reverend Father Rector at Clongowes Wood,[29] but the Rector
knew better perhaps than the Fenian the value of visits by the
aristocracy. The prestige of the college depended on more than its
academic standards, though these were not to be neglected.

The prestige of Clongowes Wood had already in the eighties extended well beyond the shores of Ireland. Perhaps the Fenian
might be mollified to learn that, for the first time in over a thousand years, students from France, Spain, and Portugal were again
attending an Irish school conducted by native Irish clerics.[30] No
one of course would compare it, either in learning or influence,
with any of the great monastic foundations of the past. Nor did
foreign students come in such numbers as to create around Clongowes a truly international or cosmopolitan atmosphere. But that
they came at all was another index of the Jesuits' success: Clongowes had tone. There was something surely to be proud of in
that.

John Stanislaus Joyce, residing in 1888 at No. 1 Martello Terrace, Bray, was perhaps more proud of it than most. The Jesuits
were the lads for him—men of the world, people of influence,
who could be of service to a chap in after years. Their college
down in Kildare was for gentlemen and the sons of gentlemen.
His oldest boy, James, was not quite of school age, but the Jesuits
were an accommodating lot. The rector there, Conmee, was as
fine and gracious a man as you'd want to meet. He'd see to it.

And it gratified John Stanislaus to think that his son, under
the guidance of the clever and influential Jesuit Fathers at Clon-

[29] "Analecta Cluenensia," *The Clongownian*, 1954, p. 68. Such visits were apparently not unusual at the college. The one mentioned here occurred on October
17, 1878. *The Clongownian* reprinted the item from an old house journal kept
by the Father Minister at Clongowes Wood.

[30] Students came to the school from places even more distant than the Continent.
Consulting the school lists given by Corcoran (*Clongowes Record*, pp. 165–291),
one finds on the first three pages alone the names of boys from Bilboa, Spain;
from Detroit, Michigan; Calcutta; Jamaica; and Melbourne, Australia.

gowes Wood, was to take his first step in life in the company of his social equals. It augured well for the future. The expense was nothing. John Stanislaus Joyce could well afford it—for the time being.

II

Joyce's age at the time may explain the arrangement, worked out between John Stanislaus Joyce and Father Conmee, whereby the boy attended Clongowes at the reduced rate of £25 per annum, "to include everything." [31] The ordinary pension was "Forty Guineas a year, payable half-yearly in advance, on the first of September and the first of February," [32] but this amount was exclusive of incidental expenses which came to about another five guineas a year. This was quite a respectable sum—at the time considerably more respectable than it is today—to invest in the education of a small boy. Not many years later it would have been prohibitive for a man in John Stanislaus's circumstances. Indeed, it soon enough became so. The arrangement remained in force during the first two years of Joyce's attendance at Clongowes. However, at the beginning of his third and last full year, the reduced rate was departed from and the elder Joyce paid the full pension by cheques of £23/17/0 on October 20, 1890, and £25/17/9 on February 25, 1891. [33] These were the last monies the Jesuits were to receive from John Stanislaus. As the expense of educating his eldest son increased, his personal fortunes began to decline. Ten years later, when the Jesuits graduated James Joyce from University College, Dublin, his father's fortunes were all talk and memories.

Joyce was the youngest and, there is little doubt, the smallest boy at Clongowes Wood at the beginning of the school year in

[31] Students' Ledger H 1886–1907, folio 132.   [32] *Prospectus,* Section V.
[33] Students' Ledger H 1886–1907, folio 132.

1888. If the college had been conducted along the lines of an English public school, his age and size could have been a serious disadvantage. William Butler Yeats, who had the added misfortune of being an Irish boy in an English school, has told of the grief and rage and general harassment he endured at the Godolphin School in Hammersmith.[34] It is difficult, and cruelly amusing, to imagine Willie Yeats, as frail and sensitive a child as young Joyce, trying to learn how to box in order to protect himself from the constant bullying of older boys. But it was necessary, Yeats claimed, if he was physically to endure the "fagging" which his father contemptuously referred to as "an English absurdity."[35] There was no such absurdity at Clongowes Wood. "To prevent bullying and for the better formation of character," Clongownians were grouped in three divisions, each with its own grounds, playrooms, and libraries, all perfectly distinct.[36] And within these separate and distinct domains the students' activities were under the constant supervision of one or more Jesuit prefects. If the cruelties of boyhood, so ubiquitous and often so sly, were not wholly eliminated by these precautions, they were nevertheless reduced to a minimum. The Irish Jesuits took seriously their claim and obligation to educate Christian gentlemen. How well they were succeeding may be indicated by the testimony of the Duke of Leinster when examined by a Committee of the House of Lords on the Catholic Question in Ireland. Referring to Clongowes, he remarked: "It is the most curious establishment I ever saw," then added, apparently as much to his own astonishment as to that of his fellow-peers: *"as the boys are well brought up!"* [37]

But in September, 1888, even the boys in the third or lowest line at Clongowes were, most of them, four or five years older

---

[34] "Reveries over Childhood and Youth," in *The Autobiography of William Butler Yeats*, p. 22.
[35] *Ibid.*, p. 23. [36] *Prospectus*, Section I.
[37] Corcoran, *Clongowes Record*, p. 111.

than Joyce. The Jesuits, therefore, prudently arranged that his contact with these older, bigger boys be limited. He did not live among them in the dormitories, but was assigned a room in the infirmary—"quite distinct from the rest of the college buildings" [38] —where a nurse, Nanny Galvin, doubling as a governess, took him in charge. Miss Galvin was not a trained nurse, but she is reported to have been fully experienced in looking after the ordinary ailments and mishaps of boyhood.[39] It was she who, during Joyce's first two years at Clongowes, seems to have acted *in loco parentis*. She did so, however, under the direct supervision of the Jesuit laybrother, John Hanly, S.J., official infirmarian.

Brother Hanly is the first Jesuit whom young Joyce could and presumably did come to know at all intimately. Brother Michael, his counterpart in the *Portrait,* is there described as a tall man— "He had a long back like the back of a tram horse"—with "reddish hair mixed with grey and a queer look." To young Dedalus, down that morning with an attack of the "collywobbles," everything looked queer, even the sunlight. But what was queer about Brother Michael was "that he would always be a brother" and "that you could not call him sir because he was a brother and had a different kind of look." Still he was "very decent," passing along to the boys in the infirmary news out of the paper about sports and politics. And in Stephen's dream it is, significantly, Brother Michael's sorrowing face and his loud voice of mourning that is heard telling the death of Parnell (P 20-21, 25).

Technically, at this point in the novel Stephen's dream pre-

[38] *Prospectus,* Section I.

[39] Father P. A. Baggot, S.J., present rector at Clongowes, supplied this information about Nanny Galvin and Joyce's residence in the infirmary in his letter to me on August 19, 1954. Baggot gives as his authority Father George Redington Roche, S.J., "who was a boy at Clongowes from 1883 to 1889 . . . and during his life as a Jesuit spent very many years at the school, being Higher Line prefect, Rector (1927–1933), as well as having a very intimate knowledge of the traditions of the College and of its past pupils."

pares the ground for the heart-rending argument over Parnell in the following episode. The implication is that Brother Michael was a Parnellite, one with Mr. Casey and Mr. Dedalus, and opposed to the full-blown clericalism of Dante. During the latter's bitter defense of priestly authority, young Stephen, in so far as he understood at all the issues at stake, could only have associated that authority with the priests and prefects at Clongowes. These gentlemen, politically impossible by tradition, represented the only such authority the boy had yet known. But Brother Michael was not like the priests and the prefects: he was not called "sir," and compassion not authority, sorrow not severity, surround his image in Stephen's troubled dream. He was a representative of that people, a race of servants, for whom Parnell had struggled and whom he might have saved had he not been betrayed by their "betters." This, too, is a reason why Brother Michael had for Stephen "a different kind of look."

His original, Brother John Hanly, was in real life a tall rugged man in his middle fifties who, before becoming a Jesuit, had been a pharmaceutical chemist.[40] At the time that Joyce came under his care he had already served the order as a lay brother for more than thirty years.[41] Like all Jesuit brothers (or temporal coadjutors, as their grade is designated in the order) he had, after entering the novitiate, received no special training. He and his fellows constitute a sort of Jesuit proletariat, and, though there would be small likelihood of any of them desiring it, they are neither encouraged nor afforded much opportunity to cultivate an intellectual life. But though they are servants, they are not menials. Guarded by their peculiar vocations from the temptations of pride, ambition, and sense of power, which are not unknown in higher circles of Jesuitdom, these humble men frequently serve their order more usefully than many of the priests and scholastics who pass as their social and intellectual superiors.

[40] Letter from Father Baggot, August 19, 1954.   [41] *Catalogus S.J.*, 1888.

Brother Hanly appears to have been such a man. In addition to his duties as infirmarian, there were a dozen other chores he might be expected to perform around Clongowes: those of porter, coachman, general handyman, and supervisor of the workmen and laborers employed on the college grounds. But the only other office, besides infirmarian, to which he was assigned in the Jesuit *catalogus* was that of sacristan. In this capacity, too, in so far as he was responsible for the corps of Clongownian altarboys, he would have had young Joyce in charge. The boy, during his first years at Clongowes, was probably considered too young to assist the priest at mass; there is no evidence that he ever did so either then or later at Belvedere. But it is quite certain that, like Stephen Dedalus, he often served as boat-bearer at Benediction of the Blessed Sacrament. As the smallest boy in the school he would have been Brother Hanly's natural choice for this minor honor, for it was an office that always devolves on tiny fellows, just as that of thurifer goes to the tall spare boys. The tall boy in this instance was George Redington Roche, later ordained a Jesuit, and later still appointed rector of Clongowes, who was in his last year at the college when Joyce was in his first. Many years later, when Joyce's notoriety had penetrated even the solemn dullness of Jesuit recreation rooms, Father Roche might add a fillip to the conversation by recalling that Joyce and he, the short and the long of it, boat and thurifer, had been altarboys together back in Clongowes Wood.[42]

III

Of the other Jesuits who are mentioned in the *Portrait,* only one, besides Father Conmee, appears under his own name. This

[42] Father R. P. Roche, S.J., rector of Belvedere College in Dublin, supplied this information about his namesake and young Joyce in an interview during August, 1954. An obituary and "an appreciation" of Father George Roche appeared in *The Clongownian,* 1954, but contained, not unexpectedly, no mention of James Joyce.

is Mr. Gleeson—William Gleeson, S.J.—a scholastic who, while a member of the Jesuit community at Clongowes Wood, was preparing for his matriculation examinations at the Royal University.[43] The description given of him is curious:

> But Mr. Gleeson had round shiny cuffs and clean white wrists and fattish white hands and the nails of them were long and pointed. Perhaps he pared them too like Lady Boyle. But they were terribly long and pointed nails. So long and cruel they were though the white fattish hands were not cruel but gentle. And though he trembled with cold and fright to think of the cruel long nails and of the high whistling sound of the cane and of the chill you felt at the end of your shirt when you undressed yourself yet he felt a feeling of queer quiet pleasure inside him to think of the white fattish hands, clean and strong and gentle. And he thought of what Cecil Thunder had said; that Mr. Gleeson would not flog Corrigan hard. And Fleming had said he would not because it was best of his play not to. But that was not why. [P 48]

The innocence of this is sinister, and sinister perhaps because ambiguous. At first reading the suggestion of effeminacy, and of something worse—a hint of perversion—seems inescapable. But there is more to it than that. The image of Gleeson's hands pick up and relate two conflicting impressions already made on Stephen's slowly emerging consciousness. The cruel pointed nails are the talons of those eagles, symbols of a Roman authority, whom Dante, defender of clerical authority, had threatened would come and pull out his eyes if Stephen did not apologize (P 2).[44] They are the instruments of a justice that is swift, sharp, and implacable. But the cruelty of the nails is mitigated by the clean strength and gentleness of the hands. They are soft and white like those of the little girl in Bray.

[43] *Catalogus S.J.*, 1888.
[44] These eagles, instruments of the "Allhighest," reappear—as what does not?—in *Finnegans Wake*, p. 80.

Eileen had long white hands. One evening when playing tig she had put her hands over his eyes: long and white and thin and cold and soft. That was ivory: a cold white thing. That was the meaning of *Tower of Ivory*.   [P 36]

This sudden association of Eileen's white hands with the Mother of God, who under another title in the same litany is also the Mother of Mercy, provides Stephen with an insight into a quite different aspect of religious authority. Though it is blinding in the obedience it elicits, it is also merciful and meaningful, an imaginative influence in the hearts of her children.[45] Mr. Gleeson represents both aspects of authority at once. As justice he is masculine and fear-inspiring, his nails pointed and cruel; as mercy he is feminine and gentle, his hands white and soft. He will flog Corrigan, but he will not flog him hard. Because it was best of his play not to? The passage ends on a note that sustains the ambiguity: "that was not why."

There was nothing ambiguous about the real-life Mr. Gleeson. He was an athlete who "excelled in all games but especially in cricket." [46] Young Joyce must often have watched him and Jimmy Magee (mentioned in the *Portrait,* p. 9), captain of the team in 1891-92, perform brilliantly at the wicket, on one occasion setting up a score of 212 which remained a record for in-matches. This talent alone was enough to make Gleeson a hero to young Clongownians. They nicknamed him "Ormonde" after the great Jacobite champion of Stuart times, and champion he was. A year or so after Joyce left the college, in June, 1893, "Ormonde," then prefect of the third line, turned in the most

[45] See Joyce's *Epiphanies,* ed. by O. A. Silverman, p. 15. The subject of the epiphany to which reference is made here is the Blessed Virgin. The full context of the reference is: "She comes from her ancient seat to visit the least of her children, mother most venerable, as though he had never been alien to her. She knows the inmost heart; therefore she is gentle, nothing exacting; saying, I am susceptible of change, an imaginative influence in the hearts of my children."

[46] "Analecta Cluenensia," *The Clongownian,* 1953, p. 76.

memorable performance of his career. The occasion was an out-match with British officers from the Curragh, Clongowes' neighbors in Kildare. The impression made upon another young Clongownian at that time reads somewhat differently from that of Stephen Dedalus, shivering pleasurably at the thought of Mr. Gleeson's fattish white hands.

We third Liners knew that Mr. Gleeson was the best cricketer in Ireland! We knew that he was on the "Gentlemen of Ireland," or that if he was not, it was simply due to the fact that he was a Jesuit [47]. . . . The match began with a calamity! In the very first over, our captain was out, l.b.w. for zero! Then, mid the encouraging cheers from the whole House, Mr. Gleeson walked calmly to the wicket. . . . With varied, brilliant strokes, he scattered the field in all directions. The score mounted rapidly. Bowlers were changed, but all in vain. We were victorious. When stumps were drawn at 5:15, the House swept across the pitch, wildly cheering Mr. Gleeson and his fellow-batsman, as they moved to the marquee. We had three or four wickets to fall, and Mr. Gleeson was 120 not out. What a victory! What a hero! [48]

One wonders why Joyce chose, and identified by name, William Gleeson, S.J., for the dubious, even if symbolic, role that he briefly plays in the *Portrait*. Gleeson had not been either his master or prefect at Clongowes. His prefect, at least on "walking-out" days, was Mr. Andrew Macardle, S.J., and during Joyce's time at the school the masters of the two lowest grades, rudiments and elements, were respectively Mr. James Jeffcoat, S.J., and Father William Power, S.J.[49]

Jeffcoat, a young scholastic barely turned twenty-two, was at the start of the Michaelmas term in 1888 beginning his first year of regency at Clongowes. When he first begins to teach, a Jesuit's patience and idealism are, like those of most new teachers, un-

---

[47] *Ibid.* At this point the editor, tongue-in-cheek, interpolates the remark that there is no incompatibility between Jesuit and gentleman. The "Gentlemen of Ireland" are the cricketing equivalents of our "All-Americans" in football.

[48] *Ibid.*, pp. 76–77.   [49] *Catalogus S.J.*, 1888.

tried and untiring. This may explain why Jeffcoat's stand-in in the *Portrait,* Mr. Harford, is described briefly as a master who was "very decent and never got into a wax" (P 48). Father Power —the Father Arnall at Clongowes, but probably not the Arnall who later directs the boys' retreat at Belvedere [50]—after twelve years of teaching small boys at Clongowes Wood, would be quite capable of getting into "dreadful waxes." But that he was also a kindly, understanding man, with a knowledge of a boy's heart and sympathy for his hurt, is indicated by his assignment as confessor to students. He is almost certainly the priest to whom young Joyce confessed in preparation for his First Holy Communion, which he would have received in the spring of 1889 after having reached the canonical "age of reason." In this connection it is perhaps significant that when, in the *Portrait,* Stephen Dedalus for the first time reflects upon the mystery of sin and the sacrament of penance (P 51), it is Father Arnall (Power) who occasions his reflections. The McGlade of the novel, the prefect whom Simon Moonan is accused of sucking up to and who leads Stephen down to the infirmary when he gets the "collywobbles" (P 6, 19–20), is Andrew Macardle, S.J. A young man in his late twenties, seven years a Jesuit, Macardle was possibly Joyce's first Jesuit teacher, in charge of his instruction while the boy was still living in the infirmary and before he was admitted on a regular basis to scheduled courses of instruction.[51] Unfortunately there is no record of these earliest studies of Joyce at Clongowes, but considering his age and circumstances at this time it is not perhaps a very significant gap in knowledge.

These three Jesuits, Jeffcoat, Power, and Macardle, were all more closely associated with young Joyce than was Mr. Gleeson; yet all three are disguised in aliases, and Gleeson is made to appear under his own name. Why? The question might be dismissed as

[50] See below, p. 128.   [51] *Catalogus S.J.,* 1888.

trivial—none of the four is of major interest or importance in the novel—were it not for the fact that the trivial was always interesting and important to Joyce. He had, moreover, an astonishing memory, nor would any serious critic accuse him of being casual or slipshod in designing and executing his effects. He had a reason for identifying Gleeson by name, and the reason would seem to be that, like Conmee who afterwards had a distinguished career as a Jesuit, Gleeson had also, though in a quite different way, made a name for himself. His reputation as an athlete, admittedly an odd sort of distinction for a Jesuit, was not confined to Clongowes Wood. It would at one time have been known and talked about all over Ireland wherever there was the slightest interest in cricket, and presumably in parts of England as well. The British officers whom he had defeated that memorable day in June, 1893, were, one may be sure, as impressed with Gleeson's performance as were the young Clongownians who idolized him for it. It is possible, then, that Joyce was trading on this reputation when he identified Gleeson by name in the *Portrait*. That it would be some years after his completion of the first draft, and years after final publication of the novel, that Irish readers might have the opportunity to read and recognize Gleeson's name, Joyce could not have foreseen.

Joyce had none of the artist-in-the-garret indifference to fame and fortune. Apart from his work, even after that work was widely acclaimed, he took pains to propagandize it further and win a still wider publicity for his current writing.[52] He knew too,

[52] Joyce at one point apparently solicited the aid of so unlikely a person as H. G. Wells. There is a letter from Wells to Joyce (now in the Lockwood Memorial Library of the University of Buffalo), dated November 23, 1928, which begins:

"My dear Joyce: I've been studying you and thinking over you a lot. The outcome is that I don't think I can do anything for the propaganda of your work. I've an enormous respect for your genius etc. . . ." (Published by Stuart Gilbert in *Letters of James Joyce*, pp. 274–75.)

See also the use Joyce made of the *transition* crowd in Paris as reported and

in blunt terms of the market place, the value of jarring his readers into a shock of recognition—or of revulsion—by means of his work. Gleeson's name is only a minor case in point, but it is a significant point. Joyce's effects were calculated, his intentions ulterior, and the results rewarding. The identities of Jeffcoat, Power, and Macardle, unlighted by the dimmest glow of fame, might be decently draped in convenient aliases. It did not matter one way or the other.

Father James Daly, S.J., the Father Dolan of the *Portrait*, was similarly disguised. He had come to Clongowes the year before Joyce entered the college, and he was to remain as prefect of studies for the next thirty years.[53] As a Jesuit he seems to have conformed perfectly to that ideal embodied in the Ignatian formula "totus ad laborem." He devoted himself single-mindedly to the task of so raising the academic standards of the college that it would be known throughout Ireland as something more than the country's most fashionable school. In this he very largely succeeded. Two years after his arrival Clongowes Wood College "went to the top of the list, and during the following score of years and more, if not absolutely first, it was always well within the very best group of Irish schools judged by the public examination records."[54] To his reorganization of the Clongowes curriculum Father Daly brought the experience gained as prefect of studies in two other Jesuit schools, Belvedere College, Dublin, and Crescent College, Limerick.[55] These were day schools, and socially not in the same class as Clongowes. But Father Daly, in his process of revitalizing the academic life of the college, would have taken small note of social distinctions. He was interested in scholarship, and scholarship is what he produced. The sons of

---

interpreted by Kenner in *Dublin's Joyce*, pp. 360–61. For other examples of Joyce's earliest efforts to publicize his own work, see Tindall's edition of *Chamber Music*, p. 20 and note.

[53] Corcoran, *Clongowes Record*, p. 149.   [54] *Ibid.*, p. 151.

[55] *Ibid.*, p. 149.

gentlemen were expected to study just as hard and as long as the sons of shopkeepers and artisans. The record indicates that they did.

Though Father Daly's success was real, it was not of a kind to bring him, even had he desired it, any appreciable fame. Fame, anyhow, is not the usual lot of schoolmasters. Their success is often in proportion to their severity, and this generally wins them little more than brief notoriety in an ephemeral community of schoolboys. Father Daly's name might still be forgotten had not Herbert Gorman chosen to identify him—the only Jesuit at Clongowes whom he does identify—as a clerical "martinet" and the persecutor of young James Joyce.[56] There would be little point in objecting to the epithet, which is gratuitous, but a reasonable doubt may be cast on the report of persecution. The account of the unwarranted punishment meted out to Stephen Dedalus (P 51–55) may possibly have some basis in Joyce's own experience at Clongowes. However, it would be a mistake to read this passage in the *Portrait* as a simple transcript of an actual event. There is at present no evidence either to prove or to disprove it. But it is worth pointing out that in the organization of a Jesuit school, the disciplining of students, especially when it is corporal discipline, is specifically excluded from the provinces of the prefect of studies. Usually some person not a master is designated for this unpleasant duty.[57] From the internal evidence of the *Portrait* itself,[58] it would seem that the man so designated during Joyce's time at Clongowes was none other than William Gleeson, S.J. This does not of course exclude the possibility that Father Daly may on occasion have taken matters into his own hands.

[56] Gorman, *James Joyce*, pp. 29, 33–34.

[57] Fitzpatrick, *St. Ignatius*, pp. 187, 206, 242.

[58] The passage describing Gleeson quoted earlier. At the time, Gleeson was not a master at Clongowes; while assigned to the Jesuit community there he was preparing for his matriculation examinations at the Royal University.

There was, finally, no reason, as there was with Conmee and Gleeson, for Joyce to identify Daly by name. As a small boy, first living in the infirmary, and then a member of the lowest line in the school, his contacts with the prefect of studies must have been few indeed. Even Daly's reorganization of the program of studies, carried out chiefly in the higher lines, would not have affected Joyce in any marked degree. Daly was only another name, remembered perhaps by a few hundred schoolboys, forgotten by hundreds of others; there was no special reason why anyone in Ireland or elsewhere should remember it. But "Dolan: it was like the name of a woman who washed clothes" (P 60).

IV

Thomas Francis Meagher, reminiscing on his schooldays at Clongowes Wood, had little good to say about the course of studies. The Jesuits, he wrote,

talked to us about Mount Olympus and the Vale of Tempe; they birched us into a flippant acquaintance with the disreputable gods and goddesses of the golden and heroic ages. They entangled us in Euclid; turned our brains with the terrestrial globe; chilled our blood in dizzy excursions through the Milky Way; paralysed our Lilliputian loins with the saggy spoils of Hercules, bewildered us with the Battle of the Frogs and Mice, pitched us precipitately into England, amongst the impetuous Normans and stupid Saxons; gave us a look, through an interminable telescope, at what was doing in the New World; but, as far as Ireland was concerned, they left us like blind and crippled children, in the dark.[59]

Joyce left no such partisan or breathless memoir of his days in the classrooms of Clongowes. He left no memoir whatever. It should be clear by now that the first chapter of the *Portrait* is not a record of actual events recollected in maturity; it is the imaginative recording of a series of immediate impressions made

[59] "Clongowes Wood," p. 271.

on the sensibility of a small boy—a boy who was to develop into a quite different kind of person from the recorder of those impressions. But had Joyce given another and more factual account of his days at Clongowes, it is doubtful that it would have been much like Meagher's either in tone or in content. Not in tone because Meagher's bias, that of a romantic Irish revolutionary relishing what he called "magnificent memories . . . of the poor old land," [60] was not that of the adult Joyce. Not in content because Joyce was not at the college long enough to be exposed to the more "disreputable" classics or become entangled in the tougher, broader nets of history and mathematics. What he did not study, is clear enough. What he did study, there is now no way of knowing fully or in detail.

But in the absence of such records as, for example, exist for his years at Belvedere, it is still possible to form a general idea of what was expected of young Joyce in the Clongowes classrooms. Since the education of any small boy barely out of his abecedarian years must be simple and elementary, this general knowledge is perhaps sufficient. Fortunately, there does exist a record, less complete than indicative, of Joyce's early instruction in religion. This instruction was also simple, elementary, catechetical. But information of this sort can do more than satisfy curiosity about the boy; it may add to a comprehension of the man. For religion, especially as emphasized at a school like Clongowes, is likely to affect the will and the imagination of the young more acutely than spelling, sums, or geography.

In September, 1890, at the beginning of his third year, James Joyce was enrolled in Clongowes as a full-fledged student for the first time.[61] This is indicated by the adjustment of the pension

[60] *Ibid.*

[61] The events narrated in the first chapter of the *Portrait*, at least from p. 25 to the end, could only have occurred during and after December, 1891. Parnell died on October 6 of that year, and his death is first mentioned on p. 25. This

paid by John Stanislaus from a reduced to a full rate. The boy
was now a member of the Third Line. For almost two years he
had lived in the infirmary under the care of Nanny Galvin and
the supervision of Brother Hanly. While there he had probably
received his first instruction from Mr. Macardle, and probably,
too, had sat in on lessons in the lowest class. But in these classes
he would not have been expected to perform as responsibly as
the older pupils in the benches around him. Now, however,
removed from the infirmary to a cubicle of his own in the Third
Line dormitory, he attended classes and study-hall regularly and
was as answerable as his fellows for his showing in the weekly
and monthly tests which were part of the school routine.

These tests were in subjects taken by all small boys in Irish
schools at the time: simple sums, spelling, writing, geography,
the rudiments of Latin, and a smattering of history. Stephen
Dedalus had been exposed to all of these.[62] Sums troubled him,
but words were a delight; geography was hard, but history was a
good thing to think back on. In *Doctor Cornwell's Spelling Book*
there were five sentences "like poetry but they were only sentences to learn the spelling from" (P 5). From Richmal Mag-
nall's *Questions* he had learned about famous people in history,
and still more about them from Peter Parley's tales about Greece
and Rome.

One might imagine from Stephen's description of it that the
latter was a single work, but Stephen has lumped together two
separate books: *Peter Parley's Tales about Ancient and Modern
Greece* and *Peter Parley's Tales about Ancient Rome*.[63] And

---

also means that the events of pp. 41–64 of the novel must be assumed as taking
place in 1892. Joyce himself was no longer at Clongowes in 1892, and had
probably left school before December, 1891.

[62] Spelling is referred to on p. 5, sums on p. 7, geography on p. 11, writing on
p. 48, Latin on p. 50, history on p. 58.

[63] The first American editions of these books were: *Peter Parley's Tales about*

these were only two in a long series of such "tales" put together by one of the earliest, most popular, and surely the most indefatigable writer of children's books in America. Samuel Griswold Goodrich, the original Peter Parley, writing for "an audience of boys and girls about ten or twelve years of age," [64] seems to have monopolized the juvenile trade during the middle decades of the nineteenth century. His books, produced at the rate of about one a year, introduced his young audience to every land under the sun and, more than that, to the sun itself and to the moon and the stars and the whole of the known and parts of the unknown universe. His success in the genre, which he did much to create, was extraordinary. His tales were translated into a number of European languages and even into Ojibwa, a curious but distinct index of the extent of their popularity.[65] It is no surprise, then, that young Dedalus, and young Joyce, too, should have been familiar with Peter Parley in the seclusion of Kildare.

It may have been on Parley's imaginative excursion into ancient Greece that James Joyce first heard of the man called Ulysses.[66] It was certainly in Parley, and not in the tough texts which Meagher struggled through, that he first encountered the gods,

---

Ancient and Modern Greece, Richardson, Lord, and Holbrook, Boston, 1832; *Peter Parley's Tales about Ancient Rome,* Carter Hendee, and Co., Boston, 1833. Dr. James Cornwell was the editor, alone and in collaboration, of an "educational series" for young people.

[64] Preface, *Peter Parley's Tales about Ancient Rome,* p. 3. This preface is identical with that to his book on Greece, except for a charmingly candid admission in a note attached: "It is perhaps proper to say that a part of this volume has been written by a friend, in the absence of the author, on account of ill health."

[65] *Abinoji Aki Tibajimouin* (A geography for beginners), 1840. Some others of Goodrich's—or Parley's—astonishing titles are: *Peter Parley's Tales about the Sun, Moon, and Stars,* 1845; *A Glance at Philosophy, Mental, Moral, and Social,* 1849; and—one should expect this—*Peter Parley's Universal History,* 1853.

[66] Goodrich mentions him only passingly in retelling the story of Troy, pp. 55–58. He makes no mention of the later adventurer of the *Odyssey.*

goddesses, and heroes of a vanished golden age. A reader of *Ulysses,* delighted or exasperated, may be struck by a passage in Peter Parley's preface to his *Tales about Ancient Rome:*

If in talking of a classical age, I have sometimes used colloquial or commonplace terms; if I have illustrated the adventures of Hercules and the Nemean Lion by a reference to Putnam and the Wolf; if I have brought Athens and Sparta into homely comparison with our own republic, and subjected even Jupiter to the test of our yankee morality; I beg the critical reader to consider two things: first, who I am, and second, who I am talking to.[67]

May not this be a dim and distant adumbration of the principle and process whereby ancient Ithaca and its wandering king were to come to life again—more in homely identity than in "homely comparison"—in modern Dublin and its meandering canvasser of public advertisements? However that may be, it is certain that in the autumn of 1890 James Joyce was not entertaining any such strange thoughts. Ulysses was no more than a name to the boy, and perhaps only a name he found difficult to spell.

There is no explicit mention in the *Portrait* of Stephen's early training in religious knowledge, but this to the Jesuits was the most important subject of all. Religion was the hub around which the rest of the curriculum turned; it was literally the *raison d'être* of the whole Jesuit system of education. No master at Clongowes doubted this for a moment; his "Masters' Rules," based on the *Ratio Studiorum* of 1599, made more than plain what was expected of him and what he might expect of his students in the matter of religious instruction. The preamble and opening section of these rules are unequivocal:

[67] Pages 3–4. The reader of *Finnegans Wake* may remark the following from the same brief preface: "It is only necessary for me to add, that I have occasionally taken a sentence, or passage from other writers, without marking it in quotations. If therefore the reader discover anything in the volume which does not suit my humble quill, I beg them to give Goldsmith or Gillies credit for it."

A Master in the Society of Jesus is a person to whom Jesus Christ has entrusted a number of children, purchased with His own Precious Blood, not merely for the purpose of being taught secular knowledge, but above all for the purpose of being made good Christians.

I. Religious instruction.

Therefore, the principal and first duty of a master, a duty of the strictest and gravest obligation, to which all others are subordinate, is to instruct his scholars in the doctrine and morality of our holy religion; to teach them to avoid and have a horror of vice; to make them know, love, and practise piety and virtue. As children pay but little heed to the instruction of those whom they do not respect, a master must in his own person be an example of the virtue and piety which he teaches, actuated by reason and justice, free from caprice, levity, and passion; polite, honourable, impartial; zealous in the performance of a duty; in a word, what the Society and his pupils expect from him.

But example alone is not sufficient. He will consider it a conscientious obligation faithfully to employ in the religious instruction of his class the whole time appointed for that purpose, never permitting any part of that sacred time to be otherwise occupied.

He will exact from all a correct knowledge of the Catechism; he will explain its meaning, and give practical instructions, particularly on the Sacrament of Penance and on the Commandments; teaching them how to assist at Mass with profit, and to perform the other duties of Religion, adding such words of exhortation as are suited to their age and needs.

He will answer such difficulties as may be seriously and for the sake of getting instruction proposed to him, bearing, however, in mind that it is dangerous to suggest objections to young persons, or to encourage them to seek for difficulties, in matters of faith. In order to fulfill so important a duty, he will carefully propose the matter for his Catechetical Instruction, consulting works of undoubted authority, as the Catechism of the Council of Trent, never advancing any doctrine of which he is not certain, and choosing his examples from the Sacred Scriptures, the Lives of the Saints, and writers of reputation.

.   .   .   .   .   .

In obedience to the *Ratio Studiorum,* masters will take care to inculcate piety and virtue in their conversations with their scholars. During class, they will seek occasions (having carefully prepared the matter of all observations) to suggest useful reflections, to extol virtue, to condemn vice and render it odious, to point out the excellence of Christianity, the folly of paganism and unbelief. They will frequently recommend their scholars to God and to His Blessed Mother, and always recite the appointed prayers both before and after class.[68]

Even when allowance has been made for the official piety and devotional rhetoric of these directions, the program they set forth is formidable as the principles on which it is based were pervasive. It was equally formidable in practise. In December, 1890, just before leaving college for their Christmas vacation, Joyce and his classmates in the Lower Line faced a lengthy examination in religious knowledge. The matter of this examination comprised the first fourteen chapters of the *Maynooth Catechism,* which were to be learned verbatim, one hundred and fifty pages of Bible history (Old Testament), and half as many pages again of Deharbe's *Catechism.*[69] The following term, in preparation for the Easter vacation, the boys continued their study of these three texts, adding the next sixteen lessons in the *Maynooth Cate-chism,* another hundred and fifty pages of Bible history, and the following seventy-five pages of Deharbe. It would seem, then, that of all the subjects studied by Joyce at Clongowes Wood none had so wide a scope or so intense a focus as that in religious knowledge. Such a course may not have produced—it was not intended to produce—a flock of learned little theologians; but the Jesuits, with an instinct for psychology quite as true as their orthodoxy in

[68] Quoted in Corcoran, *Clongowes Record,* pp. 81–82. This passage is based on "Rules Common to the Professors of the Lower Classes" of the 1599 *Ratio Studiorum,* which are reproduced in translation by Fitzpatrick, *St. Ignatius,* pp. 195–208.

[69] From a note attached to the Clongowes *Prospectus,* 1886.

theology, had now injected their young flock with a theological bias—or belief—from which few of them, however far they might wander from the piously cropped pastures of their boyhood, would ever recover. James Joyce seems not to have been one of that few.

The horizons of boyhood are limited. The boy returning to college in January, 1891, could not have foreseen that before the calendar year was out he would be leaving Clongowes Wood for the last time. He was still a small boy, still shy in company, reserved with his schoolfellows, obedient and dutiful with his masters. A slight curve of scar on his chin, left there by a mongrel dog nearly as big as he when he was only five, was still visible.[70] Years later, when his face would be familiar to the large world beyond Clongowes, that scar would still persist. But by then he would have grown a beard to hide it, a light but adequate beard, like that of a thoughtful but unsorrowing Christ. Now he was just turned nine years of age and, scar or no scar, was quite undistinguishable from the rest of the schoolboys around him.

They were a good set of fellows. Their names are set like unobtrusive stones through the first chapter of the *Portrait,* the real names of real boys—Rody Kickham, Cecil Thunder, Jack Lawton, Jimmy Magee, and the rest. But of the sixteen boys who appear or are mentioned in this chapter, the names of four are pure invention, and these are the only boys who are shown in a really unflattering light: Simon Moonan is a "suck," Athy an obnoxious goldbrick, Tusker Boyle a sissy, and Corrigan the perpetrator of a scandalous and mysterious offense bordering on sacrilege. Two other actual Clongownians, Wells and Nasty Roche, are not portrayed as the most pleasant sort of fellows, but

---

[70] "Portrait of James Joyce," edited by W. R. Rodgers, produced by Maurice Brown, broadcast by the British Broadcasting Commission, Third Program, February 13 and 17, March 22, 1950. Hereafter cited as BBC.

neither can the identity of either be established with complete certainty. Roche, a trifling snob, can be the name of any of four boys who were in school at the same time as Joyce, three of them having entered in the same year. There were two boys by the name of Wells, Charles Wells and H. Wells, who, though they also entered Clongowes in 1888, left in 1890, a year before the events narrated in the *Portrait* are supposed to have occurred. Furthermore, the Wells of the novel, something of a bully, has the decency later to apologize to Stephen for elbowing him into the ditch, and though his decency is undoubtedly motivated by fear, it is perhaps enough to redeem him in his author's eyes and in those of the reader. In the light of all this it seems not too much to claim that in writing, or in revising, the first chapter of the *Portrait* Joyce remained loyal to the ties which bound him, if only in memory, to Clongowes Wood.[71]

These were the boys with whom he shared his earliest experiences in and out of the classroom. He was only nine years old, but he had known most of these fellows for almost a third of his life. He was a good student, but this year, despite his natural shyness, he was to share in more of their outside activities. Not sports of course—he was never to be much at that—but extracurricular activities. Third Liners were not eligible for the debating society, or the sodality, or any of the other clubs at Clongowes except dramatics. Dramatics, then, it must be for young Joyce. He played his first and only role on the Clongowes stage during the Easter holidays of 1891.

It was not a spectacular role. There was an old custom at the college of presenting, on certain holidays, a program of homemade entertainments, half musical, half dramatic. The dramatic portion of these programs was usually outrageously farcical, to

---

[71] The names of the boys mentioned here may be checked on the school lists provided by Corcoran in *Clongowes Record*, pp. 165–297.

judge by the titles of some of them: *Box and Cox, Aladdin and the Wonderful Scamp,* and so on. Even when the intention was more serious, the performance was likely to take a spontaneous twist into schoolboy slapstick. On one such occasion the leading actor, an adolescent Hamlet, had to die on stage. He died so well that he was encored twice, but he "then struck and would not die any more for anyone." [72] Joyce, with his gift for mimicry and improvisation, might be expected to take naturally and happily to this sort of thing, and so he did. He was not a featured player in the Easter production of *Aladdin,* but, from a Jesuit's point of view, looking backwards, there is surely an element of irony and perhaps of prophecy in the minor role that he did play, that of an "imp." [73]

The more serious part of these programs may have stimulated Joyce in quite another way. For two years he had sat with the other Third Liners and been entertained by older Clongownians; there were piano solos and duets, quartets and choruses of trained, or at least well directed, young voices. It is possible that he experienced only small-boy boredom at these affairs, but it is more probable that he felt a small boy's admiration and envy of his elders and a desire to emulate them. The selections included many of the old favorites—"Sweet and Low," "Kathleen Mavourneen," and the rest—but Joyce also listened to Rummell's variations on *Don Giovanni,* Oesten's fantasia on *Martha,* and Althaus's on

[72] "Analecta Cluenensia," *The Clongownian,* 1953, p. 75.

[73] A scrapbook in the rector's office at Clongowes Wood contains programs of many of their entertainments. During Joyce's time there are programs for St. Stanislaus Day, 1899; Shrovetide, 1890; St. Patrick's Day, 1891, and Easter, 1891. The Shrovetide program and part of that for Easter, 1891, are reprinted in the Appendix. It is interesting to note the name "Earwig" in the first of these. Is it possible that much of Joyce's fun with words is the fun of a boy at Clongowes Wood? Finally, the burlesque program for Easter, 1891, may be distantly, very distantly, echoed by Mulligan's obscene program for "a national immorality in three orgasms" (214).

Il Trovatore.[74] It may not have been very grand opera, but it was the boy's first introduction to an art which, after literature, was to be the source of his richest and most constant satisfaction. For, whatever the quality of these schoolboy performances, they seem to have struck a responsive chord in young Joyce. At the beginning of his third year he started taking his first lessons in piano.[75]

The lessons were not to continue for long, not much longer than the end of the year. In the spring of 1891 the boy was taken ill, and his illness was serious enough to require more than the amateur nursing skills of Nanny Galvin. A physician was called in from outside, and this gentleman's fee—3/6, presumably paid by the Jesuits at the time—was duly included in the bill sent to John Stanislaus on September 1 of the same year. This was the last bill the Jesuits submitted to Mr. Joyce. His son seems to have returned to Clongowes that autumn, but he could not have remained in school for more than a few weeks. If he had, one would expect that the Jesuit procurator would have amended the September 1 bill to include such charges as might have accrued in the interval. There is no evidence of any such revision. James Joyce was withdrawn from Clongowes Wood College some time before Christmas, 1891, either because of a recurrence of the illness he suffered during the spring, or because his father's fortunes took a decided turn for the worse, or for both of these reasons combined.

Ten years later, on April 22, 1901, a conscientious procurator at Clongowes sent another copy of the September 1, 1891, bill to John Stanislaus Joyce at the Collector General's Office, 43 Fleet Street, Dublin. It was returned by the post office. Two days later

[74] *Ibid*.

[75] Students' Ledger H 1886–1907, entry for February 1, 1891; "Music 1/6/3 Piano 2/6 Pieces 4/"; for September 1, 1891: "Music 1/6/3 P 5/." These "extras," since they were never charged in advance, were incurred in the half-years beginning September, 1890, and February, 1891.

he sent it out again to the Martello Terrace address in Bray. It was again returned.[76] The bill remains unpaid to this day.

V

More important than any known fact about Joyce between his sixth and tenth year is the general atmosphere, social and religious, in which he spent the better part of those years. The influence of his home may be equally important, but less is known about his homelife than about his schooldays,[77] and he was besides "in exile" from his home during most of this time. The last fact may indeed be the most significant of all. Certainly he saw less of his own mother than of his school-mother, Nanny Galvin, and from the Jesuits he would have heard a good deal less about that mother-in-the-flesh than of his Virgin Mother, and Mother Church, and even Mother Society. So, too, the Fathers of the Society of Jesus came to represent, immediately and substantially, paternal authority. To the mind of the boy, these reverend gentlemen, more than John Stanislaus, were now his "father," as the church they husbanded was indeed his "mother"; he was, and doubtless thought himself, their "child," and as a child he relied as completely on the knowledge and authority of one as on the

[76] *Ibid*. The final entry in the ledger under Joyce's name reads:
Sept 1   HYP 21/0/0 W 2/2/0 Lib 10/ Bks 10/6 H 2/   24/4/6
         Music 2/12/6 P 5/ Med Att 3/6 H Shoes 5/   3/6/0

                                                     27/10/6

Penciled beneath the entry is this note:
      "Letter to Dublin (cir) 22/4/01
         "   to Bray 24/4/01
      Both returned by Postoffice"

[77] In *My Brother's Keeper* Stanislaus Joyce supplies an intimate but scattered account of the Joyce household. This account is more valuable for an understanding of James's adolescence and early manhood than it is for an appreciation of the period with which I am concerned here, about which ·Stanislaus has surprisingly little to say. But perhaps it is not so surprising when one reflects that Stanislaus, all but four years younger than his brother, was only six years old when James left Clongowes.

understanding and compassion of the other. Such modes of thought and feeling, impressed thus early on a nature as sensitive and responsive as Joyce's and continuing to impress him with an ineradicable sense of spiritual sonship,[78] may possibly illuminate certain significant aspects of the man's later life and work.

Joyce was not the first nor the only modern writer to concern himself with the maddening and sometimes murderous relationship of son and father: Dostoyevsky, Butler, Gosse, and, in a different manner, Synge and Yeats had all at one time or another occupied themselves with the same theme. Yet no modern writer, with the exception of Samuel Butler, has betrayed in his work such obvious and unmitigated resentment of the father. Today, after the appearance of Stanislaus Joyce's posthumous memoir of his brother, no one can longer believe that the Stephen-Simon Dedalus relationship reflects in any way, personally or symbolically, the relationship between James and John Stanislaus Joyce.[79] Nevertheless, it is possible that Joyce's preoccupation

[78] It may be helpful in this connection to recall a part of Stephen Dedalus's discourse on Hamlet (U 204–5): "Fatherhood, in the sense of conscious begetting, is unknown to man. It is a mystical estate, an apostolic succession, from only begetter to only begotten. On that mystery and not on the madonna which the cunning Italian intellect flung to the mob of Europe the church is founded and founded irremoveably because founded, like the world, macro- and microcosm, upon the void. Upon incertitude, upon unlikelihood. *Amor matris,* subjective and objective genitive, may be the only true thing in life. Paternity may be a legal fiction. Who is the father of any son that any son should love him or he any son?"

[79] *My Brother's Keeper,* see esp. pp. 237–39: "I should rather say that every man who has known the torment of thought attaches himself spiritually to one or the other of his parents, when he has left youth behind him and attained maturity, and that in the case of an author the elective affinity strongly influences his artistic production. . . . The two dominant passions of my brother's life were to be love of father and of fatherland. . . . Both passions stemmed, I believe, from his ancient love of God, and were already at that time spreading tough roots underground in a most unpropitious climate: love of his country, or rather of his city, that was to reject him and his work; love of his father, who was like a mill-stone round his neck. The roots of feeling in some men sink all the deeper for the difficulties that surround and frustrate them; and I wonder

with the theme of paternity may have its source in a different kind of personal experience, which in his work is given symbolic representation. It is possible, I say, in the light of Joyce's early and easy acceptance of spiritual sonship, to believe that when he later broke with Catholicism (a break far less dramatic, less histrionic, than that of Dedalus), he was rejecting the authoritarian father who, like the clergy—Jesuit or secular—mediating between the laity and a God accessible only through the Church, stands between him and a desiring and desirable mother. This rejection was an intellectual act, however obscurely motivated, by which Joyce cut himself off from the visible church as manifest in the words and works of the priest or spiritual father; but Joyce never completely succeeded, nor does it appear that he ever wished to succeed, in severing those emotional and imaginative ties that bound him to his spiritual mother, the Church invisible. To this extent, at least, the Jesuits never lost their hold on Joyce, paradoxical as their hold on him may now appear.

I say that it is possible to believe all this, not that it is impossible not to believe it. It is not of course offered as a "fact," but some perhaps may accept it as more than a fancy.

It is a fact, however, that the religious atmosphere around Clongowes was inseparable even from its physical surroundings. The medieval castle which housed the college was set in a sufficiently remote corner of Kildare and over the years had been converted by the Jesuits into something very like a rural monastic

---

that people do not see how much higher than the divine love, which is the preacher's theme, is that human passion which can love an unworthy object utterly without return and forgive without waiting to be supplicated." It is apparent from this passage, among others, that Stanislaus's attitude toward his father closely resembles that of Stephen toward Simon Dedalus, nor is this the only point of resemblance between Joyce's "hero" and his younger brother. It is possible that Stanislaus rather than James served as model for some of the less attractive traits of the Dedalus.

retreat. The seasons marked in the woods outside by turning leaf or drift of snow or early bloom of crocus were marked within by the pious observations of Advent and the mild austerities of Lent. During these liturgical seasons there was little change in the daily schedule. The day still began around six in the morning with a visit to the Blessed Sacrament, followed later by the celebration of Mass, and ended around nine in the evening with the school assembled in chapel for night prayers.[80] But during these seasons there was perhaps a "thickening" of the religious atmosphere. The students were urged to more frequent visits to the Blessed Sacrament, and on Fridays there were the Stations of the Cross, and on Sundays Solemn Benediction of the Sacrament. The ordinary daily routine was apparently little different from that "order of the day" observed in the Jesuit novitiate at Tullabeg, which indeed may well have served as a model for that at Clongowes Wood. Even the occasional breaks in this routine, days of special recreation, were religious occasions: saints' feastdays or days of solemn profession of vows by a member of the Jesuit community.

There was, finally, the constant example of the Jesuits themselves. Every teacher knows how easy it is to win the admiration of the young. This is often the greater part of his reward as a teacher. It is also, for the conscientious, a great part of his responsibility. For admiration begets emulation, and the very young out of the depths of their ignorance and insecurity are inevitably drawn, when they are drawn at all, to those ideals of knowledge and maturity which they see—or think they see—embodied in their teachers. The masters at Clongowes, men dedicated to their profession, represented this general idea to Joyce and his fellow students. But as Jesuit masters they represented a still more spe-

[80] For a sample of an earlier and stricter regimen at the college, see Corcoran, *Clongowes Record*, pp. 72–74.

cific ideal—that epitomized in the motto of their Society: *Ad Maiorem Dei Gloriam*—with which they tempted the latent heroism of the boys in their charge.

Boys growing up under such a regimen, confronted daily by the ideals and daily fed upon the precepts and example of their Jesuit masters, naturally—and sometimes supernaturally—develop a highly favorable view of the priestly and celibate life. James Joyce as a boy almost certainly did, and it is not hard to imagine him daydreaming of himself as a Jesuit during his years at Clongowes. He was in a sense already living the life of one. Since every Catholic boy, even those of less rigorous religious backgrounds, at one time or another suffers or rejoices in the illusion that he is called to be a priest, there was nothing unusual in that. And indeed, considering the pressures of the religious atmosphere around Joyce, it would have been more unusual if he had not at one time thought of the priesthood. But though he thought of it, he could not have thought deeply or seriously. He was still far too young and that time of decision was still far off, an eternity away in the perspective possible to a small boy.

This boy, then, must be seen in the religious light of his early Jesuit training, not in the shadow of the public, controversial figure that he later became. It is reported of him that at this time (1891) he wrote his first poem, a set of verses attacking Parnell's betrayer, Timothy Healy, and that his father, at least, thought so highly of it that he had the verses printed by the firm of Alleyn and O'Reilly in the form of a small pamphlet.[81] Though the verses are lost, the fact of their composition is interesting, relating as it does young Joyce to one of the most dramatic events in modern Irish history. But it is less often mentioned that he was at the same time writing a good deal of religious verse which appealed as strongly to the pieties of his mother as "Et Tu, Healy" appealed

[81] Gorman, *James Joyce,* p. 36.

to the political prejudices of his father.[82] None of this religious verse was ever printed, all of it is presumed to have been destroyed; but did it exist, it might prove even more interesting than the Healy item. For the content of these lost verses might successfully measure the depth and extent of the boy's actual religious experience—or what passed for religious experience—more successfully, at any rate, than the Healy verses could possibly reveal a ten-year-old's political experience or passion. One can dismiss a child's politics, but not always his religion; what he learns and what he knows about history and geography is less important to the person he will or will not be than what he feels and has been taught to feel about God and his soul.

No one will exaggerate the influence of these early years on Joyce's work. There is the first chapter of the *Portrait,* about which enough has been said to show that, though it is far from being an accurate record of Joyce's schooldays, the spirit and tone of Clongowes Wood are faithfully preserved in the impression made on Stephen Dedalus. Before he left the college Joyce had a passing and distant acquaintance with the classics, no more intimate than that of any small boy, and had at least heard the name of the adventurer Ulysses. He had been introduced to music and there first began his study of it. He learned what parody and satire were, and the fun and joy of teasing words in and out of meaning, not from books or lectures but from the exuberant performance of his fellows at school entertainments. At one of these an "Earwig" dropped into his ear and, after fifty years of gestation, was to be delivered full-blown as H. C. Earwicker, analogue to the blubbering giant of *Finnegans Wake.*

In the perspective of Joyce's threescore years, in the light of all that he later accomplished and all that afterwards happened to him, the few years he spent at Clongowes Wood tend to lose

[82] BBC.

themselves in a blur of childish innocence. But in the more innocent and more human moments of his life, the effect of these
years was not lost. Joyce remained always under the emotional
influence of the faith he abandoned. His daughter-in-law recalls
a time when Nora Barnacle was hospitalized for a fortnight in
Paris: during those two weeks Joyce, who, though not permitted
to see Nora, had insisted on putting up in the room next to hers,
never left the hospital except to visit a nearby church or to make
small purchases of food, cigarettes, and newspapers.[83] The incident
may be dismissed as a blind act of superstition—Joyce was certainly a superstitious man—or an empty symbolic gesture of which
any man, under the pressures of love and fear, may once be guilty
and afterwards ashamed. Perhaps so, and perhaps not. But there
is no doubt that all his life he remained a firm traditionalist, empty
or insignificant as those traditions may now appear to some.
Among his family, for example, he preserved the custom, to which
he was introduced at Clongowes Wood, of celebrating certain
days in a special manner. Many of these occasions coincided with
religious feasts (his own birthday, for example, fell on Candlemas
Day), but the celebrations, from all accounts of them, were far
from religious. St. Patrick's Day he always observed, but this of
course was a patriotic piety which he shared with all Irishmen
the world over. No one will seriously think of reading any residual
religious significance into this family custom of celebrating birth-
days and holidays, which were never more than the occasion for
a good party. But what is one to make of the fact that on each
December 13, the feast of St. Lucia, Joyce solemnly lighted a holy
candle for his talented and unfortunate daughter? [84] The habits

[83] Conversations with Helen Joyce.
[84] BBC. Lucia's first mental breakdown occurred in the summer of 1932. For
an account of this, see Colum, *Life and the Dream*, pp. 395–99. Her family's
hopes for her eventual recovery were never realized, and she is now permanently
institutionalized.

instilled in one's boyhood die hard, and in Joyce many of these habits never died at all.

To the modern secular mind, bemused or repelled by the vagaries of religious experience, Joyce's immersion in the religious atmosphere of Clongowes Wood may be simply unfortunate. It was never to appear so to Joyce. In his mature years, settled with his family in Trieste and looking back on his days at Clongowes, he still felt, as his friend Svevo reports, "admiration and gratitude for the care of his educators—whilst," Svevo continues, "his sinister Dedalus cannot find time to say so." [85] Another friend, Frank Budgen, who knew Joyce during the hard days at Zurich, attributes much of the moderation and self-discipline he showed with respect to the minor annoyances of life directly to his Jesuit training.[86] But Joyce's life was filled with more than "minor" annoyances: long periods of privation, chosen as deliberately as any Jesuit ever elected the vow of poverty, in order to preserve his integrity as an artist; acute physical pain, largely brought on by his work, that ended in near-blindness; years of tragic anxiety caused by the shattering illness of his daughter. He faced up to these things, too, and if one looks for an explanation of his endurance and fortitude, it is perhaps best stated by his brother Stanislaus, who seldom in his life had a kind word for the Jesuits or for things Jesuit.

I confess I have no better explanation to offer of his triumphant struggle to preserve his rectitude as an artist in the midst of illness and disappointment, in abject poverty and disillusionment, than this, that he who has loved God intensely in his youth will never love anything less. The definition may change, the service abides.[87]

[85] *James Joyce. A Lecture Delivered in Milan in 1927 by his Friend Italo Svevo*, trans. by Stanislaus Joyce.

[86] *James Joyce and the Making of Ulysses*, p. 192.

[87] BBC. For a somewhat different expression of the same sentiment, see *My Brother's Keeper*, p. 153.

2

The Belvederean Exhibitioner

We've had our day at triv and quad and writ our bit as intermidgets. Art, literature, politics, economy, chemistry, humanity & Duty, the daughter of discipline. . . .   [FW 306]

Father Conmee, walking, thought . . . of the book that might be written about jesuit houses and of Mary Rochfort, daughter of Lord Molesworth, first countess of Belvedere.   [U 220]

BELVEDERE COLLEGE, Dublin, was a far cry from the college at Clongowes Wood. Had Father Conmee had time to write the book he contemplated, he would have found little in the history of the Dublin school to equal the legendary and romantic past of Clongowes. That history was brief enough. Belvedere House was built in 1786 by George Rochfort, second earl of Belvedere, who, dissatisfied with the family mansion on Ormond Quay, desired a place in comparatively rural surroundings but at the same time not too far removed from the Dublin world of fashion. The site he chose was in Great Denmark Street on a rise of ground that then afforded a fine and full view of the city. The view was framed by lines of trees standing on either side of North Great George's Street, a broad avenue known at the time as "Eccles Lane," that opened into Great Denmark directly opposite the huge wooden doors that fronted Belvedere House. Rochfort's choice was so admired that he soon had a host of noble imitators. Within a few years his neighbors, settled in newly built houses along the same street, included among others the earls of Charleville, Norbury, Fingall, and Erne. Prosperity ran high in those years when Grattan's Parliament still sat in College Green, and the affluence and excitement of the period expressed itself culturally in a flurry of architectural activity that provided Dublin with some of its most stately and impressive houses. Of these Belvedere House was, and is still considered, an excellent example.[1]

But the excitement did not last long, nor did the affluence. The Dublin Parliament voted itself out of existence, Ireland was bound into legislative union with Britain, and the country settled slothfully into the political and economic morass of the nineteenth century. One of the men responsible for this Act of Union, an act tantamount to national suicide, was George Rochfort. After a show of patriotism, too vehement to be genuine, he sold his vote and those of his supporters in Commons to Lord Castlereagh, architect of the Union, for a consideration of £15,000. In 1815, a year after he died, his widow remarried, and she and her second husband, Abraham Boyd, K.C., continued to reside in Great Denmark Street until her death in 1835. Her son, George A. Rochfort Boyd, inherited the property but did not then or later take up residence in Belvedere House. The place was closed down on his retiring to the Rochfort estates in Westmeath, and some time later was sold to one Sylvester Young, from whom the Jesuits acquired possession in 1841.[2]

There is little excitement or romance in such a history, and Joyce, if not Father Conmee, knew it. And yet Conmee in *Ulysses* (p. 220), a kindly, moralistic dreamer whose mind dwelt fondly on smiling noble faces in beeswaxed drawing rooms, is made to

---

[1] Scantlebury, "Belvedere House," *Dublin Historical Record,* XIII (An Tóstal, 1953), 128.

[2] *Ibid.,* pp. 130–31.

summon up out of the past at least one romantic figure, that of Mary Rochfort, first countess of Belvedere.

A listless lady, no more young, walked alone the shore of Lough Ennel. Mary first countess of Belvedere, listlessly walking in the evening, not startled when an otter plunged. Who would know the truth? Not the jealous lord Belvedere and not her confessor if she had not committed adultery fully, *eiaculatio seminis inter vas naturale mulieris,* with her husband's brother? She would half confess if she had not all sinned as women did. Only God knows and she and he, her husband's brother.
[U 220]

But this sad lady had no connection with Belvedere House, Dublin. Married in 1736, as a girl of sixteen, to Colonel Robert Rochfort, she was accused, sometime after her husband was created earl in 1753, of intrigue with her brother-in-law, Arthur Rochfort. When the case was brought to trial and a verdict given in favor of the earl, the brother, unable to met the damages of £20,000 awarded by the court, hastily left the country. The wife was not so fortunate. Enraged by his brother's escape, Lord Belvedere imprisoned his wife on the Rochfort estate near Gaulstown, County Westmeath. There some years before he had built a mansion, the original Belvedere House, close by Lough Ennel, then renamed Lake Belvedere. The countess, however, was not lodged in the new mansion, but was instead shut up in the older Gaulstown residence, where she remained until her husband's death in 1774. She then returned to Dublin, a pitiful friendless woman, who a few years after her release died at the home of her son-in-law and daughter, Lord and Lady Lanesborough.[3]

These events may be considered "romantic," and it is interesting to see what use Joyce made of them when in *Ulysses* he dwelt briefly on the history of his old school. He obviously knew the general outline of the Molesworth-Rochfort story, and so it could

[3] *Ibid.,* p. 129.

be set conveniently among Father Conmee's romantic reveries.
There the reader naturally relates her, as Father Conmee does, by
a loose association of ideas, with Belvedere House, Dublin. But
when he first wrote this passage Joyce seems to have suspected
that there was no actual connection between the two. His suspicion
may explain why, in the late summer of 1921, between the first
appearance of this episode in the *Little Review* (June, 1919) and
the first edition of the novel (February 2, 1922), he wrote to
Father Charles Doyle, S.J., then stationed at Belvedere College,
enquiring about the possible occupancy of Belvedere House by the
unfortunate first countess of Belvedere.

Father Doyle answered Joyce's enquiry on October 3, 1921: [4]

Dear Sir:

The Christian name of the wife of the first Earl of Belvedere
was Mary. She was the daughter of Lord Molesworth. She never
lived in Belvedere College, however. After the divorce court proceedings she was confined in Gaulstown, Co. Westmeath, the old
seat of the family, near Belvedere House by the shore of Lough
Ennel, a new residence just completed by the Earl. The Countess
Mary died about 1790. Belvedere House (now Belvedere College)
was not completed and occupied by the second Earl (the builder
of it) until 1786.

> Yours faithfully,
> Charles Doyle, S.J.

In his first draft of this episode, that which appeared in the
Little Review, Joyce had written "Ellen" for "Mary" and "Lough
Owel" for "Lough Ennel." On receipt of Doyle's letter he corrected these minor inaccuracies. Moreover, he now knew that there
was no historical basis for associating Mary Molesworth any

[4] This letter may be found in The James Joyce Collection, In Memoriam Philip
J. Wickser, Lockwood Memorial Library, University of Buffalo. Joyce's letter to
Father Doyle seems not to have survived.

more intimately than he had with Belvedere House. But the temptation to do so may once have been great. For the rumor of the lady's "romantic phantom" still haunting the old school persisted in Joyce's time and constituted the sort of legend that might profitably have been accommodated to the romantic pattern of Conmee's thought. But the legend, as Joyce knew, was more groundless than most: it was due to the confusion of Belvedere House, Dublin, with the Belvedere House near Lough Ennel, and to the mistaken idea that Lady Belvedere spent her captivity in the former. But that Joyce wrote to Doyle about so apparently trivial a matter is still another indication of the pains he took for the sake of an accuracy which only his own artistic conscience demanded of him. The further point that Mary Molesworth was a Protestant and so would hardly be confessing or "half-confessing" her sins to any priest cannot, in the light of this, be thought an inadvertence on Joyce's part; it is quite in keeping with the cast of Father Conmee's mind, professionally preoccupied with the matter of moral theology.

Belvedere College, then, unlike Clongowes Wood, was less a preserve of history than a relic of the past. By Joyce's time the site of the building was no longer rural. Modern Dublin had grown up around the house and college with an urban insistence whose impulse was not aristocratic magnificence but middle-class necessity. In 1884 the Jesuits, in an effort at expansion, acquired Killeen House, the adjoining town residence of Lord Erne, and in the rear erected a gymnasium and a boys' chapel which formed against the back of Belvedere House a rough cramped quadrangle less than half the size of one of the lower line cricket grounds at Clongowes. In the center of this small yard, which had once been a flower garden, stood a worn, waterless fountain with no tears now to shed for the perished splendors the house had known in the days of the second earl. Confined here between classes and in

periods of recreation, Belvedereans had more in common with
yardbirds than with the schoolboys who ran free on the spacious
grounds at Clongowes Wood. There was no football, cricket, or
outdoor game of any kind. In place of the private pool at the disposal of Clongownians, boys from Belvedere who wanted to swim
—it is hard to imagine Joyce among them—had the Tara Street
public baths.[5]

Belvedere House itself was less changed. The Jesuits did what
they could to preserve the Georgian, or "Irish-Classical," grace
of line and decoration inherited from a happier era. In one instance
they actually improved upon it. The great wooden coach-house
doors that in Joyce's time led into the main hall have since been
replaced by iron gates which add appreciably to the appearance of
the building. Beyond these gates the main stairway and the ceilings of the rooms on the first floor are covered with the elaborate
plastic decoration work of Michael Stapleton, a Dublin craftsman,
whose skill was such that for a long time this work was freely
attributed to Italian artisans and, more specifically, to the Vene-
tians. The two mantlepieces in the parlor and boys' dining room
on this floor, were executed by Bossi, an Italian who invented a
special plaster—the secret of which died with him—which achieved
all the effects of the most delicately colored inlaid marble. On
the second floor, in addition to the community chapel, which was
formerly Lord Belvedere's study, are three large rooms connected
by folding doors which, when open, connect the whole into one
spacious L-shaped room. These three rooms, used for classes during Joyce's time at the school, were known, respectively, from
Stapleton's plaster designs on the ceilings, as the Venus, Diana,
and Apollo Rooms. In converting them into classrooms certain
changes were inevitable. The organ, for example, whose painted
panels are supposed to be the work of Angelica Kaufmann, was

[5] Sheehy, *May It Please the Court*, pp. 1, 10–11.

removed from the Apollo Room to what is now the Community Chapel. And the opulent Venus whose curvilinear figure once adorned the ceiling of the drawing room was chastely concealed beneath a simple floral and geometric design.[6] It might be quite true, as Gorman remarks, that the Jesuits themselves had no fear of Venus; but, charged with the care of young boys, they had a healthy respect of that concupiscence of the eye that stirs incontinently in the twilit imagination of adolescence.

To this house, and to this college, James A. Joyce, trailed by his awed and admiring younger brother Stanislaus, came in early April, 1893.[7] He was a blond frail boy—"the thinnest thing you ever saw"[8]—just past his eleventh birthday. He had trouble with his eyes and already wore glasses. His shyness, while probably not so marked as that of Stanislaus, who had never seen a Jesuit before, was the shyness of any small boy coming into a new school and having to adjust to new companions and new surroundings. The rector at Belvedere, Father Thomas Wheeler, S.J., was probably expecting their arrival.

According to the account given in the *Portrait* (pp. 78–80) of how Stephen and Maurice Dedalus came to attend Belvedere, their father Simon Dedalus chanced to meet Father John Conmee, Provincial of the Irish Jesuits, on the corner of Mountjoy Square, and the two men arranged the matter between them.

Such a meeting between Father Conmee and John Stanislaus Joyce is altogether plausible. In 1893 the Joyces lived at 14 Fitzgibbon Street, not six blocks from Belvedere. Just around the corner of Mountjoy Square, on Upper Gardiner Street, was the Jesuit

[6] Scantlebury, "Belvedere House," pp. 131–32.

[7] The Prefect of Studies Book, Belvedere College, folio 65, records that "James Augustine Joyce, born 2 Feb. '82" and "John Stanislaus Joyce, born 17 Dec. '85" were enrolled in the school on April 6, 1893, the former in Third of Grammar, the latter in Elements.

[8] Hutchins, *James Joyce's Dublin*, p. 33, quoting an unnamed contemporary of Joyce at Belvedere.

church of St. Francis Xavier, and adjoining it the residence of the
Jesuit Provincial. As parishioners, the Joyces would be known
to the Jesuits on Gardiner Street, and more than likely John Stanislaus was constantly encountering members of the order, both
from the Parish house and from the college. Father Conmee, as
his son's former rector, was certainly a familiar figure, and Mr.
Joyce, a man who believed in making "connections," may be
credited with making the most of this one. In April, 1893, however, Father Conmee was not Irish Provincial; his appointment
was not made until August, 1905.[9] The position he did hold at the
time was, for young Joyce, even more significant, and otherwise
substantiates the account given in the *Portrait*. He was then prefect
of studies at Belvedere College.

But there is no evidence for the statement that "through some
wangling with influential personalities, James and his younger
brother . . . would be admitted without the payment of the cus-
tomary fees." [10] The pension for one boy per term was only £3,
for two brothers £5/10.[11] Since there were three terms in the
scholastic year, the total cost of sending James and Stanislaus to
Belvedere was not more than £16/10 per year. Even granting
that their father's fortunes had declined from modest affluence
to imminent poverty, this cannot be considered a prohibitive
sum.[12] Indeed, it was less than the value (£20) of the exhibition

[9] *Catalogus S.J.*, 1893, 1905.
[10] Gorman, *James Joyce*, p. 139. Stanislaus Joyce (*My Brother's Keeper*, p. 52)
says only that "we were sent free of fees at the invitation of the Jesuit Father
Conmee . . . to Belvedere."
[11] The Account Book at Belvedere College has inscribed in ink on the flyleaf:
"One boy—£3 per term
Two brothers—£5/10 per term
Three brothers—£7/0 per term
Four brothers—£9/0 per term."
[12] In 1891 or 1892, according to Stanislaus (*My Brother's Keeper*, pp. 49–50),
the Office of the Collector General of Rates and Taxes, in which his father was
employed, was permanently abolished and Mr. Joyce was pensioned off at one
third of his regular salary, amounting to about eleven pounds a month.

won by Joyce at the end of his first full year in the Preparatory Grade. And there was no "wangling with influential personalities." The most that can be said to have happened was that some Jesuit, very probably Father Conmee, arranged that the Joyce boys, instead of having to wait until September and the start of a new school year, might be admitted to the college at the beginning of April. There was nothing exceptional in that, and that would seem to be the extent to which "influence" was brought to bear on their behalf. As at Clongowes, young Joyce had special consideration from the Jesuits at Belvedere, but he was not in any sense a charity case.

Equally unfounded is the myth that the boy was given meals at the college, a rumor long current in Dublin, where gossip still abounds.[13] It seems to have had its origin in the habit of the new Rector, Father William Henry (appointed August 15, 1894) of calling young Joyce into his office around midday and spending some time in conversation with him. That is the only discoverable basis for the later gossip which the denials of relatives and friends have not yet put to rest. But that it is empty talk is evident. One notices that Stanislaus Joyce, who did not achieve the notoriety of James, is not reported to have shared in the Rector's largess— presumably because he was less hungry or hungry-looking.[14] But not even Jesuits can be expected to have distinguished so in their charity. That Father Henry frequently called Joyce in to see him is altogether probable, and the reasons why he should have done so will shortly be made clear. Finally, such gossip leaves out of account the boy's own sense of himself. What can one imagine

---

[13] Hutchins, *James Joyce's Dublin*, p. 36.

[14] He may have been a good deal hungrier looking: "I was a scraggy, underfed boy with arms like the shins of thrushes, and too conscious of my weakness to be quarrelsome," he writes of himself at the time in *My Brother's Keeper*, p. 55. Later (p. 67) he denies again and *in toto* Miss Hutchins's report of breakfasts at Belvedere.

would have been the reaction of young Joyce, who the gossip-mongers are agreed was already touched with a kind of satanic pride, had Father Henry offered him a mess of pottage?

Myth and gossip can only obscure what Joyce's true feelings and real person may have been at this time. Belvedere was not Clongowes. Even a less sensitive boy than Joyce, remembering Clongowes Wood, would soon be conscious of the differences between his old school and the new, and of what these differences must mean to himself and others. The course of studies would be much the same, organized as in every Jesuit school around a nucleus of religious ideals. But there the similarity ended. At Clongowes education was the right of the privileged and fortunate; at Belvedere it was a necessity for those less fortunate but equally intent on getting ahead in the world so that someday perhaps they might be in a position to send their own sons to schools like Clongowes Wood. To pass from one to the other was to take a perceptible step down the social ladder. There was little likelihood of a boy at Belvedere asking another if his father was a gentleman or a magistrate, or of boasting of an uncle who was a judge or a general in the army. The pretensions of the Clongowes gentry were foreign to a school where most of the boys, unaccustomed to anything else, placidly accepted their status as member of the middle or lower middle class.

On the surface Joyce, too, seems to have accepted his status placidly enough. But unlike most of the others, unlike even his brother Stanislaus, he had been used to something different and better. Even had his home not provided him now with evidence enough of the family's social deterioration, his new school, cramped and cheerless, a sorry refuge from the troubles undermining his home, was a constant reminder that he no longer moved among those whom at an earlier age he had been taught to consider his social equals. In time, with the adaptability of boyhood, he would grow used to his new surroundings and new companions. Outwardly he would conform, and the placid surface of his existence would, to the eye of a Jesuit preceptor, be little different from that of other Belvedereans, except perhaps that it shone with a brighter promise. Nor would his conformity, his obedience, piety, and excellence in studies, be a sham or a mask behind which he plotted, unsuspected by any about him, a secret and different destiny. He was not a hypocrite, he was a young boy protected now by his own innocence. After the first minor shock of his passage from Clongowes to Belvedere, he adjusted himself consciously to his new world and largely forgot the old.

But was there a part of him, beyond his own awareness, deeper even than innocence, that had been irreparably if ever so lightly shattered by this initial shock? And in the trivial wound made in that sensibility was there secreted a broken grain of pride that, lodged early and deep in the dark of the boy's soul, began thus early its slow and magnificent irritation?

I

After a single term, or trimester, in Third of Grammar, Joyce entered the Preparatory Grade at Belvedere in September, 1893. His education now began in earnest, and in earnest the boy applied himself to it. His schooling at Clongowes, significant though it was, had been cut short by circumstances; in his years at University College he was seldom to allow studies to interrupt the wayward course of his education. But during these five years at Belvedere Joyce showed himself a serious and ambitious student, submissive to the intellectual discipline of the Jesuits and obedient to their moral and religious counsels. What they had to offer he accepted without question and, more than that, with gratitude.

What the Jesuits could offer, however, at least in secular courses of instruction, was conditioned by a secondary school system then in the hands of a group of well-meaning, muddled bureaucrats corporately known as the Intermediate Education Board for Ireland. The Board had been founded in 1878 with a capital endowment of £1,000,000 drawn from the disposable surplus funds of the Church of Ireland disestablished a few years earlier. The income from this invested capital, some £30,000 a year, was distributed in cash prizes to students who excelled in secular subjects of examination at the end of each academic year. In order that their students might qualify for these prizes, Irish secondary schools had to gear themselves to the new educational machinery operated by the Board. Before 1890 most Irish schools had done so.[15] As a result the upper school at Belvedere College in Joyce's time was divided into four grades roughly equivalent to the four years of an American preparatory school, known respectively as the Preparatory, Junior, Middle, and Senior grades. Within this new system a new emphasis was placed on the study of mathematics and the natural sciences, and such subjects as drawing, bookkeeping, and shorthand were introduced into a curriculum which until then, in Irish Catholic educational practice, had been exclusively humanistic. The teaching of the humanities themselves underwent change. Formerly the study of literature, classical and modern, was centered on considerations of structure, style, and idea, with a view to personal composition, based on imitation, in the language studied. Now translation was considered an end in itself, and the approach to language, by way of syntax, etymology, and even historical grammar, was linguistic rather than purely or properly literary.[16]

These changes effected by the IEBI in Irish secondary education were at best a mixed blessing. Culturally their implications are clear. The changes signified a departure, in theory and practice,

[15] Corcoran, *Clongowes Record*, p. 145.   [16] *Ibid.*, p. 144.

from those educational principles which had always prevailed in Catholic schools on the Continent and, until 1890, in Ireland. Substituted for these principles were a set of standards derived chiefly from English and Irish Protestant contemporary practice. Irish Catholic students of education have been at times aggrieved by this policy. The older forms of Catholic secondary education were, to them, "the last element in our natural culture to be brought fully under the process of anglicisation. . . ."[17] But true as this may be, there were immediate practical advantages in the new system which partially compensated for whatever may have been the cultural loss. Chief among these was the awarding of substantial cash prizes or "exhibitions" to students of superior talent and industry. When, many years later, a schoolfellow of Joyce referred to the system as "Bumbledom,"[18] he was only expressing common impatience with bureaucratic falderal. Certainly to weigh trivialities like bookkeeping and shorthand in the same scale with Horace and Homer is educational nonsense. But despite these absurdities, the principle, however misapplied, was sound. It was also to prove generally advantageous, and James Joyce, among others, benefited appreciably from it.

Until shortly before Joyce's time at Belvedere, Jesuit schools had adhered closely to the precepts of the original *Ratio Studiorum*. From the close of the sixteenth century until the suppression of the Society in 1773, this plan of studies had been the Jesuits' official and authorized code of liberal education. It was essentially a *plan*, in no sense a pedagogical treatise; that is, it assumed certain moral and religious principles as indispensable to the education of a Christian mind, and starting from this assumption it set down a body of explicit and highly detailed instructions and regulations for the government of schools, colleges, and universities. The plan was practical, systematic, and compre-

---

[17] *Ibid.*, p. 145.   [18] Sheehy, *May It Please the Court*, p. 2.

hensive, and for almost two hundred years, during those centuries of transition which transformed medieval into modern Europe, the *Ratio* remained essentially the same. In 1814, however, after the restoration of the Society, it was apparent to Jesuit educators that the changed conditions of intellectual life necessitated changes in their plan of studies. These were effected in the revised *Ratio* of 1832.

Of the changes then introduced few were of major importance. Some, however, were more substantial than others. Among these were "the new emphasis on the vernacular, the specific recognition of scientific subjects as such, and the removal of Cicero from his dominant position in language study." [19] Yet even these changes were advisory rather than mandatory, for the revised *Ratio* did not possess the force of law throughout the whole society.[20] In the Irish province, moreover, the currents of conservatism seem to have coursed as strongly in education as in politics, and it was not until the eighties that the full effect of the revised *Ratio* made itself felt. Then the impulse to revision of the curriculum came from outside the Society rather than from within, through the "reform" of Irish secondary education introduced by the newly established Intermediate Education Board for Ireland. Some of the changes effected by the latter, notably the promotion of mathematics and science, coincided with the recommendations of the new *Ratio*. The Irish Jesuits thus found themselves in a happy educational circumstance: obeying the letter of the law set down by the state, they were at the same time abiding by the spirit of the law of their own Society.

Such were the circumstances prevailing at Belvedere College during Joyce's years in the school. The new system—and it was

[19] Fitzpatrick, *St. Ignatius*, p. 36.
[20] *Ibid.* The revised *Ratio* would have had to be approved by a decree of a general congregation of the Society in order to be universally binding. Such a decree, however, was not passed.

still very new—had not yet dimmed the spirit of the old *Ratio*.
That spirit had been redefined as late as 1892 by the Jesuit General,
Luis Martin. "The characteristics of the Ratio Studiorum," Father Martin wrote, "are not to be sought in the subject matter,
nor in the order and succession in which the different branches
are taught, but rather in what may be called the 'form,' or spirit
of the system. This form, or spirit, consists chiefly in the training
of the mind [*efformatio ingenii*], which is the object, and in the
various exercises, which are the means of attaining this object." [21]
It is clear even from so dry and bare a definition that the Jesuit
General saw the *Ratio* as an instrument of what is now generally
known as a liberal education. A student so trained was intended
to be more than a mere wage-earner, however successful, or a
mere specialist, however skillful. He was marked for intellectual
salvation, and this salvation was to be achieved through the gradual
integration and harmonious development of the "faculties" of
memory, imagination, intellect, and will, so that, whatever the
circumstances of his existence, an educated man's interest and
understanding were constantly challenged and seriously engaged
by the more fundamental problems of life, moral, philosophical,
religious, and aesthetic.

The object of the *Ratio* is, then, one with that of any system
of liberal education properly so called. The Jesuits, however, had
long ago settled upon special means—the "exercises" noted by
Father Martin—to attain that object and realize that end. It was
through these exercises that the mind of Joyce received its first
intellectual impulses, and from them that it first acquired that
discipline which was afterwards to serve it in such good stead. For
this reason alone, it would be important to review here the characteristic methods of Jesuit pedagogy, familiar though these meth-

[21] Quoted by Schwickerath, "Ratio Studiorum," in *The Catholic Encyclopedia*,
XII, 655.

ods are to many. In addition to this, such a review affords some idea of Joyce's experience from day to day in the classrooms at Belvedere.

In the spring of 1898, at the end of his last year in the college, Joyce made the following translation of Horace's *Ode* III.13:

> Brighter than glass Bandusian spring
>   For mellow wine and flowers meet,
> The morrow thee a kid shall bring
>   Boding of rivalry and sweet
> Love in his swelling forms. In vain
> He, wanton offspring, deep shall stain
> Thy clear cold streams with crimson rain.
>
> The raging dog star's season thou,
>   Still safe from in the heat of day,
> When oxen weary of the plough
>   Yieldst thankful cool for herds that stray.
> Be of the noble founts! I sing
> The oak tree o'er thine echoing
> Crags, the waters murmuring.[22]

This is interesting as the earliest of Joyce's extant writing, and it is something more than "a rather charming curiosity." [23] Not only does Joyce translate the Latin with great accuracy, he remains remarkably true to the spirit of Horace. The seven-line stanzas, triple-rhyming to a close as gently as the flow of fountains, still suggest the undercurrent of excitement just below the placid somnolence of the Horatian surface. Compare the last three verses with the Latin original:

> fies nobilium tu quoque fontium,
> me dicente cavis impositam ilicem

---

[22] Text from Gorman, *James Joyce*, pp. 45-46. "Forms" in line 5 should probably be emended to "horns."   [23] *Ibid.*

saxis, unde loquaces
lymphae desiliunt tuae.

Be of the noble founts! I sing
The oak tree o'er thine echoing
Crags, the waters murmuring.

One is reminded of Joyce's remark about a much more ambitious project: "I'm not looking for the *mot juste,* I've got them all. What I'm looking for is the order of words in the sentence." [24] The same care for the "order of words" is evident in the schoolboy who locates his "crags"—"echoing" at the end of the preceding verse—so that they beetle over the murmuring waters of his last line. The translation is a schoolboy exercise, the poetics—contraction, inversion, archaism—obviously and easily borrowed from a genteel tradition of versifying. But it is also an exhibition of skill, grace, and accuracy that reveals, prophetically perhaps more than precociously, a sense of language that was to mature into genius.

But of more immediate interest than Joyce's verse is the pedagogical process that preceded it. The boy was not set to work on this ode of Horace on his own. In the classroom on the day the ode was assigned, Joyce's instructor first read the poem aloud, distinctly, accurately, according to meter, in a tone adjusted to convey the mood and "feel" of Horace. He then interpreted it, giving either a paraphrase or, more probably, a translation of the Latin. Following the translation, he identified the meter and, writing one or two lines on the blackboard, scanned them, marking off the long and short quantities and locating the caesura. If any linguistic difficulties occurred that had not been met with before, he offered an explanation of these and parsed the more knotty passages for syntax. When the text had been this thoroughly

[24] "Portrait of James Joyce," edited by W. R. Rogers, produced by Maurice Brown, broadcast by the BBC, February 13, 17, and March 22, 1950.

examined, he spoke to the students about the background of the poem; of Horace's Sabine farm, perhaps, or of the ritual sacrifices of the Romans, or the seasonal significance of the Dog Star—in short, of any historical, literary, biographical, political, or religious detail that might be pertinent to the text just read.

This "prelection," as it is called in the *Ratio,* is perhaps the most characteristic feature of Jesuit pedagogy.[25] The five steps in the process—reading, translation, explication, analysis of poetic or rhetorical structure, and *eruditio*—insured a systematic handling of a text from every possible point of view.

A similar process, with special emphasis on the first, third, and fifth steps, is involved in any useful attempt to teach or study *Finnegans Wake* and much of *Ulysses.* The second and fourth steps, involving considerations of "meaning" and form, are possible only when a section of Joyce's work is *heard,* its multiple implications simultaneously perceived, and its allusive texture recognized as integral to the central theme and not as mere pedantic embroidery. To a mind trained, as Joyce's mind was trained, in this way, *Finnegans Wake* is not the doorless labyrinth it has appeared to some. Neither is it a locked treasure chest whose lid snaps open on ghostly riches at the mere touch of a skeleton key. It is a consciously wrought "classic"—Joyce was as self-consciously a great poet as Yeats or Milton—demanding of the reader an effort of imagination which, however difficult, is never wholly impossible. The work must perhaps be "prelected" before it can be read, for Joyce is also the schoolmaster requiring of his readers a schoolboy's docility. Indeed, without such docility —the humility proper to the experience of a great work of art— there is no comprehending *Finnegans Wake* at all. One can only

---

[25] It is treated in the *Ratio Studorium* of 1599 under "Rules Common to the Professors of the Lower Classes," Section 27. See Fitzpatrick, *St. Ignatius,* pp. 201–2. See also "Rules for Professors of Rhetoric," Section 8 (*ibid.,* p. 212).

talk and write about it, but never experience it. To experience it, one must approach the work in much the same way that the schoolboy Joyce was taught to approach classical literature.[26]

This approach, or prelection, was an exhaustive process. Its virtue lay in the cultivation of the intellectual habits of thoroughness and accuracy which Joyce was later to exhibit abundantly in his work. But as ordinary classroom routine the prelection could, and in the hands of uninspiring masters undoubtedly did, tend to become mechanical and dull. Its defects were then more apparent than its qualities. Accuracy degenerated into pedantry and thoroughness burgeoned into boredom. And there are critics more conscious of these defects in Joyce's work than of his corresponding virtues.

But a more serious criticism of the system is that the master, having exhausted the possibilities of the text in his prelection, left nothing seriously to challenge the interest of his students. A predigested text, so to speak, was offered, accepted, and returned to the master without the student's having extracted from it any real intellectual nourishment. Consequently real growth was inhibited; students were guarded from rather than guided into maturity. They remained children of the Jesuits, incapable of assuming intellectual responsibilities and discouraged from exercising true independence of mind. The criticism is in general justified, at least so far as mediocre students are concerned. But it may be offered in defense of the system that the Jesuits did not envision their schools as foundations dedicated to the care and cure of scholastic mediocrities. Quite the contrary was true.

The Jesuits first ventured into education to save thinking men, the potential intellectuals, for the Church. But at the time of this venture, in the middle of the sixteenth century, education was far

---

[26] "Joyce a creé un monde et ce monde ne nous est accessible que si nous ne savons obéir humblement." Soupault, *Souvenirs de James Joyce*, p. 16.

from being universal. At the end of the nineteenth century it was a good deal more so. Its base had broadened, and in proportion to its breadth were the number of mediocre students who attended all kinds of colleges, Jesuit colleges included. Consequently, the potential intellectual was now the exception rather than the rule, but for this exceptional student the Jesuit system could still serve as a stimulating and effective instrument of education. James Joyce was certainly such a student. As such, his defection from the Church shortly after he left Belvedere was itself a gesture of intellectual independence made possible, at least in part, by his training at Belvedere.[27] In his case the system may be said to have worked more efficiently than could be anticipated by his Irish Jesuit masters, and in a way hardly contemplated by the framers of the *Ratio Studiorum.*

Two other procedures, though not as significant as the prelection, may also be mentioned as characteristic of Jesuit educational method. These are repetition and emulation.[28] *Emulatio* is the term used in the *Ratio* to cover all appropriate means for stimulating a wholesome spirit of scholastic rivalry. In the *Portrait,* for example, Stephen Dedalus, in the class of Elements at Clongowes, wears pinned to his jacket a little silk badge with the white rose of York on it; Jack Lawton across the aisle wears a similar badge bearing the red rose of Lancaster. The two boys

[27] The paradox here is more apparent than real. The Jesuits certainly opposed "originality" in faith and morals, which, according to their lights, could only be equated with heresy and libertinism. For the same reason, they were opposed to that "independence" of mind which, in the guise of free thought or rationalism, set itself apart from and above the truths of Revelation. But stated so, the issues are philosophical or theological. The only issue here is pedagogical.

[28] For "emulation" see "Rules Governing Awards" (Fitzpatrick, *St. Ignatius,* pp. 192–95); "Rules for Prefect of Lower Studies," Section 36 (*ibid.,* p. 187); "Rules Common to the Professors of Lower Classes," Section 31 (*ibid.,* p. 203). For "recitation" see the last two sets of rules, Sections 8 (articles 3–4) and 25, respectively (*ibid.,* pp. 178, 200), and "Rules for Professors of Rhetoric," Section 3 (*ibid.,* p. 210).

compete during the hour for sums under their master's exhortation: "Go ahead, York! Go ahead, Lancaster!" In a brief daydream afterwards Stephen muses on "White roses and red roses: those were beautiful colours to think of. And the cards for first place and third place were beautiful colours too: pink and cream and lavender" (P 8). Later, too, at Belvedere, Stephen's schoolfellow Heron is described as his friend and also as his "rival"—that is, his scholastic rival (P 84).[29]

These are typical examples of *emulatio,* a stimulus to friendly rivalry, in which Joyce himself participated fully while at Belvedere. Its purpose was to engage the interest of slower students by disguising study as a game, and to whet the ambition of superior students by the testimonials, premiums, and prizes awarded for excellence. The custom was common enough in most systems of education, especially on the elementary levels, and the *Ratio,* a compilation of the best educational practices of the time of its formulation, simply adopted the custom to its own ends. While the method was not to be especially welcome to modern educational theorists, it was generally approved of in Ireland during the last decades of the nineteenth century. In any event, the theory behind it was endorsed by the government when, in 1878, a series of annual exhibitions was instituted.

Emulation was not, then, a pedagogical innovation. Repetition was even less new. It was as old as, perhaps older than, the Horatian dictum *decies repetita placebit.* But the Jesuits adapted it with new emphasis on daily and weekly repetitions of material covered in the classroom. In the higher grades students were even exempted

[29] Compare the roles assigned here to Stephen and Heron—"It was they who went up to the rector together to ask for a free day or to get a fellow off"—with that of "Chief Decurion or Praetor" as given in the Ratio: ". . . let him be honored with some privilege, and let him have the right, with the approval of the master, of begging off some lighter penalties for his fellow pupils." *Ibid.,* p. 189.

from class work in the final weeks of the term, during which time they were expected to review the year's work in preparation for the final examinations. The purpose of these repetitions was twofold: first, to insure a thorough grasp of the material; second, to accomplish this through the constant exercise and development of the powers of memory. The Jesuits were not content to expose their students to literature, religion, and philosophy; their intention was so to saturate young minds with the matter of these disciplines that they became, according to their capacities, literary, religious, and philosophical minds. The daily memory lesson—a passage from one of the Latin poets, an English or French lyric, the versified rules of Latin prosody [30]—was intended to develop and, where memory was naturally strong, to strengthen further the powers of retentiveness and recall. Joyce's own innate powers of recall were considerable. He seems never to have forgotten anything once committed to memory, and thirty years later he could astonish Dublin friends by reciting verbatim lessons that he had learned as a boy at Belvedere.[31]

The mind of Joyce was, then, accustomed early not merely to touch upon a theme but to dwell on it, to roll and re-roll it through memory till the theme itself became part of the texture of his own thought. To the objection that this may be a sound way to train a parrot but a sorry way to educate a boy, the same answer must be given as to the objection against prelections. If the boy is bird-brained, the method is anyhow appropriate; if he is more capacious of mind, it is surely well to store that mind with worthy and useful knowledge. But even this is not enough. Not the possession of knowledge, but the manner in which it is pos-

[30] On his morning walk across Dublin (P 208) Stephen Dedalus runs one of these rules through his head: *Contrahit orator, variant in carmine vates.* From such memory lessons, Stephen reflects, "he had learnt what little he knew of Latin verse."

[31] Colum, *Life and the Dream,* p. 392.

sessed is what matters. The contents of a poem, for example, may be readily accessible to memory in paraphrase or summary; but the form of the poem—its cadence, rhythms, its *this*ness rather than its *what*ness—is more than a mere possession of the mind. It might indeed be truer to say that the mind is the possession of the poem, taking on the being of the poem and expanding through poetic possibilities to new kinds of awareness. This is the real value of memorization, and this is the value that Joyce began to make his own at Belvedere. No one today can read *Finnegans Wake* without being aware of the artist's unfailing sense of the shape of words, the form and cadence of sentences, the structural rhythms embodying whole pages of this extraordinary work. So true is this that even where the content of a passage remains obscure to the mind, the ear recognizes rhythms and cadences re-echoing from earlier passages. One is not surprised at this in a work so structurally conceived; it is a commonplace of the Joyce commentaries. But there are more distant echoes, extrastructural echoes, so to speak. To take but one example, and that the most obvious: the solemn voice of the retreat master in the *Portrait*— "Time is, time was, but time shall be no more" (P 129, 141)— emerges through the transfigured rhythms, their sadness turned through hope to joy, of "Anna was, Livia is, Plurabelle's to be" (FW 215). The link is memory, but the memory is of form not of mere fact.

To point this out is not to claim that while Joyce's work was in progress he was making conscious use of what was impressed on him at Belvedere decades before. But sufficient ground may have been cleared for the statement—made often, but seldom substantiated—that the workings of Joyce's mind, conscious or unconscious, were so conditioned by his early Jesuit training that the effects of the training may be felt in almost everything that he afterwards wrote. The works of Ibsen, Aquinas, Dante, Vico,

Freud, and a dozen others are all relevant to an understanding of Joyce. They are all influences, but they are tributary influences. The sources of Joyce are more remote; they rise in Jesuit country, where they were given a shape and a direction—as the hills and valleys of Kildare direct the course of the Liffey—which was formative rather than tributary. The boy felt the "influence" of the Jesuits even before he was capable of recognizing it as an influence. He would of course recognize it in time, and in time, too, he would recognize the *Scienza Nuova,* the *Summa,* and the *Divina Commedia.* But none of these great works could have the initial impact or enduring effect of a small book which Joyce himself had probably never read, the *Ratio Studiorum* of 1599.

II

Mark Hopkins on one end of a log and a student on the other is an educational ideal that may have much to recommend it. It is not, however, the sort of ideal that would find unqualified favor among Jesuit educators. In drafting the *Ratio,* the Fathers of the Society intended to construct a closed but not inflexible system, one that would insure a uniform performance in their widely scattered schools and colleges and still operate effectively even when the quality of instruction was less than inspired. Their plan of studies was, then, a sort of educational sacrament, intended to operate *ex opere operato.* Inspiration was not contemned, but neither was it considered a *sine qua non;* much depended on the instructor, but more depended on the system or plan of studies. This was especially true on the elementary levels where, like the trivium (whose linguistic orientations it incorporated and preserved long after they had disappeared elsewhere) the *Ratio* achieved its best results. One does not lecture to schoolboys, one puts them through grammatical paces, moving from grammar through rhetoric to logic.[32] On this triple foundation the whole educational structure of the *Ratio* is based. But even here, where the importance of inspirational guidance may be thought to be minimal, the values implicit in the plan of studies are not wholly separable from the intellectual discipline imposed by the instructor.

"During my time in Belvedere," J. F. Byrne writes, "the teachers could not have been characterized as outstanding members of their profession. Indeed, it might well be questioned whether there was, or ever could be, such a thing as a great teacher. I have my own opinion on this point. I think none of the clerical teachers in Belvedere was deserving of a high rating as a teacher. . . ."[33] Byrne, the Cranly of the *Portrait,* is a man of obstinate, even oppressive, honesty. One senses this on almost every page of his autobiography, where, disagree as one will with his opinions, his candor and integrity go unquestioned. But though his book fairly bristles with honesty, Byrne's memory is not always to be trusted. For example, his detailed and straightforward account of how, on leaving Belvedere in 1895, he entered University College through the generous intervention of its rector, Father Thomas Wheeler, S.J., is quite convincing as given.[34] It is marred only by the hard fact that Father Wheeler was at no time rector of University College.[35]

That Byrne could be so mistaken about a former superior to whose kindness he was indebted may weaken one's confidence in his opinion of other masters whom he would have less reason to remember. And yet he disarms doubt by admitting quite

[32] Grammar, rhetoric, and logic, or dialectic, comprise the matter of the trivium. In the Jesuit system, however, logic served as an introduction to philosophy and so was taught at the university rather than at the secondary level.

[33] Byrne, *Silent Years,* p. 23. [34] *Ibid.,* pp. 27–28.

[35] Father Robert Carberry, S.J., was rector from April 10, 1888, to March 25, 1897. See *Catalogus S.J.* for these years.

candidly his prejudice; no one who starts from the premise that there can be no such thing as a great teacher is likely, when recalling persons and events of sixty years before, to tug out of memory an example to the contrary. One can, moreover, assent to Byrne's judgment on the teachers at Belvedere if by "outstanding" he means men whose names are widely remembered for what they were or did as teachers or because of the fame of other men whose minds they influenced significantly. For it is surely doubtful that any of the masters, lay or cleric, who taught at Belvedere College in the last decade of the nineteenth century would be remembered today if their names had not been meanwhile associated with the genius of Joyce. It is the disciple who reflects honor upon his masters, and this too is in the spirit of the *Ratio,* which was designed to produce not great teachers but good and great students.

Joyce mentions none of his Belvedere masters by name in the *Portrait.* George Dempsey, his English teacher, appears briefly as Mr. Tate: he points out a near heresy in one of Dedalus's essays (P 88), chats quietly with Vincent Heron (Albert Connolly) during the famous retreat (P 143), and is not seen or heard of again. Physically, Mr. Dempsey appears to have been an imposing figure. A tall thin man with gray hair and a mustache the color of old hay, he reminded Eugene Sheehy of a retired brigadier and J. F. Byrne of Mr. Justice Holmes.[36] The accounts agree in the impression of dignity conveyed, a dignity that seems not to have been impaired by the slight stoop, becomingly pedagogical, with which he moved among the boys at Belvedere. But he is remembered best for the caustic judgments pronounced on the English themes read in class on Monday afternoons. It is easy now to imagine him standing by one of the great second-floor windows overlooking Great Denmark Street, staring down on the broad tongue of

[36] Sheehy, *May It Please the Court,* p. 4; Byrne, *Silent Years,* p. 147.

pavement that George's Street dips into the pool of Dublin, listening with feigned inattention to a schoolboy's voice elaborating more or less grammatically the praises of A Favorite Hero or Heroine.[37] And while the boy read, Mr. Dempsey's right hand would be working the hay of his mustache, twisting it into a sugan and shaping and reshaping it with patient care. Almost under the shadow of that mustache, in the first seat in the first row next to the great window, sat young Joyce, a small blond boy, delicate but not unmanly, precocious but strangely simple, listening, too, to the schoolboy voice repeating the theme, observing the odd behavior of Mr. Dempsey, waiting for the end and the flick or flash of the master's comment. The boy was a favorite of Dempsey's, for he was personable as well as proficient, and when his turn came to read the master, more deliberately attentive now, "would literally wriggle and chuckle with delight." [38] George Dempsey was indeed Joyce's first critical and appreciative audience, and he was to remain so long after the boy had gone from Belvedere. According to Gorman he continued always a strong partisan of Joyce, forwarding reference books when the latter was in the midst of work in progress and urging publication of Joyce's verse in the college magazine.[39]

Dempsey's brother-in-law, P. Bertram Foy, who taught chemistry and physics (known in the curriculum of the day as "natural philosophy") has been singled out by Byrne as the best of the teachers then at the school.[40] But, Byrne admits, his judgment in this may well have been guided by his predilection for the subject matter of Foy's course. Joyce, whose grades in natural phi-

---

[37] This title is included in a comic list of essay assignments in *Finnegans Wake*, p. 306. Gorman says (*James Joyce*, p. 45) that for this assignment Joyce wrote on Ulysses, and so indeed he may have. But it is unlikely that the boy's choice of subject was thought "not quite orthodox, at least from the point of view of the Society of Jesus."

[38] Byrne, *Silent Years*, p. 147.   [39] Gorman, *James Joyce*, p. 42.

[40] Byrne, *Silent Years*, p. 23.

losophy indicate a profound lack of interest in the subject, did not, one feels sure, think one way or the other about P. Bertram Foy. Nor could he have worked up any great enthusiasm for the physical culture program of Sergeant Major Wright. Athletic boys like Byrne and Sheehy might be expected to enjoy their sessions in the new gymnasium behind Belvedere House, twirling Indian clubs and hoisting dumbbells and playing monkey on parallel and horizontal bars. But poor Joyce was no gymnast. "His legs just wouldn't behave in the ordinary way, no muscles at the hip you see." [41] It is easy to believe that, like Dedalus, he got through these sessions by assuming the painless role of "secretary to the gymnasium" (P 81).

With the exception, then, of George Dempsey, Joyce seems to have had little to do with any of the lay instructors at Belvedere. On the evidence of the *Portrait* alone, it would also seem that he had about as little to do with his Jesuit instructors. All the Jesuits in the Belvedere chapters of the novel, with the exception of the retreat master, are cast in minor roles. Only one is introduced by name; all the others, even the rector, remain anonymous. The Jesuit who is named is the object of Heron's contemptuous irreverence—"Will you tell Doyle with my best compliments that I damned his eyes?" (P 92)—an irreverence not shared on the occasion by Stephen Dedalus. This Doyle is described as "a plump freshfaced jesuit" (P 94) in charge of the Whitsuntide play at Belvedere who, in contrast with the cold unconcern of Dedalus, is in "a great bake" about his young actor. His original is Charles Doyle, S.J., a scholastic assigned in 1897 to teach Third of Grammar at Belvedere.[42] He was not, then, one of Joyce's teachers (Joyce having completed this grade of Grammar in 1893), but he

---

[41] Hutchins, *James Joyce's Dublin*, p. 33. For a different account of Joyce's athletic abilities, see Stanislaus Joyce, *My Brother's Keeper*, pp. 41–42.

[42] *Catalogus S.J.*, 1897.

was well enough remembered by Joyce that, twenty-five years later, the artist could write to the Jesuit, long since ordained and assigned again to the same college, enquiring into the past history of Belvedere House. Father Doyle's answer, already quoted, appears to have been prompt and cordial, and one wonders now how well the priest remembered Joyce as a boy or whether he recognized the sketch of himself in the *Portrait,* had he the luck to read it.

The Jesuit whom Joyce probably knew more intimately than any other at Belvedere was the rector, Father William Henry, S.J. He is unnamed in the *Portrait,* where he is introduced only to announce to Dedalus and his school fellows the schedule for the retreat and to deliver a brief devotional exhortation to the boys on St. Francis Xavier. But Father Henry seems to have played a somewhat larger part in Joyce's life at school. He was not only rector of the college, he served also as procurator, prefect of studies, and instructor in Latin in the higher grades.[43] It was his prelection in Horace that prepared Joyce for his translation of *O Fons Bandusiae* into English verse. It was to his office, as prefect of studies, that he summoned Joyce to receive the prizes won in scholastic competition. It was in the same office, but now in his capacity as rector, that Father Henry discussed with Joyce, prefect of the sodality and virtual head of the school, plans for college activities and perhaps, at times, more personal plans for the boy's future. For in addition to their various official connections, a friendly, even familiar relationship seems to have existed between the boy and the priest.

In the *Portrait,* on the night of the Whitsuntide play, Heron suggests that "it would be a ripping good joke" (P 83) if Dedalus took off the rector in the part of the schoolmaster. There is no indication in the novel that Dedalus did so, for Joyce does not

[43] *Ibid.*

allow this solemn adolescent to step out of character even for a moment. But the mimicry that was foreign to the solemnity of Dedalus was natural and spontaneous in Joyce. On the occasion of one such Belvedere play the boy, cast in the role of a farcical pedagogue, did turn his performance into an impersonation of the reverend rector. The story is that Father Henry, a small, precise, bewhiskered man, master of the cliché and the Delsarte gesture, sat in the front row of the audience that night and, before the assembly of students, parents and friends, laughed as heartily at the joke against himself as any of the boys or parents present.[44] It may be true that, under the circumstances, there was not much else he could do without appearing even more ridiculous than Joyce had made him out. But it is more probable that he honestly enjoyed the jape, for Joyce was not reprimanded then or later for this piece of talented impudence.

If one wonders why he was not reprimanded, the answer must be, first, that Belvedere was an Irish school. It is difficult to imagine Dr. Arnold of Rugby reacting like Father Henry of Belvedere. It is even more difficult to imagine an audience of Victorian parents joining in a laugh had at the headmaster's expense. Indeed, it is quite impossible to imagine a contretemps of this kind even occurring at an English public school, where, however much the boys might bully or jolly or fag one another, the attitude toward masters was one of relentless respect stamped into the students by a code of behavior as stiff and confining as an Eton collar. But Irish schoolboys were not groomed by so fine or stern a code. They were trained to reverence rather than respect, the impulse of belief starting from the heart being held more significant than the gesture of the hand touched to one's cap. Disrespect was not to be condoned, but neither was its appearance

---

[44] Sheehy, *May It Please the Court,* p. 8. Stanislaus Joyce (*My Brother's Keeper,* p. 88) identifies the play as Anstey's farce *Vice Versa* and corroborates Sheehy's report of the rector's amusement.

to be mistaken for irreverence. Joyce and Father Henry and the audience present at the Whitsuntide play knew what reverence was, took it indeed for granted, and so did not have to make a great show of respect for themselves or for each other. Joyce's mimicry of the rector, juxtaposing a show of disrespect against this fundamental reverence, struck among them the essential note of laughter—*on se moque de ce qu'on aime.* The same note is sounded throughout Joyce's work where too often the respectable reader, lacking perhaps in reverence, responds to it in shock or in outrage—if indeed he is aware of it at all.

The most immediate significance of this episode is the light it casts on the relationship between Joyce and Father Henry. Even in an Irish school boys are not likely to joke or trifle with an unpopular master, and no master, unless he is sure of his students' devotion, will endanger discipline and decorum by submitting to schoolboy bantering even when it is less pointed and public than that reported of Joyce. Father Henry, then, may be supposed to have known his boy, to have liked him, to have been on easy and cordial terms with him, and even perhaps to have been more than ordinarily interested in his future. On his part, Joyce was certainly fond of Father Henry, and though he had reason to believe that he was the rector's favorite, he also knew that he was not his toady. He could ape his mannerisms because he admired his man. And the characteristic trait of this man, like that of Joyce's former rector, Father Conmee, was fairness, that quality in a master valued above all others by schoolboys.

There is another story told of Father Henry that in class one day, receiving what he thought to be a wrong answer from a pupil, he ordered the boy to write out the correct answer a hundred times. When the boy stubbornly insisted that he was right, the rector doubled the penalty. When the boy still refused to yield, the rector raised it another hundred—agreeing, however, to write out the penalty himself should he be proved wrong and the boy right. So it turned out, and before classes were dismissed that afternoon Father Henry presented the boy with several sheets of paper on which the penalty was inscribed three hundred times in a neat priestly hand.[45]

This was not the act of a "harsh and warped" character, as Father Henry is depicted by Joyce's biographer.[46] It was the act of a man whom boys could recognize, beneath his mask of professional severity, as eminently just and fair, worthy of admiration and even of affection. This estimate of the man would seem closer to Joyce's opinion of Father Henry than Gorman's dismissal of him as "a fanatical Roman Catholic convert who wore whiskers."[47] That the boy who figures in this story was a lad named Lenehan and not Joyce himself, as one version has it,[48] does not alter the point of the story.

None of the other teachers at Belvedere appears to have known Joyce quite so well at this time, and their influence on him was probably negligible. Of some all that is now known is their names, and in at least one case even this may be inaccurate. For example, there was a layman called Loup who is said to have first taught Joyce Italian at the age of twelve.[49] Of this Mr. Loup there is now no trace, but it is interesting to note that his name may be anglicized as "error" or "trick" (literally "wolf"), and Joyce, who

---

[45] Sheehy, *May It Please the Court*, p. 5.   [46] Gorman, *James Joyce*, p. 41.

[47] *Ibid.*; echoed by Stanislaus Joyce: "a fanatical convert from Protestantism." *My Brother's Keeper*, p. 68.

[48] Hutchins, *James Joyce's Dublin*, p. 48.

[49] Gorman, *James Joyce*, p. 43. The biographer also states that only one other boy, "Albrecht" Connolly, was studying Italian at this time. If this is so, there seems to have been a superfluity of Italian masters at Belvedere—each with one pupil apiece. To add to the confusion, Stanislaus Joyce speaks of "a young Jesuit, MacErlaine, the professor of French . . . whose best pupil my brother was in those years . . ." (*My Brother's Keeper*, p. 89). But, according to the official records, there was no Jesuit of that name at Belvedere during the year in question, 1897–98.

was presumably Gorman's authority in this, was not beyond having a bit of fun at the expense of his biographer. But if Mr. Loup did exist, he shared the burden of teaching Italian to not more than three or four out of approximately one hundred and twenty boys [50] with Father Francis Ryan, S.J., who was officially assigned to teach Italian and French at Belvedere from 1894 to 1898.[51] Another Jesuit, Father Richard Campbell [52]—"whom some of the boys called Lantern Jaws and others Foxy Campbell"—is mentioned only in passing in the *Portrait* (p. 187), where Stephen Dedalus remembers him as "eyeless and sourfavoured and devout." But such descriptions, it should be remembered, are Stephen's impressions, invented rather than recollected by Joyce himself. So, in the first chapter of the novel, the author can locate another Jesuit, the scholastic Patrick Barrett, at Clongowes Wood where he is depicted as one of the more ingenuous and formidable of the prefects (P 29, 46). Actually, Barrett was stationed at Belvedere, and though he was not one of Joyce's own masters, he taught his younger brother Stanislaus in the class of Elements in 1893–94.[53]

In the novel the Belvedere Jesuits are dimly, vaguely drawn. They are names without faces, like Charles Doyle, or faces without identity, like Richard Campbell, or personifications of authority without name or definition like William Henry. None of them is a person in his own right—neither a pleasant person, like Father Conmee, nor unpleasant, like Father Dolan. They exist only as modifications of Stephen's consciousness. At Clongowes the child Stephen had sensed the opposition between ego and non-ego, between self and the world, and though it had puzzled and

[50] Sheehy, *May It Please the Court*, p. 1.
[51] *Catalogus S.J.*, 1897. This would appear to be the same Ryan who is mentioned in "An Encounter."
[52] *Ibid.*   [53] *Catalogus S.J.*, 1894.

frightened him, he had not had to choose between them or to deny one or the other. His innocence preserved the world within and the world without in delicate balance, and the latter world was peopled by real persons who had names and faces and identities of their own. But at Belvedere, after a futile attempt at religious surrender of self, the frightened adolescent drew more and more into himself: "he drew less pleasure from the reflection of the glowing sensible world . . . than from the contemplation of an inner world of individual emotions" (P 194). The balance tipped inward, the conflict resolved in favor of ego, and the nonego then appears as a *veiled, grey, dim haze* (P 194). In this progressive idealization of experience, the identity of individual Jesuits blurs and becomes lost, for in the world in which Stephen Dedalus now moves the only individual that really exists is Stephen himself, and the only identity that matters is his own.

James Joyce was not the philosophic idealist or solipsistic aesthete that Stephen Dedalus became. But it may be true that, like Dedalus, he found the world of Jesuits less immediate at Belvedere than he had at Clongowes. With Father Henry he seems to have preserved a close and cordial relationship, but with most of the others there was no longer the intimacy there had been a few years before at Clongowes Wood. This, however, was not because of any serious change in the boy's attitude toward the Jesuits, or in their attitude toward him. It was due to a change in circumstances. At Clongowes, a boarding school, Joyce had been under the constant daily supervision of Jesuit masters and prefects. He arose in the morning to their salutation, "Laudetur Jesus Christus," and went to bed at night to their benediction, "Deo Gratias." In between he prayed, studied, played, walked, talked, and ate always in the company of Jesuits. Now he was older and less dependent on them physically, but, more than that, he was now attending one of their day schools where his contact with Jesuits, though still considerable, was far more limited than it had been at Clongowes. He was still very much under their influence once he had climbed the steps of No. 6 Great Denmark Street, but when he left again in the late afternoon, with the dark coming down on the Dublin streets, he was physically free of them. Still, of course, he was never wholly free. Their spirit followed him into the streets, accompanying him like a conscience or a curse, through the dusk of his way homeward. So, when he was older, it was to follow him still, more dimly and from farther off, when for the last time he left church, home, and country, to meet the challenge of exile and creation.

III

On December 21, 1922, Joyce wrote to his Aunt Josephine (Mrs. William Murray), then mystified by *Ulysses,* suggesting that the best introduction to his novel was Charles Lamb's *Adventures of Ulysses.*[54] It still may be. Certainly it is the primary source of his interest in and meditation on the Ulysses theme. "I was twelve years old," he told a student in Zurich, "when I studied the Trojan War but the story of Ulysses alone remained in my recollection. It was the mysticism that pleased me." [55]

It would seem that Joyce was here again referring to Lamb's *Adventures.* But Lamb's book had, of course, no more to do with the Trojan War than had the *Odyssey* itself. Barring the possibility that the comment is inaccurately reported, all that Joyce could have meant by his Zurich remarks is that *by the time* he was twelve he already knew the story of Troy, having read about it at Clongowes in *Peter Parley's Tales about Ancient and Mod-*

---

[54] "Some Unpublished Letters of James Joyce," *Envoy,* V (April, 1951), 47; reprinted in *Letters of James Joyce,* ed. by Gilbert, p. 198.

[55] Gorman, *James Joyce,* p. 224.

ern Greece, and that *when* he was twelve he learned in somewhat greater detail the story of Ulysses. It is a matter of record that he studied the story in the Preparatory Grade at Belvedere where, in the Intermediate examination in English, he was responsible for a knowledge of Lamb's *Adventures of Ulysses.*

This examination included matter not usually associated with the study of English. In addition to grammar, composition, and literature, a knowledge of history and geography was also required. To each of these five divisions of the subject the Intermediate syllabus allotted a specific number of points, and it is worth noting that fewer points were allotted to Lamb (150) than to history (250) or grammar (200), or than were allotted to composition (250) or geography (200). The results of the examination in 1894 further show, interestingly enough, that Joyce did less well percentagewise in English, where he scored 455 out of a possible 1,200 points, than in Latin, where his score was 700 out of 1,200, or in French (400 out of 700), or even in arithmetic (430 out of 500). The significance of this should not be missed. A schoolboy, anxious to excel in his examinations—in actual need, perhaps, of one of the cash prizes awarded for excellence—may be expected to have concentrated his efforts on those subjects, and on those particular divisions of a subject, in which he could most surely accumulate the greatest numbers of points. Young Joyce was an ambitious and practical boy, and one should not be too quick to read into his scholastic interest in Ulysses *at this time* anything more than is warranted by the ambition and practicality of his twelve years.

But what is to be made of his remark that "it was the mysticism [in Ulysses] that pleased me"? It should be said at once that by "mysticism" Joyce could not have meant the ascetical, though the boy was probably more responsive to asceticism than most twelve-year-olds. "Mysticism" in its secondary and more literal sense, as "spiritually allegorical, of occult meaning," would seem the more probable definition. This way of interpreting Homer began as far back as Theagenes of Rhegium (525 B.C.), flourished among the Alexandrians, the Neoplatonists, and the Fathers of the Church, and it did not wholly fade from view until the eighteenth century and the dawn of deistical and scientific optimism.[56] The Romantics, consequently, found Prometheus and Ossian more acceptable heroes than the wily Ithacan, and their Victorian successors, Joyce's immediate predecessors in the Ulysses tradition, produced portraits of the hero quite untrammeled by "mysticism." Joyce, a Greek-less schoolboy of twelve, could not have been familiar with the older tradition of Homeric exegesis, but in Lamb's redaction of the Ulysses story, based on Chapman's pre-Augustan translation of the *Odyssey,* he found the spirit of that older tradition still sufficiently alive to start him to wonder.

In his preface Lamb acknowledges his debt to Chapman, but almost apologetically and without mentioning him by name. He refers there only to "the obligations which I have had to one obsolete version." [57] But twenty years later he feels less need of caution or apology; writing to Barton, in 1827, he asks: "Did you ever read my 'Adventures of Ulysses,' founded on Chapman's old translation of it, for children or men? Chapman is divine, and my abridgment has not quite emptied him of his divinity." [58] The quality here praised by Lamb is that scorned earlier by Pope

[56] Stanford, "The Mysticism That Pleased Him," *Envoy,* V (April, 1951), 62–65. It was not until my own independent research at the IEBI in Dublin had been completed that my attention was called to this rewardingly suggestive article.

Though my use of IEBI materials is here a good deal more extensive than Stanford's, I am in this and the paragraphs immediately succeeding much in his debt, especially for his relation of Lamb's book to the whole Ulysses tradition. Stanford's larger work, *The Ulysses Theme,* is indispensable for an understanding of the significance and development of that tradition.

[57] Preface to *The Adventures of Ulysses,* in *Mrs. Leicester's School and Other Stories,* ed. by Ainger, p. 90.

[58] *Ibid.,* p. 394.

in the preface to his own translation of Homer. Pope scores Chapman's "strong affectation of extracting new meanings out of his author" and expresses impatience with the older translator's predilection for "mysteries" and his efforts "to strain the obvious sense." [59] Lamb, and possibly Keats, did much to rescue Chapman from that oblivion to which Pope's criticism had confined him in the eighteenth century.

Lamb, however, in following Chapman, had before him a very different kind of audience from the sophisticated courtiers of Elizabeth and James. He was writing for "young readers," and so he sought to give "a rapidity to the narration" and an "air of romance" that might attract and hold the interest of the young.[60] In his attempt to do so, he very wisely avoided the subtleties of allegory and "sacrificed in many places the manners to the passion, the subordinate characteristics to the essential interest of the story." [61] But the magical and wondrous remained dominantly in the foreground:

The agents in this tale, besides men and women, are giants, enchanters, sirens: things which denote external force or internal temptations, the twofold danger which a wise fortitude must expect to encounter in its course through this world.[62]

Lamb further emphasized this aspect of his story by omitting entirely the Telemachia and beginning with Ulysses' strange adventures among the enchanters (lotus-eaters) and giants (Polyphemus and the Cyclops). The Intermediate syllabus added to this emphasis by prescribing only the first seven chapters of Lamb's *Adventures* for examination. Perhaps the Intermediate Board felt that the last three chapters, especially the account of the slaughter of the suitors, was meat too strong for the tender

[59] Pope's preface to the *Iliad*, in *The Iliad and Odyssey of Homer*, ed. by Buckley, p. 1.
[60] Preface to *The Adventures of Ulysses*, p. 89.　　　[61] *Ibid.*　　　[62] *Ibid.*

sensibilities of twelve-year-old boys. Accordingly, the students' final view of Ulysses was of the hero standing under the shadow of Mount Nerytus, aware at last "that he was arrived in his own country, and with the delight which he felt he could not forebear stooping down and kissing the soil." [63]

Joyce himself doubtless read beyond the seventh chapter to the end of Lamb's *Adventures*. The book, as Lamb conceived and executed it, although not elaborately or obviously allegorical, could suggest to a sensitive and imaginative boy meanings as "mystical" as those which Joyce commentators have since professed to find in his own work. Much of Joyce's later reading—Dante ("For every true born mysticist / A Dante is, unprejudiced . . ." [64]), Max Muller, Victor Bérard—would serve to clarify and confirm the "mysticism" inherent in the Ulysses theme. For Joyce, they would all be grist to his mill. But the beginning was at Belvedere with Charles Lamb and the Jesuits.

IV

Belvedere was the beginning of much else besides. Scholastically, Joyce was to prove himself a more than competent student, and the studies in which he excelled—as, to a lesser degree, the subjects in which he showed an increasing lack of interest—were to indicate this early where his real talents lay and the direction of his future success. At the end of his first year he won an exhibition, actually an award for general excellence, valued at £20. He was one of only four boys at Belvedere to do so, and he was the only Belvederean that year to win a prize in Latin (£2). This was clearly his best subject and his score (700 out of a possible 1,200 points) remained his best showing in any division of the four Intermediate competitions in which he participated.

[63] *The Adventures of Ulysses*, p. 149.
[64] James Joyce, "The Holy Office," in *The Portable James Joyce*, ed. by Levin, p. 657.

The following year Joyce retained the exhibition won in 1894, but by the slimmest of margins. There were 164 names on the Honors List in 1895, and Joyce's name was the 164th. In the Preparatory Grade, out of 132 boys, he had ranked 103d in order of merit. The explanation of this near fall from excellence is probably to be found in the marks he received in natural philosophy (i.e., physics) and chemistry, where out of a possible total of 1,000 Joyce scored just 200 points. He had not competed in either of these two subjects in the previous year, and after 1895 he dropped chemistry completely. It is possible that he was not permitted to drop natural philosophy, but for all the good the subject did him on subsequent examinations it would have been just as well if he had.

In June, 1895, Joyce had completed his first two full years at Belvedere College. (The date, incidentally, corresponds to that of the Whitsuntide play in the *Portrait*.) Now at the end of his Junior year, he would under ordinary circumstances be expected to pass into the Middle Grade in the following September. He did not, however, do so.

"Joyce," a fellow-Belvederean wrote many years later, "was under age for the junior grade and was held back a year. The plan was that he would secure first place in the succeeding year. He didn't! Although he was high on the list." [65] The quotation is interesting as an example of what might be called the "approximate accuracy" of the so-called Joyce-people. With perhaps the best of intentions (though one wonders at the envious exclamation point in the quotation just given), schoolmates, acquaintances, friends, and relatives of Joyce have blurred the facts about his early life by relying too casually upon powers of recall that are altogether too fallible. Caution will usually demand that such "facts" be disregarded unless they can be substantiated by more

[65] W. G. Fallon—named on p. 189 of the *Portrait*—in a letter dated December 7, 1954, to the Very Reverend R. F. Roche, S.J., Rector of Belvedere College.

reliable, documented evidence. The present "fact" is a case in point, albeit a minor one. For it is true that Joyce was held back for a year, and it is true that he was under age, and it may be true that he and the Jesuits planned with an extra year of preparation to win first place the following year. But it is not true that he was under age for the *Junior* Grade, for he had won an exhibition as a Junior in 1895. The truth is that, since he would not be fifteen until February 2, 1897, he was not old enough for the *Middle* Grade competitions in 1896. This year, then, 1895-96, was a sort of scholastic interlude during which young Joyce, on the edge of adolescence, was probably left more to himself than at any time during his years at Belvedere.

It was probably during this year that he began to read widely on his own. It is unlikely that *Robinson Crusoe* or Scott's *The Lord of the Isles,* the assigned readings for the Junior Grade, absorbed much of his attention this second time round. Possibly he anticipated the assignments for the Middle Grade and began reading Goldsmith's essays (selections from *The Bee* and *The Citizen of the World*) and Gray's poetry ("Elegy," "The Bard," "Ode on a Distant Prospect of Eton College"). But more than either of these, he would have taken to Milton's early poetry— "L'Allegro," "Il Penseroso," and especially "Lycidas." Lines from the last were to be introduced as part of the lesson Stephen Dedalus set his pupils in Mr. Deasy's school (U 26-27) and one line— "through the dear might of Him that walked the waves"—was to stick into Stephen's memory like a thorn. Twenty-five years later Joyce, sitting with Frank Budgen over a glass of Nostrano, could recite "Lycidas" from beginning to end and after it repeat the whole of "L'Allegro." [66] It was no accident that Joyce, this early and late, should have found much to admire in Milton. The two men had much in common: music, scholarship, a mastery

[66] Budgen, *James Joyce and the Making of Ulysses,* p. 176.

of the English language, a high sense of dedication, and extraordinary gifts of memory. Both, too, were to suffer a similar fate at the hands of biographers: Johnson believed as firmly that Satan was Milton as Gorman believed Dedalus was Joyce.

During 1895–96 Joyce certainly must have read much more than was prescribed by the Intermediate syllabus, but in the absence of evidence it would be profitless now to speculate on what that reading may have been. It is more tempting, perhaps, to imagine what his life was like away from books. He did not have to work very hard at Belvedere and, being thrown much on his own, he possibly discovered, as others had before him, that idleness may nurture pleasures other than literary. Did he take advantage of this unwonted leisure to investigate, as Stephen Dedalus later did, the seamier side of Dublin life? He had the opportunity, but it is more than probable that he took no advantage of it. He was, first of all, only fourteen years old and, even granted that the Irish are a precocious lot—though much in Joyce is suspiciously "postcocious"—this is not an age when young men are normally seeking, or made welcome in, establishments of night. In any event, this period cannot be made to correspond to Stephen's season of debauch in the *Portrait*. Stephen there confesses that he is only sixteen (P 166)—young enough, God knows, to be initiated into the rites of the bordello—an age which Joyce did not reach until his final months at Belvedere.

But this may be the time at which another incident occurred which, according to Stanislaus Joyce, became the basis for one of the stories in *Dubliners*:

"An Encounter" [Stanislaus writes] is based on an actual incident that occurred to my brother and me when we planned and carried out a day's minching together. He was about twelve and I was about ten years of age at the time, and we did not understand what kind of individual we had encountered, but our suspicions were aroused.

We thought he was a "queer juggins"—some kind of escaped lunatic —and we gave him the slip. Later, my brother put him into the book as a by-product of English educational methods.[67]

Stanislaus Joyce was ten years old on December 17, 1895, and James was four years, less two months, his senior. Even by Stanislaus's hazy reckoning, then, the incident is to be located during the year that Joyce was repeating at Belvedere. Moreover, though possible, it is unlikely that a student as serious and ambitious as Joyce would be "minching"—playing truant—during a term of regularly scheduled classes. Stanislaus, whose masters complained that he was "late to school often" and "not working as he could," [68] was apparently not the kind of student to worry over an occasional unscheduled holiday. But James was of a different sort, and a day's minching for him, under the circumstances, could hardly be considered even technical truancy.

The Jesuits, aware by Joyce's third year at Belvedere that they had a highly talented student on their hands, and knowing how talent may be endangered by idleness, probably tried to keep him as occupied as possible. They may have recommended further reading to him, but in a school where only a year or two before one of the Jesuit masters had been reprimanded for recommending *Ivanhoe*—"my God, A NOVEL!"—to his students,[69] that reading may have been, aside from established classics, safe to the point of dullness. The Jesuits, practical men, may also have found another way of keeping Joyce busy. In the Belvedere Cash Book, now in the rector's office at the college, there appears, under the date of October 15, 1896, the following entry: "Mr. Joyce (tutor) Sept.

---

[67] "The Background to 'Dubliners,' " *The Listener*, LI (March 25, 1954), 526. The word Joyce uses in "An Encounter" is "miching," not "minching" as Stanislaus has it, but in both cases the word means truancy.

[68] Notes penciled in a Belvedere College Account Book under date of October 14, 1900.

[69] Byrne, *Silent Years*, p. 22.

2–Oct. 15 (inc.) £2/18/4." [70] If this Mr. Joyce is James A.—
though there is no proof that he is—it may indicate that during
the previous year the boy was profitably occupied in tutoring other
Belvedereans younger and less talented than himself.

Whatever may be the truth of this, Joyce in the Middle Grade
in 1896–97 turned in the best performance of his scholastic career
at Belvedere. But if he and the Jesuits had really planned on his
winning first place in the Intermediate examinations, both were
disappointed. Not deeply, however. The names of only 34 boys
appeared on the Honor List in 1897, and of these Joyce was 13th
in order of merit. In attaining this rank he scored a sum total of
2,927 (out of a possible 5,800) points, the highest score he ever
made in the examinations. Again he did best in languages (English, Latin, French, and Italian), and again mathematics and
physics conspired against his doing better. His great success,
however, came in English composition. In all Ireland only three
boys won English prizes in the Middle Grade examination, and
Joyce was first of the three. For this he received, in addition to an
exhibition worth £30, a cash prize of £3. Father Henry and the
Jesuits at Belvedere could not have been too deeply disappointed
at their pupil's showing, and they were perhaps human enough
to take a certain partisan satisfaction in the thought that Joyce, in
winning first place in English, had topped a Protestant boy (John
L. Moore) from the Royal Academical Institution in Belfast.
Joyce himself, pocketing his prize money, may have found the
occasion gratifying for reasons more private than the Jesuits' pride
in him or the prize money in his pocket.

His scholastic success in 1896–97 was repeated in the Senior Grade

---

[70] The first entries in this Cash Book date from 1861. There is no order of
regularity in the accounts and it is far from clear whether the "Mr. Joyce" mentioned here was the payee or payer of the £2/18/4. The name does not occur
again before or after October 15, 1895. I am personally very dubious about
identifying the name with James Joyce.

the following year, his last at Belvedere. But there was a difference. Though he was again on the Honor List and so retained the exhibition won in 1897, he now ranked 53d among 64 boys so honored. The reason for this drop in the order of merit is clear. In the Intermediate examinations Joyce all but ignored the sections devoted to science and mathematics. In physics, where the year before (when he was apparently *trying* for first place) he had exerted himself sufficiently to score 175 out of 500 points, his score this year was 10! In plane geometry it was 20 out of 700, and in Euclid 40 out of 600. Only in arithmetic and algebra (combined for a maximum of 900 points on the Intermediate examinations of 1898), did Joyce make any show of effort, and that effort, represented by a score of 145 points, was not especially impressive. This lack of interest in mathematics and science, revealed in his examination, doubtless reflects a similar attitude toward these subjects during the whole of his last year at Belvedere. At some time during that year the boy seems to have made up his mind to concentrate on what really interested him and to develop what he considered his real talents. If "natural philosophy" and the like had as a consequence to go by the board, then so much the worse for the world of science.

What Joyce's real interests were, and what were the talents he was developing during this year, are equally clear from the records of the Intermediate examinations. As in previous years, his forte was languages. But where he had previously been strongest in Latin and modern languages, there was in 1898 a slight falling off. This was more than compensated for by the striking gains made in English, which now was clearly his best subject. This Senior examination, in which he scored 650 out of 1,200 points, was his best single performance in any of the four Intermediate competitions in which he took part. The boy's personal satisfaction with his exhibition—and the £30 that went with it—was probably less intense than the pleasure he felt in winning first place in English composition for the second successive year. It was not the extra £4 prize that was awarded, though this was not to be despised; it was not the smiles and congratulations of the Jesuits for whom he had again beaten out two Protestant boys from the same Royal Academical Institution in Belfast. The pleasure was, perhaps, more than private—it was secret. Exhibitions, prizes (Joyce this year also won a "third class prize [in books] value £1") were public acknowledgment of schoolboy competence or excellence. They were distinctions, but distinctions shared by many in a small, generally undistinguished world of scholastic effort. The boy was pleased, of course, but undeceived by this public proof of his industry. For what he had proved to himself was still more important, and the secret of his pleasure started deep in the root of a new consciousness of his talents, of potentialities that might yet be powers, of promised mastery of the word, through which alone as artist he might celebrate the mysteries of the world in which he was born.

Father Henry, sitting in the gray light of his Belvedere office, reading the results of the Intermediate examinations, may also have let his mind wander to celebrations and mysteries—though not to those of this world. It was not difficult, with the proof before him, to think of James Joyce as some day celebrating the mystery of the Mass. For the boy, Father Henry knew, was more than a gifted student. During his time at Belvedere, and especially during the past two years, he had given every sign of being a dedicated and even perhaps chosen spirit.

"Jesuit Bark and Bitter Bite"

Whatever he had heard or read of the craft of Jesuits he had put aside
frankly as not borne out by his own experience. His masters, even
when they had not attracted him, had seemed to him always intelligent and serious priests, athletic and highspirited prefects. . . .
During all those years he had never heard from any of his masters
a flippant word: it was they who had taught him christian doctrine
and urged him to live a good life and, when he had fallen into
grievous sin, it was they who had led him back to grace. [P 180–81]

. . . the soulcontracted son of the secret cell groped through life at
the expense of the taxpayers, dejected into day and night with jesuit
bark and bitter bite. . . .   [FW 182]

READERS OF *Finnegans Wake,* on first encountering the passage
quoted above, are likely to read it simply as metaphor—vaguely
suggestive perhaps of curs and kennels, or possibly of seas and
sailingships. No doubt it is open to either interpretation, or to
both at once. But Jesuits' bark, before becoming a metaphor, was
of course a fact, an early designation for the skin of the cinchona
tree from which are extracted the febrifugal properties of quinine.
Mindful of this, one may find Joyce's reference less contemptuous
than it at first appeared. The man is remembering the Jesuits of
his boyhood not as a contemptible breed (whose bark is worse
than their bite) but as physicians of the soul who were concerned
that the fevers of adolescence should not be soulcontracted into

a chronic disease of life. They may have succeeded all too well. This bitter bite (in *Ulysses* "the agenbite of inwit"), under Jesuit medication, resulted in a form of spiritual cinchonism from which, it would appear, Joyce was never fully to recover.

While at Belvedere, the boy's response to the Jesuit prescription was pronounced. Even Dedalus had been infected briefly by the virus of Jesuit idealism and in his quieter moments could reflect dispassionately, even admiringly, on those "intelligent and serious priests and highspirited prefects" who had guarded and guided him thus far through life. James Joyce cannot be thought less sensitive or intelligent or responsive than Stephen Dedalus, and his thought about his Jesuit masters and about himself as a Jesuit must be taken at least as seriously, and perhaps a good deal more seriously, than the somber solipsistic reflections of the Dedalus. In want of any more intimate record, the quality of his response at this time may be deduced from what is known of his experience—apart from his purely scholastic achievements—while at the college. What, to begin with, were his relations with his fellows, his family, and his superiors in the schoolboy world of Belvedere?

Of all the boys who are mentioned in the Belvedere chapters of the *Portrait* only one may be said to figure more than incidentally.[1] This is Albert Connolly, who appears under the *nom de guerre* of Vincent Heron. The name is significant because of the impression the boy makes on Stephen Dedalus:

He had often thought it strange that Vincent Heron had a bird's face as well as a bird's name. A shock of pale hair lay on the forehead like

[1] J. F. Byrne entered Belvedere on September 3, 1892, and, according to his own account, left the school in 1895 after he had taken and passed the autumn matriculation examination in the old Royal University. His last two years at the college coincided, therefore, with Joyce's first two; but, though the two boys were doubtless acquainted at this time, they did not become close friends until they met again at University College.

a ruffled crest: the forehead was narrow and bony and a thin hooked nose stood out between the closeset prominent eyes which were light and inexpressive. [P 84]

This description of Heron relates him to Dante's eagles (P 2) and to Mr. Gleeson (P 48), both taloned symbols of authority. But where Dante symbolized domestic authority (with strong clerical overtones), and Gleeson is an obvious representative of ecclesiastical authority (whose justice is tempered with gentleness), Heron stands for a kind of self-justifying lay or civil authority. Stephen—"this heretic"—is delivered into his power by his two henchmen and fellow inquisitors, and the punishment that Stephen had trembled to consider at the hands of Mr. Gleeson is in fact meted out at Heron's hands (P 91). And during this caning the exchange between Stephen and Heron ("Admit," "No," "Admit," "No. No.") distantly echoes the cruel antiphon of the encounter with Dante: "Apologise, / Pull out his eyes, / Pull out his eyes, / Apologise." The episode does point up the cowardice and cruelty of Heron and his two lieutenants, Nash and Boland; and Stephen at the time is reduced to tears by their malice. But, though the details of the incident are painfully clear in Stephen's recollection (it is presented in the *Portrait* as a flashback; P 87–91), "the memory of it called forth no anger in him." This is because Stephen is already beginning to feel the stirrings of a more profound unrest which is eventually to carry him beyond the bounds of all authority.

But this does not mean that Joyce is branding his own companions at Belvedere as fools and cowards. Who Nash and Boland were is not known, nor does it now seem of much importance. But Albert Connolly's relation with Joyce would seem to be much like that between Dedalus and Heron in the *Portrait:*

The rivals were school friends. They sat together in class, knelt together in the chapel, talked together after beads over their lunches.

As the fellows in number one were undistinguished dullards Stephen and Heron had been during the year the virtual heads of the school. It was they who went up to the rector together to ask for a free day or to get a fellow off. [P 84]

Albert Connolly was in fact Joyce's scholastic rival at Belvedere. The two boys appear to have been in the same class until 1896. That year, the year in which Joyce was held back because of his age and did not compete in the Intermediate examinations, Connolly won an exhibition. This he retained the following year when Joyce and he were the only boys from Belvedere so honored. The closeness of their rivalry may be measured by their respective ranks in the order of merit: of the 64 students who won honors in 1897, Joyce was 54th and Albert Connolly 57th. The rivalry was, however, friendly. They did "kneel together in the chapel" where Joyce served as prefect of the Sodality and Connolly was his first assistant prefect: [2] the former led one group of boys in recitation of the Little Office B.V.M., and the latter led another group in antiphonal response. As prefect and assistant prefect respectively, they were indeed "virtual heads of the school."

As the Jesuits in the Belvedere chapters of the *Portrait* are more dimly drawn than the Clongowes Jesuits, so too are the schoolboys in their charge. Only one student, W. G. Fallon, is clearly identified by name (P 189), but the passing mention of him is of no significance to the narrative.[3] Moreover, one must again be constantly on guard against confusing Dedalus's response to the "undistinguished dullards" around him with the attitude of the adolescent James Joyce to his own schoolfellows.

[2] Annals of the Congregation of the Blessed Virgin Mary, a record of the sodality at Belvedere, now in the Rector's archives at the college.

[3] This William Fallon was frequently one of Joyce's fellow guests at the Sheehy parties on Belvedere Place. During one evening of charades he and Joyce did a burlesque of *Hamlet,* Joyce playing the queen mother to Fallon's Ophelia. See Sheehy, *May It Please the Court,* p. 22.

Dedalus at Belvedere goes into a solipsistic spin in which the objective realities of existence recede from the tightening center of his sensibility like a universe of fading stars. When he does not deliberately shun the community of his fellows, he is enduring their company passively and reluctantly. Only once is he drawn back briefly into a sense of oneness with those about him. The occasion is again the Whitsuntide play.

> Another nature seemed to have been lent him: the infection of the excitement and youth about him entered into and transformed his moody mistrustfulness. For one rare moment he seemed to be clothed in the real apparel of boyhood: and, as he stood in the wings among the other players, he shared the common mirth amid which the drop scene was hauled upwards by two ablebodied priests with violent jerks and all awry. [P 95]

This "rare moment" in Dedalus's experience would seem to have been the more habitual mood of Joyce himself. The other nature here lent to him may well be Joyce's own nature, "clothed in the real apparel of boyhood," and the passage, contrasting the living boy with the literary portrait, may be read as more authentically autobiographical than other more dramatic passages in these Belvedere chapters. For if Joyce, like Dedalus, was different from his fellows, it was not that he stood apart from them in mysterious and surly aloofness, but that he stood superior to most of them in ways at once understandable, acceptable, and admirable in their eyes and in the eyes of their Jesuit masters. *At this time* the boy is not to be thought of as a budding artist whose Dedalean eccentricities were also at the bud; he was an exceptional schoolboy of proved scholastic superiority, of sound if fragile health, and, to all outward appearances, of substantial moral and religious disposition. As such, he had all the physical, intellectual, and moral qualities prerequisite for a vocation to the priesthood.

I

"His mother," Gorman writes, *"an unreasoningly pious* woman whose piety increased as she aged, would have been pleased to see her oldest son reveal a vocation for the church. With the influence of his Jesuit teachers *subtly directed on him* and the emotional instigation of his mother *pushing him towards the Holy of Holies* there was a period during the Belvedere years when Joyce actually entertained the idea of entering the Jesuit order. Father James Joyce, S.J. At least, it was alliterative." [4]

These unabashed clichés—pious women are always unreasoning, Jesuit influence always subtle—serve here only to contradict Gorman's own curious image of Dedalus-Joyce. This impossible young man, whom Gorman has endowed with an "independent and restless will," [5] is now pushed about by a pious old woman. That inquisitive mind, that found in "subversive writers . . . an acidulous antidote to the dogmatic precisions of Jesuit philosophy," [6] is now the innocent object of jesuitical guile. Finally, one is asked to believe that young Joyce, though "impatient of stupidities," [7] at one time actually thought of a vocation to the priesthood in terms of an alliteration! In the light of this, one can understand why Joyce should afterwards refer to Herbert Gorman as his "biografiend" (FW 55).

If the boy's thoughts on the priesthood were now more serious than his daydreaming about it back at Clongowes, there was good reason why this should be so. But one is likely to miss the whole point of this first major decision in Joyce's life if the crisis resolved by that decision is thought nothing more than the convergence

---

[4] Gorman, *James Joyce,* p. 47. Italics mine.   [5] *Ibid.,* p. 44.

[6] *Ibid.* It is hardly necessary to point out that Joyce studied no philosophy at Belvedere, "Jesuit" or other kind.

[7] *Ibid.,* p. 46.

of two external pressures brought to bear by his mother and his masters.

Stanislaus Joyce, in his recent memoir of James, felt it necessary to deny emphatically that there was ever any hostility between his mother and her oldest son. James remained always her favorite, even after his repudiation of the faith to which she owed so deep a loyalty. Before that time—and, according to Stanislaus, his own rejection of Catholicism was earlier and more overt than his brother's—the relation between James and his mother was especially intimate and untroubled. As a child, soon after leaving Clongowes, James used to have his mother assign him lessons in his old schoolbooks and examine him on them. The custom continued long after he entered Belvedere, despite the fact that by then Joyce's childhood was already a thing of the past and other children (a new brother or sister appeared almost every year) were present to claim the attention and affection of his mother. It was his mother, too, who accompanied him to early morning Mass in the Jesuit chapel and, when the boy remained after Mass to continue his prayers, whispered to him to hurry, that breakfast was waiting.[8]

This intimacy between mother and son was not confined to lessons at home or visits to chapel. On Sunday evenings the two would walk over together to Belvedere Place where every week their friends the Sheehys held open house. Mr. David Sheehy was a member of Parliament whom Joyce thought a bit pompous, but who was really no more than patriarchal—quite unlike John Stanislaus Joyce—in the midst of a large, happy, and rather handsome family. Mrs. Sheehy, moreover, was a great favorite of the boy. Frank, the oldest of the six Sheehy children and a classmate of Joyce at Belvedere, had first brought him to one of these parties at the beginning of their last year, and Joyce continued to

[8] *My Brother's Keeper,* pp. 45, 80.

attend them, though less and less regularly, until the end of his final year at University College.

The Sheehys appear in *Stephen Hero* as the Daniel family, among whom Stephen Daedalus, whom no company could cheer, was moodily ill at ease. Priggishly shy, he objected chiefly to what he considered too great a familiarity presumed too soon by the various Daniels. "In this house," it is reported, "it was the custom to call a young visitor by his Christian name a little too soon . . . though Stephen was spared the compliment" (SH 36). But this hardly reflects Joyce's own attitude toward the Sheehys, or theirs toward him. Mary Sheehy, Frank's younger sister and afterwards the wife of Joyce's college friend Tom Kettle, remembers him quite differently. On his first visits to Belvedere Place the boy did appear diffident and withdrawn, seldom venturing more than a *sotto voce* aside to Frank in a corner of the Sheehy parlor. This naturally caused some amusement among the older Sheehy girls and their friends, and they were not above mimicking his too-serious attitudes. But he was easily enough teased out of silence and, once drawn into the group, became quickly enough the center of their evenings' entertainment—the charades, the singing, and the dancing. One evening in particular stands out in Mary Sheehy's memory. She was herself a more than ordinarily shy girl, more so than her sisters or their friends, and when young Joyce approached her that evening and invited her to dance she was accountably, consciously flustered. Courteously he tried to put her at ease, but when she stood up her shyness stretched such a distance between them—she was too shy even to take his hand— there was little chance of their managing a waltz at all. In a gentle mumble James whispered to her: "Take hold of my hand, Mary." And Mary looked up at him aghast, blushing, a little bewildered, and exclaimed weirdly: "Take hold of your *tongue*, is it!" Joyce's eyes opened wide, then back went his head in a great whoop of laughter, and catching the girl up in his arms he swirled her around her father's parlor in a tumultuous and most original waltz.[9]

These parties on Belvedere Place must also have been particularly happy occasions for Mrs. Joyce. She came with her son —not always, but often enough for it to be remembered years later—because her son wanted her with him. Besides Mr. and Mrs. Sheehy themselves, she was usually the only other parent present. Nor was she present as spectator only. Often mother and son would entertain the company together, she taking her place at the piano and accompanying him as he sang the songs they were both especially fond of: "I Will Arise from Dreams of Thee," "A Pair of Sparkling Eyes," "Blarney Castle." The Sheehys and their guests were delighted by the old music, but no less by the young mother and her son. And some of the girls present, those who had been put off at first by Joyce's apparent reserve, were easily won over, no doubt sentimentally, by what they then thought his most endearing quality.

Mrs. Joyce during these years—hearing her son's lessons, visiting with him the silent morning chapels, sharing his gay and innocent evenings with friends—must surely have taken great and forgivable pride in the boy. He seemed to have inherited many of her own qualities: a frailness of body that in her was delicateness (how vain would be the man Joyce of his fine hands and tiny feet!), a seriousness and reserve of manner that was almost shyness and welcomed silence, and a marked love for the arts, especially poetry and music. She may be forgiven for not guessing then that, though the flesh and feeling of the boy seemed so

[9] From conversation with Mrs. Thomas Kettle in August, 1954, and a personal letter from her two months later. Stanislaus Joyce, *My Brother's Keeper*, p. 150, identifies Mary Sheehy—"young, happy, and very handsome"—with the girl E.C. in the *Portrait* and as the inspiration of two poems (XII and XXV) in *Chamber Music*, an honor which Mrs. Kettle has graciously declined.

much hers, the spirit of the man—jovial, boisterous, unbounded, all but chaotic—was wholly the inheritance of her husband. (Her second son, Stanislaus, seemed then more his father's son in body and mind; yet in the end it was Stanislaus and not James who was to be a mother's boy, but tough not gentle, recalcitrant not resigned.) She may be forgiven too for thinking that the boy had also inherited her own unaffected and ineradicable piety. At the time he gave every sign of it, and these signs might well point to the hope that in him she had a son who was destined for the priesthood. The degree of her hope now would be the measure of her disappointment later. The boy's piety, like hers, was unaffected; it was not, like hers, ineradicable.

But her hopes, whatever else they might have been, were not coercive. Mrs. Joyce was not, morally or temperamentally, a person who could push or drive the boy—or his father or anyone else—against his will. She was the antithesis of dominating woman or possessive mother. Like any woman with her faith, "unreasoning" perhaps but not unreasonable, she would have been pleased and proud to see her son a priest, but her religious awe of the priesthood was such that she would never have presumed to decide for another what she piously considered was God's holy will.

II

The Jesuits at Belvedere almost certainly shared Mrs. Joyce's pious hopes. And with good reason. The boy's scholastic record at the college had been impressive, but what they found even more impressive was his deportment. He showed every sign of being not only an exceptionally bright boy, but an extraordinarily good boy. He took his religion as seriously as he did his studies, and in the religious life of the school he was as much a leader as in scholastic life. This was especially true during his last two years at the college.

On Saturday morning, December 7, 1895, the eve of the Feast of the Immaculate Conception, Joyce and twenty-one fellow students "were admitted members of the Sodality." [10] Nine months later, on Friday, September 25, 1896, Joyce was elected prefect of the same sodality, and his friend and rival, Albert Connolly, first assistant prefect.[11] The significance of this for Joyce is only apparent when one understands the importance of the sodality and its prefecture in the schoolboy world of which he was then a part. In a little book called *The Sodality Manual,* a book which was Joyce's constant vade mecum during his last years at Belvedere, rules are set down for the election *"once* (or at most twice) *a year"* of sodality officers. The director, in this case Father Joseph McDonnell, S.J., and the outgoing officers were to "select out of the whole Sodality three eminent among the others for the example of their virtues and their reputation for goodness." The names of the three were then proposed to the full membership of the sodality; the sodalist who obtained the most votes was declared prefect, and the others first and second assistants, "according to the number of votes given for each." [12]

The sodality, older even than the *Ratio Studiorum,* is one of the most characteristic and cherished traditions in the Jesuit educational system; to be prefect of the sodality is one of the highest distinctions to which a Jesuit student can attain. Joyce's nomination, therefore, by the director meant recognition by college authorities of his "eminence"; his election by his fellows a mark,

[10] See, under the date given, Annals of the Congregation of the Blessed Virgin Mary. The names of the twenty-two boys are not given in alphabetical order; if, as seems probable, they are arranged "in order of merit," it is significant that Joyce's name is first on the list.

[11] *Ibid.*

[12] *The Sodality Manual,* ed. by the Rev. J. A. Cullen, S.J., p. 45. Italics in original.

if not of eminent virtue, certainly of general popularity. He was now recognized by masters and students alike as *primus inter pares*. Against the towering international reputation the man later won for himself, a schoolboy distinction of this sort may pale into insignificance, but in the small world of Belvedere sixty years ago the distinction was real and immediate. And, of course, no other world yet existed for the boy. He now served a religious ideal with the same sense of complete dedication that within a few years he was to bring to literature.

Joyce's election, then, represented a real triumph, a triumph which may have been heightened by the circumstances surrounding it. The first of these was the fact that of the officers elected with him he was the youngest; the other three boys—Connolly, Leo Wilkins, and Michael Cassidy—had all been admitted members of the sodality a year or more before him. Secondly, and more significantly, though the prefecture because of its "eminence" was almost always held by a senior student, Joyce was in his next-to-last year, was indeed just beginning the Middle Grade, at the time of his election. Finally, Joyce remained as prefect not one but two years: on Friday, December 17, 1897, he was reelected to his "post of honor" and served in it until he departed Belvedere College in June, 1898.[13] This in itself was unusual and points up both the esteem in which Joyce was held at Belvedere and the conscientiousness with which he performed his duties as prefect.

These duties were clearly outlined for him in the sixth chapter of the "Rules and Constitutions" of the sodality as given in *The Sodality Manual*. Of these the most important is the first, with its strong emphasis on personal example:

As the Prefect takes precedence in rank and office, and claims the first place after the Director, so should he excel the other members of the Sodality in virtue. Wherefore, he should observe with the

[13] Annals of the Congregation B.V.M.

greatest diligence not only the rules of his own office but also the common rules, those especially that relate to the frequentation of the sacraments, confessing his sins, and receiving the Blessed Eucharist more frequently than the others; and he should take care to advance the Sodality in the way of virtue and Christian perfection, more by example even than by words.[14]

Joyce, reelected prefect in December, 1897, may be presumed to have fulfilled, satisfactorily and even exemplarily, the obligations of his office until at least that date. And this office and its obligations also explain, as was indicated previously, the close and constant contact between Joyce and the rector of Belvedere, Father Henry. For on the prefect of the sodality, more than on any other boy, the rector would depend for the advancement of the religious and spiritual ideals, as well as the general morale, of the school—ideals which, in the Jesuit scheme of things, always took precedence over all other objectives. Joyce, then, as prefect, played a more significant role in the life of the school than might, for example, his modern counterpart, the president of a student council. The latter is commonly supposed to act as a sort of liaison between administration and student body; but the prefect of a sodality, like Joyce, was in a sense the spirit of the rector among his fellow students. Indeed, at the weekly meetings of the sodality he was something more: he served in place of the rector. While it would be too much to claim that the functions of his office—administering the sodality, exhorting the sodalists by word as well as by example, and leading them as a priest might lead his congregation in recitation of the litanies and the Little Office B.V.M.—were in any sense sacerdotal, it is still true that, like minor orders, the prefecture was quasi-sacerdotal, and its functions approximated in their own way those of the priest. And it is at least possible that the "sacerdotalism" of Joyce's writings,

[14] *The Sodality Manual*, p. 47.

remarked by his commentators, traces its origin, in part, to the sodality at Belvedere. The thoughts on the priesthood which may have been entertained by the child Joyce at Clongowes were generated out of the fervid religious atmosphere in which he was then confined, and they took no more solid shape than the vague daydreams with which any child might amuse himself. But now, though he was less confined and though the religious atmosphere pressed in on him less relentlessly than before, young Joyce, his thought not yet mature but maturing rapidly, had occasion to think of the priesthood not as a dream but as a definite possibility, the reality of which he had some slight foretaste in his services as prefect.

Joyce at Belvedere was certainly not the rebel some have thought him. For that matter, neither was Stephen Dedalus. The latter, for example, despite Heron's spirit of quarrelsome comradeship, never allows himself to be seduced "from his habits of quiet obedience" (P 93). Obedience, significantly, is that characteristically Jesuit virtue to which St. Ignatius especially exhorted his companions. "Above all," he wrote to the scholastics at Coimbra, "I desire that you be most outstanding in the virtue of obedience. . . . Let other religious orders surpass us in fasts and vigils and in all things else that, according to their own rule and discipline, they piously undertake; but in true and perfect obedience, and in the abdication of your own will and judgment, I especially desire that you who serve God Our Lord in this Society, be outstanding." [15] Again and again Ignatius stresses the im-

[15] "Atque ego sane . . . imprimis obedientiae virtute praestantissimos esse cupio. . . . Ab aliis religiosis ordinibus facilius patiamur superari nos jejuniis, vigiliis, et cetera victus cultusque asperitate, quam suo quique ritu ac disciplina sancte suscipiunt: vera quidem ac perfecta obedientia, abdicationeque voluntatis atque judicii maxime velim, fratres charissimi, esse conspicuos, quicumque in hac Societate Deo Domino nostro deserviunt." "Epistola S. Ignatii de virtute obedientiae," in *Thesaurus Spiritualis S.J.*, pp. 428–29.

portance and preeminence of obedience, and his words are fully
familiar to Stephen Dedalus who, observing the Jesuit dean of
studies at the University, can repeat to himself the original
simile of Ignatius from the *Summarium Constitutionum:* [16]
"Similiter atque senis baculus, he was, as the founder would have
had him, like a staff in an old man's hand . . ." (P 217).

But if Stephen at the University was already beyond the bounds
of obedience, he was never so at Belvedere, and the Jesuits, sensible of the boy's merits, might naturally be expected to see in him
a prospective candidate for the order. For here was a young
man of obviously superior intellectual capacity, who enjoyed a
reputation for solid and unassuming virtue, and who, though not
robust, was in unquestionably good health. Unless one believes
that every call to the religious life must, like that of St. Paul,
be accompanied by a bolt of thunder and a flash of lightning,
these three qualities—brains, character, and health—are in the
natural order and in an otherwise uninvolved Catholic all that
is necessary for a vocation. And in the supernatural order they
will also be deemed sufficient when there is evidence of a sincere
desire to devote such talents to the service of God. Joyce clearly
had all the necessary qualifications, and the Jesuits may well
have believed that there was sufficient evidence for a vocation in
the boy's habitual demeanor. For a firm habit of obedience—that
virtue by which the order was supposed to be especially distinguished—was indeed especially marked in Joyce, and seemed to
indicate a vocation not merely to the religious life in general, but
quite specifically to the Society of Jesus.

In the *Ratio Studiorum* Jesuit masters are urged to converse
frequently with their students about spiritual things, but at the
same time they are admonished not "to entice anyone into our

---

[16] ". . . vel similiter atque senis baculus, qui ubicumque et quacumque in re
velit eo uti, qui eum manu tenit, ei inservit." *Ibid.*, p. 397.

order." [17] The admonition, however, as any Jesuit alumnus might testify, is one of those more honored in the breach than in the observance. One of the annotations to *The Spiritual Exercises* also forbids the director to urge upon his retreatants any special advantages of the religious life over another. But the same annotation continues: "Outside the Exercises, it is true, we may lawfully and meritoriously urge all who probably have the required fitness to choose continence, virginity, and religious life, and every form of religious perfection." [18] The director is further advised that he should act "as a balance at equilibrium, without leaning to one side or the other, and that he should permit the Creator to deal directly with the creature, and the creature directly with his Creator and Lord." [19]

In the *Portrait* it is, appropriately, the director who, after the retreat, speaks to Stephen about the possibility of a vocation. He is acting entirely in the spirit of *The Spiritual Exercises,* and he presents the life of a Jesuit in terms calculated to affect the imagination and idealism of an adolescent. His simple arguments are weighted on the side of a vocation, but toward the close of his remarks he makes a gesture of restoring "a balance of equilibrium": "But you must be quite sure, Stephen, that you have a vocation because it would be terrible if you found afterwards that you had none" (P 185). The balance is more than restored and, with a pious promise and exhortation to pray, the director releases Ste-

[17] Fitzpatrick, *St. Ignatius and the Ratio Studiorum,* p. 196.

[18] *Thesaurus Spiritualis S.J.,* p. 23: "Decima quinta, ille, qui tradit exercitia, non debet ea accipientem movere magis ad paupertatem neque ad promissionem quam ad opposita, neque ad unum statum vel modum vivendi quam ad alium: quia licet, extra Exercitia, possimus licite ac meritorie movere omnes, qui probabiliter idoneitatem habeant, ad eligendam continentiam, virginitatem, religionem et omnem modum perfectionis evangelicae. . . ."

[19] *Ibid.,* p. 24: ". . . qui tradit Exercitia, non divertat, nec se inclinet ad unam neque ad alteram partem; sed consistens in medio, ad instar bilancis, sinat Creatorem cum creatura, et creaturam cum suo Creatore ac Domino immediate operari."

phen in order to "permit the Creator to deal directly with the creature, and the creature directly with his Creator."

In the *Portrait* the issue is never in doubt. The opening lines of the episode, descriptive of the director, adumbrate the decision that is already in the back of Stephen's mind and which later, passing the Jesuit residence in Gardiner Street, he does not so much *will* as recognize.

The director stood in the embrasure of the window, his back to the light, leaning an elbow on the brown crossblind, and, as he spoke and smiled, slowly dangling and looping the cord of the other blind, Stephen stood before him, following for a moment with his eyes the waning of the long summer daylight above the roofs or the slow deft movements of the priestly fingers. The priest's face was in total shadow, but the waning daylight from behind him touched the deeply grooved temples and the curves of the skull.   [P 178]

The embrasure (that is, recess or crypt), the crossblind, the other blind, the waning daylight, the total shadow, the skull, all of these evoke a joyless, sepulchral mood in which the person of the priest suggests to Stephen a figure of death, and his invitation to the priesthood a temptation to deny nature and life. The director's "back to the light" contributes to the same effect. The repetition of the image of the waning daylight, of the words "crossblind" and "blind," and later of the words "gravely" and "grave," deepen the mood with incantatory echoes as if indeed this were the opening of a chant for the dead. One wonders whether Joyce, in presenting the Jesuit director here as a symbol of death, had again in mind that passage in the *Summarium Constitutionum* from which Stephen afterward quotes. Just preceding the simile of the old man's staff, the *Summarium* presents a far more graphic image of Jesuit obedience. "Let each one," it reads, "persuade himself that he ought to allow himself to be ruled and governed . . . as if he were a dead body that suffers itself to be turned this way and that and to be treated in any manner whatsoever."[20] If the *Summarium* did suggest to Joyce his treatment of the director, then the significance of the latter "slowly dangling and looping the cord of the other blind" is abundantly clear and may be rightly identified as the central image, the epiphany of the interview.[21] Stephen is indeed receiving an invitation to death, to hang himself on the crossblind of obedience, and his executioner is that representative of the *"dio boia,* hangman god" (U 210), the Jesuit director.

But Stephen, who even before this interview acknowledged that "to merge his life in the common tide of other lives was harder for him than any fasting or prayer" (P 175), was temperamentally incapable of following this ideal or of accepting this destiny. It was not for him to be "made obedient unto death, even to the death of the cross."[22] After the interview, on his way homeward, he wondered vaguely "at the frail hold which so many years of order and obedience had on him" (P 188) when once his personal freedom was threatened. And at home, in the squalor and disorder of the family kitchen, the weary voices of his brothers and sisters sounded for him a note which, "like the voice of nature herself" (P 190), despite pain and weariness, gave utterance to a kind of hope which was not to be heard in "the voice of the director urging upon him the proud claims of the church and the mystery and power of the priestly office" (P 188). That voice was the voice of death, to be echoed a little later by the mocking voices of his schoolfellows on the beach at Dollymount. But by

[20] *Ibid.,* p. 397: "Quisque sibi persuadeat, quod qui sub obedientia vivunt, se ferri ac regi a Divina providentia per Superiores suos sinere debent perinde, ac si cadaver essent, quod quoquoversus ferri, et quacumque ratione tractari se sinit. . . ."

[21] Kenner in *Dublin's Joyce,* p. 113, does so identify it, but without calling attention to this relevant passage in the *Summarium Constitutionum.*

[22] A significant text *(Phil.* 2:8) quoted by St. Ignatius in his "Letter on Obedience" with which Joyce was doubtless familiar.

then Stephen's "soul had arisen from the grave of boyhood, spurning her graveclothes" (P 197). He heard now only the affirmative cry of his own heart, and listened now only for the wild cry of the voice of Nature herself. This came to him in the image of a girl standing, alone and still, by the sea, in "the likeness of a strange and beautiful sea-bird" (P 199). Always before the image or suggestion of a bird—Dante's eagles, Gleeson's taloned hands, Heron's ruffled crest—had symbolized a cruel and repressive authority. All these are now submerged and transmuted in the dark-plumaged dove of a girl rising, like love, from the sea. The symbols are transmuted—authority into loveliness, obedience into liberty, repression into joy. Stephen is transfigured. The call, the vocation he had awaited has come to him: "Her eyes called him and his soul had leaped at the call. To live, to err, to fall, to triumph, to recreate life out of life!" (P 200). Out of the death of the priest who might have been is now born the artist who is never entirely to be.

III

Stanislaus Joyce has said that his brother, after a boyish lapse from virtue, went through a brief period of religious fervor during which, under Jesuit pressure, he did entertain the thought of becoming a Jesuit.[23] The statement supports, if indeed it was not suggested by, the account given in the *Portrait* of Stephen's fall from grace, reform of life, and ultimate refusal of a vocation. But this account is perhaps a little too neat, and does not seem to fit the realities of Joyce's experience at Belvedere. It does not fit either what are the known chronological facts or what may rightly be presumed to have been the psychological truth of that experience.

On the assumption that Joyce is Dedalus, consider the follow-

[23] *Recollections of James Joyce*, p. 7.

ing facts of chronology. When Stephen "drew forth his orders on
the government bank of Ireland for thirty and three pounds"
(P 108), the date of this transaction—in the Joyce chronology—
is to be fixed in October, 1897. (The month is also designated in
the *Portrait*, p. 109: "A keen *October* wind was blowing round
the bank.") The Intermediate prize lists were published annually
each September, and the only year in which Joyce won precisely
"thirty and three pounds" (an exhibition worth £30 and an addi-
tional prize of £3 in English composition) was in 1897. This,
then, fixes the date of the incident in the *Portrait*. It is shortly after
this that Dedalus—and the presumption here is still that Dedalus
is Joyce—first visits a brothel. He is fifteen years and eight months
of age. After a "swift season of merry-making" during which he
squandered all his prize money in a futile attempt "to build a
breakwater of order and elegance against the sordid tide of life
without him and . . . the powerful recurrence of the tide within
him" (P 110), he yields quickly to those tides which "began once
more to jostle fiercely above the crumbled mole" (P 111). In the
Portrait, therefore, it seems clear that Stephen's "orgiastic riot"
started on these "autumnal evenings" of 1897 and moved to a
speedy climax in the three remaining pages of the second chapter.

The following chapter opens with "the swift December dusk"
(P 115), and one would naturally assume—so rapid has been the
course of events—that this was December, 1897. Unfortunately,
one would be wrong. On the evidence in the *Portrait* itself this
year could only be 1898. A few days before the retreat, which oc-
cupies almost the whole of this central chapter of the novel, the
rector informs the students in his catechism class: "The retreat
will begin on Wednesday afternoon in honour of Saint Francis
Xavier whose feast day is Saturday. The retreat will go on from
Wednesday to Friday" (P 121). Xavier's feast is celebrated on
December 3, and during the years in question December 3 fell

on a Saturday only in 1898. But, of course, in December, 1898, Joyce had finished at Belvedere and was already attending University College.

Out of this chronological confusion, one fact is quite clear: Stephen Dedalus, in point of time, is not James Joyce, nor in terms of time may his experiences—his fall, reform, and refusal of a vocation—be considered a duplicate of Joyce's own.[24] Moreover, the time-sequence of Stephen's experiences is confused in itself without any reference to Joyce's chronology. When, for example, he confesses his sins (P 166), he admits his debauch has been going on for "eight months." But the date of this confession is Friday, December 2, the eve of the feast of St. Francis Xavier; therefore, according to this reckoning, Stephen's fall from grace would have to have occurred around the beginning of the previous April. But this springtime month cannot be made to square with "the veiled autumnal evenings" (P 111) which, in the preceding chapter, mark the beginning of Stephen's transgressions.

This distortion of time and apparent confusion of chronology is not to be thought a defect in the *Portrait*. It is the sort of thing that readers have since come to expect in the impressionist novel whose hero is conscious of the time-space universe around him only in so far as the limitations of that universe are apprehended as modifications of his own sensibility. So in the *Portrait* Stephen's four years at the university are telescoped into a single final chapter, while his years at Belvedere occupy the greater part of three chapters. This might at first seem a disproportion in the novel itself, but of course it is not. It is not, because the pace of the novel is determined by the rate of development of Stephen's conscious-

---

[24] This confusion may have been deliberately planned by Joyce. One might like to believe that he distorted the chronology of his school years in order to indicate that, on close examination, Dedalus was not indeed an exact duplicate of himself. But ingenious explanations of this kind seem remote from the authentic ingenuity of Joyce.

ness. Since all action must be sifted through that consciousness, the movement of the first chapter is understandably slow, but it picks up in the second chapter and toward the end races to an orgiastic climax. In the third chapter, the dead center of the book, the movement is again retarded while Stephen's consciousness is in the paralyzing grip of the terrors of retreat. For a moment it even seems that the paralysis may prove incurable and that all movement will come to a dead standstill. But Stephen succeeds in surmounting this crisis, the movement again picks up, and the story now rushes to its climax in the episode on the beach at Dollymount. There Stephen is consumed in a blaze of consciousness, sparked by the electrifying vision of a young girl, and he is suddenly and forever aware of himself, of the world around him, of the meaning of life, and of the ends which he now must serve. This episode occurs at the very end of the fourth chapter. At the beginning of the fifth and final chapter Stephen's consciousness is as fully developed as it is to become. He is to admit that he may be mistaken, but the fear of making a mistake, even an eternal mistake, does not dull the consciousness of what he now knows he must and will do. The pace of the novel, accordingly, is accelerated. Time contracts tightly under the onrush of impressions, and the unwary reader is often left bewildered by the sudden shift of mood and swift change of pace. The four years at the university are over almost before they have begun, and at their end Stephen stands ready to encounter the reality of whatever experience may bring and out of that experience, realized in his own soul, to forge the uncreated conscience of his race.

Time, then, is of little importance in a novel so conceived and executed—of so little importance that, even if the novel were meant to be read as essentially autobiographical, any attempt to straighten out the details of its chronology would prove futile. But there remains the spiritual crisis through which Stephen passes during and following the Belvedere retreat, and one may ask whether the psychological truth of this experience fairly represents—or at all represents—Joyce's actual experience while at school. Stanislaus Joyce would say that it does and that his brother's weighing of a vocation was consequently never more than penitential, arising and subsiding, like Stephen's, during a brief period of fervor and remorse. The truth of the matter, however, would seem to be different.

The retreat is presented as a unique and terrifying experience in the consciousness of Stephen Dedalus. Its effect is to shrink that consciousness into the straight confines of orthodox morality and to hold it there—for as long as it is held—by fear. While it is thus in check, a Catholic conscience takes over the government of Stephen's life. But this is no more than an interregnum. When the effects of the retreat wear off Stephen repossesses his own soul with a vengeance. But what had made the retreat terrible was fear, and what had made it unique was the abdication of Stephen's intellect to fear. Even as a child at Clongowes, though shaken with fear, he had not capitulated to the pandy-bat morality of Father Dolan. To that same morality, more formidable now in Father Arnall's sermons, he does capitulate at Belvedere—but only this once. There were to be no further surrenders.

The director of the retreat, Father Arnall, was Stephen's former master at Clongowes Wood—identified in an earlier chapter as Father William Power, S.J. But though the Father Arnall of Clongowes is undoubtedly William Power, it is highly doubtful that this same William Power is the Father Arnall of Belvedere. A tradition among Irish Jesuits identifies the latter as Father James A. Cullen, S.J., and the tradition seems to be supported by facts. During the whole of Joyce's time at Belvedere, Father Cullen was a member of the Jesuit community stationed at No. 6

Great Denmark Street.[25] But he was not at any time assigned to teach in the school. His principal duties were to act as director of the Apostleship of Prayer and editor of *The Irish Messenger,* a pious, unimpressive magazine dedicated chiefly to popularizing devotion to the Sacred Heart. The catalogue also defines his status as "operarius," that is, one who is expected to take on those specifically spiritual tasks (sermons, missions, retreats, visitations) which the burden of teaching or administration makes it difficult or impossible for his fellow priests to assume. Both as operarius and director of the Apostleship of Prayer, Father Cullen was for years busily engaged in retreat work, and during those years he established, in and beyond Dublin, a considerable reputation as a zealous and effective director of souls.[26] Finally, in September, 1897, a few months before the putative date of the retreat in the *Portrait,* Father Cullen was assigned, in addition to his other duties, the office of "spiritual father" at Belvedere College.[27]

At Jesuit schools the spiritual father is not necessarily, or ordinarily, the director of the annual retreat. The usual custom is to bring a priest in from outside the college so that, supposedly, the solemnity of the occasion will not be threatened by the students' familiarity with the director. But Father Cullen, though long a member of the Jesuit community on Great Denmark Street, had until the fall of 1897 little or nothing to do with the students at Belvedere. He was, therefore, as acceptable on these grounds as he was desirable on grounds of his reputation, and the fact that he was newly appointed spiritual father made it even more advisable that he conduct a retreat at the beginning of his first year in that

[25] *Catalogus S.J.*

[26] Father Cullen's biography has been written by Lambert McKenna, S.J., published by Longmans, Green and Co., New York, 1924.

[27] *Catalogus S.J.*

office. For the retreat would also be an opportunity of introducing himself to the students in his new role, and of judging for himself the general spiritual temper of the school.

Evidence from the *Portrait* also supports this view that it was Cullen, not Power, who was the original of Father Arnall at Belvedere. Father Power was at the time still teaching at Clongowes. Even granted that he temporarily set aside his teaching chores at one school to give a retreat at the other—which is most unlikely—he would certainly have returned at once to those chores at the conclusion of the retreat. But in the *Portrait* the director is still at Belvedere when, some time after the retreat, he speaks to Stephen Dedalus about a vocation.[28] He is, moreover, acquainted with Stephen's virtuous way of life, either by personal observation or by report of other Jesuits in the Belvedere community. Father Cullen's status at Belvedere fits these various requirements of the novel so aptly that it seems there can no longer be any question as to his identity.

But the question does remain: Why does Joyce make a point of having Stephen's former master at Clongowes the director of the retreat at Belvedere? The sentence in the *Portrait* which so identifies him is unmistakable and may also provide a clue to the answer. "The figure of his old master, so strangely rearisen, brought back to Stephen's mind his life at Clongowes . . ." (P 123). The key word here is "rearisen." Father Arnall has just been described as shrouded in a heavy cloak, his face pale and drawn, his voice broken with rheum. He is strangely rearisen not as one dead returned to life, but as one still dead intruding upon the living. He is a figure of death, clothed in the habiliments of

[28] The priest who here interviews Stephen is identified only as "the director." It is possible this was the director of the B.V.M. Sodality—in Joyce's time Father Joseph McDonnell, S.J. But Father Cullen was also the director of another sodality at Belvedere, the sodality of St. Ignatius. He was, moreover, in his role of spiritual father, the logical person to speak to Joyce about a vocation.

the grave, but no more is seen of him than this. From now until the retreat's end he is no more than a voice sounding dire tidings of another world.

But the mere sight of him reminds Stephen of his life at Clongowes, and "his soul, as these memories came back to him, became again a child's soul" (P 123). This is the soul of innocence, but it is also the soul of a terrified child, alone and unfriended in a world he does not comprehend, abused and mocked by his fellows, cowering in momentary blindness from the upraised pandy bat of an angry Father Dolan. Father Arnall had then acquiesced in a cruel and unjust act and by his acquiescence shared equally in Father Dolan's guilt. He is now, at Belvedere, in the place of Father Dolan. He raises aloft a more terrible pandy, one that will afflict Stephen's soul more dreadfully than his flesh was afflicted at Clongowes. Stephen now reverts to what he had been before his consciousness had begun fully to develop, he returns in spirit to that dead past out of which Father Arnall has rearisen, and he is again a half-blind child defenseless against the shattering blows to be delivered by that broken and rheumy voice.

It was necessary, then, or at least expedient, for Joyce to make the director of the retreat Stephen's former master at Clongowes. The story gains, as a result, in greater psychological as well as narrative tightness. The writer is little interested in the persons of William Power or James Cullen, who in the novel are no more than half-reflections of shadows in a mirror. He might have been interested had he been writing autobiography, but since he is writing fiction it is Father Arnall, and neither of his real-life counterparts, who alone is important.

The retreat itself is based on the five meditations of the First Week as given by Ignatius in the *Spiritual Exercises*. These exercises, divided into Four Weeks and proceeding from meditations on sin in the First Week to the *contemplatio ad amorem* in the

Fourth, were originally intended to be made over a period of approximately thirty days. But this is usually impracticable except for members of a religious order, and so the common practice in retreats for laymen is to confine the exercises to meditations of the First Week: sin and hell.[29] St. Ignatius made express provision for this in his introductory remarks to the exercises. "The Spiritual Exercises," Ignatius wrote, "must be adapted to the condition of the one who is to engage in them, that is, to his age, education, and talent."[30] This provision also helps to explain the detailed, vivid, and concrete descriptions as well as the naive and simplistic tone of Father Arnall's sermons. He was after all talking to schoolboys, and his appeal was to the imagination and conscience of schoolboys. More sophisticated minds may be amused by Father Arnall's hyperboles failing to measure an immeasurable eternity, or by his picture of a hell whose walls are exactly four thousand miles thick. But such is the stuff likely to impress immature minds which demand verisimilitude as well as wonder in their fairy tales. There is no doubt that it impressed Stephen Dedalus. His spirit is lashed into temporary submission by the priest's grotesque and sweeping eloquence. In such a state he is incapable of reflecting that the moral dimension of life

[29] It is interesting to note how closely Joyce follows the plan of this first week of the *Spiritual Exercises*. In the *Portrait* the meditations on death and judgment, unlike those on sin and hell, are not given in Father Arnall's direct discourse, but are reported indirectly (P 127–31). This subordination of material appears to be cued by St. Ignatius who, omitting specific exercises on death and judgment, adds a note to those of the first week, saying: "If the one giving the exercises judges that it would be profitable for the exercitant, other exercises may be added here, for example, on death and other punishments of sin, on judgment, etc. Let him not think it is forbidden, though they are not given here." (Si visum erit ei, qui tradit Exercitia, expedire ad profectum eorum, qui exercentur, alias meditationes his adjicere, ut de Morte, ac aliis peccati Poenis, de Judicio, etc., non se putet prohiberi, licet hic non adscribantur.) *Thesaurus Spiritualis S.J.*, pp. 75–76.

[30] *Ibid.*, pp. 25–26: "Decima octava, juxta dispositionem eorum, qui volunt exercitia spiritualia suscipere, id est, secundum eorum aetatem, doctrinam, vel ingenium, applicari debent talia Exercitia."

as outlined by Father Arnall would preclude the flight of his own free spirit, that the materiality of the priest's hell denies by implication the reality of any corresponding heaven. But the whole experience of the retreat has been so terrifying that Stephen now renounces his own will and thinks to entrust his spirit to an unfamiliar and most improbable heaven.

For James Joyce a Jesuit retreat was neither a terrifying nor a unique experience. During his years at Belvedere the boy made at least five such retreats, and he may also have made a sixth during his first term at University College, though this is doubtful. It is certain that he did not make any more than this. The nature of the retreat was, then, so familiar to Joyce that it is extremely unlikely that one of the last he was ever to make struck him with the same devastating and original impact as overpowered Stephen Dedalus. It is unlikely even on the assumption that the boy wallowed for a time in mortal sin and, conscious of his state, was then especially susceptible to the terrors that a vision of hell and damnation may evoke in the fervid imagination of a young sinner. For this supposedly sinful boy would not need a retreat to torment his conscience and frighten him into repentance. At Belvedere the ordinary course of talks, sermons, and exhortations —on virtue and sin, and especially on the sin of impurity and its direful consequences—were more than enough to keep a sensitive young conscience in a constant state of apprehension. It is also to be remembered that Joyce, as prefect of the sodality, was expected to and presumably did set an example to his fellow sodalists in frequent reception of the sacraments. Any prolonged absence from them would be certain to be remarked and impossible to explain. Explanations might of course be avoided if he continued to receive the sacraments unworthily. But to the Catholic conscience there is nothing more heinous than thus to compound sin into sacrilege. Even Dedalus, after his rejection of Catholicism, refuses to commit this particular sacrilege, though Cranly's logic urging him to do so seems unanswerable (P 285). Joyce, who years later when a drinking companion casually proposed a toast "to sin," replied curtly "I'll not drink to that!"[31] must be thought as a boy to have been at least as adamant as Stephen Dedalus under similar circumstances.

The latter's experiences, therefore—his sin, his repentance, and his temptation to the priesthood—cannot be accepted as a fair reproduction of Joyce's own. For they cannot be adapted to the objective facts and psychological truth of Joyce's experience. Finally, a better guide than the *Portrait* as to what Joyce's attitude toward a vocation may have been is the little book, already mentioned, called *The Sodality Manual*.

IV

The full title of this book reads: *The Sodality Manual or a Collection of Prayers and Spiritual Exercises for Members of the Sodality of the Blessed Virgin Mary*. By coincidence, it first appeared, under the *imprimatur* of Thomas P. Brown, S.J., Irish Provincial, on Joyce's birthday, February 2, 1886. Father James A. Cullen, S.J., compiled the work and saw it through the press at the office of *The Irish Messenger,* which he then edited, at No. 5 Great Denmark Street, directly adjoining Belvedere College. The book went through five editions in ten years, and it is probable that a copy of it was in Joyce's hands as early as December 7, 1895, the date on which he was first received into the sodality. The evidence for this is provided by the manual itself. According to the order of exercises to be followed at the reception of new members: *"When the Act of Consecration has been recited, the celebrant gives a medal, already blessed, and a Manual of the Congregation* [i.e., of the Sodality] *to each Candidate, saying:*

---

[31] Williams, *Autobiography,* p. 189.

Receive this medal and Manual of the Blessed Virgin Mary as a safeguard and defence for your body and soul, that, by the grace of the Divine goodness, and the assistance of Mary, your Mother, you may deserve to obtain eternal happiness." [32] If, for any reason, Joyce did not receive a copy of the manual at this time, he was certainly in possession of it by September 25, 1896, when he was elected prefect of the sodality at Belvedere.

The contents of the manual are fairly indicated by its full title. The book ran to some six hundred pages, which included, in addition to much else, not only the history, rules, and ceremonial of the sodality, but a complete text of the Little Office B.V.M., the Office of the Dead, a wide variety of hymns and prayers ("only those familiar to the faithful and sanctioned by general use have been introduced" [33]), and, significantly, the Ignatian form of meditation and examen of conscience.[34] In his preface the editor, Father Cullen, says that it was also intended "as a prayer-book in after life." James Joyce in after life may not have used it with Father Cullen's pious intention in mind, but that he did make use of it for ends of his own there can be no doubt.

The fourth chapter of the *Portrait* opens with an account of Stephen's reform of his way of life.

Sunday was dedicated to the mystery of the Holy Trinity, Monday to the Holy Ghost, Tuesday to the Guardian Angels, Wednesday to Saint Joseph, Thursday to the Most Blessed Sacrament of the Altar, Friday to the Suffering Jesus, Saturday to the Blessed Virgin Mary.
[P 170]

---

[32] *The Sodality Manual*, p. 77. Italics in original.   [33] *Ibid.*, p. 1.

[34] These are presented (pp. 394–402) as simple synopses of the methods proposed by St. Ignatius in the *Spiritual Exercises*. Joyce was doubtless familiar with the latter work, though, for his purposes in the *Portrait*, the *Manual* would seem to have sufficed. The "old neglected book written by Saint Alphonsus Liguori" (P 176) which Stephen used in his private devotions, may have been either Liguori's *Way of Salvation* or his *Preparation for Death*, both of which are readings suggested by the *Manual*, p. 397.

The whole of this opening paragraph is adapted from *The Sodality Manual*. There, under "Devotions for Every Day in the Week" (pp. 301–13), it is explained how "it was an ancient and pious practice among the faithful to dedicate every day in the week to some particular devotion." Following this brief explanation, each day is assigned its special devotion, and to this is added an appropriate prayer which, according to the *Manual,* is less important in itself "than in the practical instruction it contains." So "Sunday . . . is called the day of the Lord, and is chosen to render homage in a more special manner to the Most Holy Trinity" (p. 301). Under "Monday" the *Manual* reads: "Although the three adorable Persons of the blessed Trinity concur unanimously in the sanctification of our souls, our spiritual regeneration and all the graces we receive from heaven are, nevertheless, attributed more especially to the operations of the Holy Ghost . . ." (p. 303). And so on through Saturday the *Manual* supplies Joyce with specific devotions to which Dedalus dedicates each day of his week.

Dedalus's further habit of praying "that one of the seven gifts of the Holy Ghost might descend upon his soul and drive out of it day by day the seven deadly sins that had defiled it in the past" (P 171–72) may also have been suggested by the exhortation for Monday which reads in part: "What abundance of light and strength does He not communicate by His seven gifts . . . let us continually follow the motions of our hearts; let us follow those which the Holy Spirit produces, and which alone can vanquish every evil inclination excited in us, either by the corruption of our nature, or the machinations of our spiritual enemy" (p. 303). Unfortunately, the *Manual* does not instruct the sodalist how to distinguish between "motions of the heart" inspired by the Holy Spirit and those inspired by less beneficent agents. As things turned out, Stephen Dedalus could have profited from such in-

struction. Meanwhile, his acceptance of the "august incompre-
hensibility" (P 172) of the Trinity echoes the *Manual's* prayer of
thanksgiving for "this glorious and incomprehensible mystery"
(p. 302).

On page 323 of the *Manual*, in an introduction to "Pious Reflections for Every Day of the Month," the reader is urged to "suffer
a good thought to take possession of your mind before the business of the day is entered upon." This advice Stephen also follows: "Every morning he hallowed himself anew in the presence
of some holy image or mystery" (P 170). Then, after repeating
"The Morning Offering," the boy is off to early Mass and Communion—devotions constantly urged throughout the *Manual*. At
Mass, the two candles on the altar symbolize for him "the old and
the new testaments" even as *The Sodality Manual* (p. 16) says
that they "signify the light of faith revealed to the Jews and
Gentiles."

"A Rule of Life" as given in the *Manual* (pp. 360–69) seems to
have provided Stephen with the general plan whereby "his daily
life was laid out in devotional areas" (P 170). This "Rule" begins
with the exhortation to "elevate your heart to God by fervent
ejaculations," and "ejaculation and prayers . . . for the souls in
purgatory" are mentioned as the first of Stephen's devotional
practices. This practice of amassing indulgences, Stephen's feeling
that "his soul in devotion [was] pressing like fingers the keyboard
of a great cash register" (P 171), is, on the level of irony, an obvious parody on the doctrine of the economy of grace. But the
literal surface of the passage was available to Joyce in the *Manual*
where indulgences are carefully explained (p. 20) and a list of
ejaculations provided (pp. 100–1) with a precise number of days'
indulgence attached to each. The devotional arithmetic involved
in totaling up these figures might pose a problem for one less
naive and more patient than Stephen Dedalus.

"A Rule of Life" further contains individual sections devoted to "Mass," "Spiritual Reading," "Visiting the Blessed Sacrament," "The Presence of God," "A Spirit of Mortification," "Communion," "Ruling Passions," "Duties of Our State in Life," "Crosses and Afflictions," and several more. Each of these subjects finds a place in Stephen's plan of life and the execution of that plan on pages 170–78 of the *Portrait*.[35] The "Rule" treats of these subjects in so general a way that no sure and firm connection can be made between them and what seem to be corresponding passages in the novel. Many books of devotion treat of the same subjects in much the same way. On the other hand, it is known that Joyce owned this particular book, that he made particular use of it,[36] and that his surrogate also owned and used the same book.[37] The presumption, then, must be that *The Sodality Manual* is the primary, if not the exclusive, source of this entire section of the *Portrait*.

It may also have been the source of another part of the novel. Consider the following parallels. The quotations on the left are from Father Arnall's sermons in the *Portrait*, those on the right from *The Sodality Manual*.

[35] The correspondences between the *Manual* and the *Portrait* are as follows (page numbers immediately following topics refer to the *Manual*, italic page numbers to the *Portrait*): Mass, 360, *170*; Spiritual Reading, 362, *172, 176*; Visiting the Blessed Sacrament, 362, *176*; The Presence of God, 363, *173*; A Spirit of Mortification, 363, *174, 175*; Communion, 365, *176*; Ruling Passions, 366, *172–73, 176–77*; Duties of Our State in Life, 367, *171*; Crosses and Afflictions, 368, *177*.

[36] That is, in his adaptation of devotions for every day in the week.

[37] At a meeting of the sodality (P 118) Stephen reads "in a veiled voice, lulling his conscience to its music" a passage from Ecclesiasticus (24. 17–20). The passage is found on page 489 of the *Manual*, where it is part of the third lesson of Matins in the Little Office B.V.M., recited weekly by the sodalists at Belvedere. Joyce's variations from the text of the *Manual*, which is that of the Vulgate, are negligible; *Libanon* for *Libano*; *cupressus* for *cypressus*; *Gades* for *Cades*; *uliva* for *oliva*.

. . . we have been sent into this world for one thing and for one thing alone: to do God's holy will and to save our immortal souls . . . What doth it profit a man to gain the whole world if he suffer the loss of his immortal soul? [P 124–25]

The important and the only affair, therefore, is to serve God, and thereby save our souls: the whole good, the whole perfection of man, consists in this . . . *"What doth it profit a man, if he gain the whole world and suffer the loss of his own soul?* [pp. 334–35]

The blood seethes and boils in the veins, the brains are boiling in the skull, the heart in the breast glowing and bursting. [P 139]

. . . —the blood boiling in our veins, the marrow in our bones! . . . rage, anguish and despair eternally rooted in our heart. [p. 330]

O think what pain, what anguish it must be for the poor soul to be spurned from the presence of the supremely good and loving Creator . . . This, then, to be separated forever from its greatest good, from God . . . this is the greatest torment. [P 147]

But nothing more keenly gnaws them than the impossibility of forgetting that God whom by their own fault, they have miserably forfeited . . . To be banished from the presence of God! —to be accursed of God! Can any misery be like it? [pp. 330–31]

The first sting inflicted by this cruel worm will be the memory of past pleasures. [P 147]

The recollection of their past pleasures is one of their most grievous torments. [p. 331]

They will repent indeed: and this second sting of conscience, a late and fruitless sorrow for sins committed. [P 148]

Oh, repentance of the damned, how rigorous art thou! but ah! how fruitless! [p. 330]

This is the last and deepest and most cruel sting of the worm of conscience. The conscience will say: You had time and opportunity to repent and would not. [P 148]

These wretches are outrageous, as having had so many opportunities of saving themselves, and for having neglected them. [p. 330]

But while they [the pains of hell] are everlasting they are at the same time, as you know, intolerably intense, unbearably extensive. To bear even the sting of an insect for all eternity would be a dreadful torment. What must it be, then, to bear the manifold tortures of hell forever? [P 148]

Is it not enough that the evils of the damned are extreme? Must they still, besides this, be eternal? To be hurt by the point of a pin is trifling in itself; yet, were this pain to last always, it would become insupportable. What shall it be then? etc. [*sic*] [p. 331]

Eternity! O, dread and dire word. Eternity! . . . Try to imagine the awful meaning of this. You have often seen the sand on the seashore . . . Now imagine a mountain of that sand a million miles high . . . if it so rose and sank as many times as there are stars in the sky, atoms in the air, drops of water in the sea, leaves on the trees . . . at the end of such a period . . . eternity would have scarcely begun . . . O, what a dreadful punishment! [P 151–53]

O Eternity! when a damned soul shall have shed tears enough to make up all the rivers and seas in the world, did he shed but one tear in every hundred years, he shall not be nearer to the end of his punishment, after so many millions of ages, than if he had only just begun to suffer . . . and when he shall have begun as often as there are grains of sand on the sea-shore, or atoms in the air, or leaves on the trees, he shall still be as far off from the end of his sufferings as ever . . . Oh, cruel thought! Oh, deplorable condition! [pp. 331–32]

The points of resemblance between these parallel passages are obvious. But the resemblance does not by itself indicate that one passage is the direct source of the other. In at least one instance both have a common source, and so are cognates rather than derivatives. Thus the first quotation is simply a restatement of the opening sentence of the "First Principle and Foundation" of the *Spiritual Exercises:* "Man was created to praise, reverence, and serve God our Lord, and by this means to save his soul." [38]

[38] *Thesaurus Spiritualis S.J.,* pp. 34–35: "Homo creatus est, ut laudet Deum

The content of the subsequent passages had been part of the common possession of devotional writers for hundreds of years before Joyce or the *Manual,* and the dominant mode of expression—hyperbole—is only what might be expected from an attempt to concretize such concepts as hell and eternity. This is especially true when these abstractions are presented to the very young, an audience generally more imaginative than intellectual, more emotional than reflective. Both the *Manual* and Father Arnall's sermons were intended for precisely such an audience.

Nevertheless, the similarity and, in some cases, the identity of image and example (blood boiling in the veins, the sting of an insect and prick of a pin, sand on the seashore, atoms in the air, leaves on the trees); the specification in both works of the nature of pain (banishment from God's presence, the triple sting of conscience); and in both the same devotional rhetoric and balanced rhythms of piety (parallelism, repetition, the exclamatory shock and stop of movement, questions dropped dramatically in a void that returns no answer); all these argue a more than incidental connection between the sermon in the *Portrait* and the "Pious Reflections" of the *Manual.* The argument seems conclusive when one again considers that, whatever other devotional literature Joyce may have read, he certainly read the *Manual,* and that there can be no doubt the book supplied him with material used elsewhere in the *Portrait.*

It has been generally assumed that Joyce's early familiarity with Catholic ceremony and ritual, so richly invested with symbolic gesture and meaning, constituted a sort of novitiate in which the embryo artist was prepared for the adoption and employment in his mature work of the technique of his European predecessors in the symbolist tradition. *The Sodality Manual* now provides a

---

Dominum nostrum, ei reverentiam exhibeat, eique serviat, et per haec salvet animam suam."

more particular confirmation of that assumption. Pages 11 to 19 are given over to an explanation of the principal feasts and ceremonies of the Church, more especially to the ceremony of the Mass. "All the visible rites," the *Manual* reads, "employed in and about the sacrifice of the Mass tend to instruction . . . this is plainly to be observed in the altar and its ornaments, as likewise in the garments with which the priest is vested." There follows a list of such ornaments (including the candles mentioned above) and vestments, and a brief explanation of the symbolic meaning of each. Under "Principal Festivals Explained" the *Manual* states: "6th January—*The Epiphany of Our Lord,* is a feast solemnised in memory and honour of Christ's manifestation to the Gentiles by an extraordinary star." In the light of this there is no longer reason to believe, as one reputable scholar, relying on the authority of Oliver St. John Gogarty, appears to believe, that Joyce, who knew no Greek, did not learn the meaning of "Epiphany" until Father Darlington's Latin class at University College.[39]

The *Manual,* then, is important because it provided Joyce with material and suggestions for his work, and because it may provide his critics with interesting sidelights on the Joyce text. But it is also important for another reason. The schoolboy Joyce was hardly aware, even remotely, of the use to which he would one day put many of the strange and familiar matters to be found in this little book. To him it was primarily a prayer book, a book of devotions. It was as such that he read it and meditated upon its contents at least weekly, and perhaps daily, often enough, at any event, to become so thoroughly familiar with it that years later large portions of it would remain fresh in his memory. It seems

---

[39] *Stephen Hero,* ed. by Spencer, Introduction, p. 16, note. Spencer's introduction and note are allowed to stand unchanged in the most recent edition of *Stephen Hero* by Slocum and Cahoon. Father Darlington taught English and later philosophy at UCD; Latin was taught by Father Henry Browne, S.J. See below, pp. 161, 168.

certain that at this time, during his most impressionable years, there was no book with which he was more familiar. Though less than a history of his soul during these years, the *Manual,* read and reread constantly, may be taken as an indication of the boy's religious and spiritual orientation. It supports the impression given by his industry and excellence as a student, by his zeal and distinction as prefect of the sodality, the impression made upon his mother and his Jesuit masters, and indeed the impression he probably had of himself, as a serious-minded, ambitious, obedient, and decently pious young man who for all of these reasons might be expected to enter the priesthood. It makes a less exciting story— far less exciting than Stephen Dedalus's adolescent soul-wrestling and final escape from religious gloom to profane joy. But James Joyce's thoughts on the priesthood were the sensible thoughts of a reflective boy whose habitual attitudes of piety and obedience remained unbroken during all the time he was at Belvedere.

In making his decision Joyce possibly consulted those pages of the *Manual* (pp. 454–55) which dealt with "The Choice of a State of Life." It is doubtful, however, whether the general remarks and recommendations which he found there were of any great help. But perhaps he did follow one of the *Manual's* more specific directions and seek the counsel of his Jesuit superiors— if indeed they did not approach him first. These conversations, like that between Stephen Dedalus and the director, would naturally revolve around the prerequisites and prerogatives of the priesthood, though Joyce, like Stephen, was certainly aware that a Jesuit vocation would also afford him "a life without material cares" (P 186). To be thus offered the best of both worlds—a life of sacrifice and a life of security—is doubly attractive to adolescents generally endowed with equally generous shares of insecurity and idealism. To James Joyce at sixteen, as to many other Catholic young men, the appeal of the priesthood was real and immediate, a sort of divine temptation to which the soul might gladly surrender its infinite possibilities. But unlike others, Joyce, during his last year at Belvedere, had been building up, without perhaps fully realizing it, a specific resistance to such temptation. His scholastic record supplies the clue to what that resistance may have been. During this last year his apparent disregard of all nonliterary subjects, his growing preoccupation with literature, and his intense concentration on English composition indicate a developing and deepening interest that was to suggest a quite different way of life. This other vocation was to present itself not as a temptation, but as a challenge. To accept this challenge was to overcome the divine temptation and to reject for good a religious vocation. So it turned out. In the end the boy's overpowering desire to write, to celebrate the word, proved stronger than any desire he may still have had to renounce the world. And yet that which was now rejected was to linger on in the artist's mind; no longer, it is true, as desire, but as the ghost of desire, *desiderium desiderii.*

This refusal of a vocation is not to be confused with Joyce's later rejection of Catholicism. The two are separate and distinct experiences, though in the *Portrait* they are made to appear as practically simultaneous. In his work, Joyce's apostasy (about which much remains to be said) may have supplied the emotional pattern for those acceptance-rejection themes and their ensuing tensions, which are particularly evident in the first three stories of *Dubliners,* everywhere throughout the *Portrait,* in the Dedalus-Bloom relationship in *Ulysses,* and, to name but one instance here, on the final pages of *Finnegans Wake.* But the refusal of a vocation seems to have had other effects upon his work—effects sufficiently large to justify the belief that his thoughts on the priesthood at Belvedere were not merely the passing thoughts of adolescence.

The most pronounced of these effects is what has been called

Joyce's "sacerdotalism." It is usual to find the origins of this in the intellectual atmosphere of *fin de siècle* Dublin. Not long after he left Belvedere Joyce would have been aware of what was being thought and said at meetings of the Dublin Theosophical Society; he would have met AE, its guiding spirit, and he had already read Yeats, whose work suggested to him ways of adapting esoteric speculations to the requirements of literature. At the same time, perhaps even before he left school, he may have read and recognized the Symbolists as kindred spirits. Young Rimbaud, for example, conceiving of the artist as Hermetic priest, may be a prototype of Stephen Dedalus in his aesthetic posturing as priest of the eternal imagination. But though it be accepted as true that "theosophy provided a doctrine, symbolism an aesthetic, which could be harmonized with the symbolic bent of Catholicism," [40] the primary impulse behind Joyce's sacerdotalism is neither aesthetic nor intellectual, traditional nor revolutionary. It is primarily personal and emotional. It is the ghost of the priest Joyce did not become who is constantly guiding the hand of the artist in the act of becoming. The priest is preoccupied with thoughts of sin and the redeeming effect of grace; the artist is busy portraying the sinner and parodying the ways of grace. For parody is his mode, as prayer is the mode proper to the priest. So the murmurous streams of sin poured in at the priest's ear, the work of the confessional, are measured out by the writer in a work which is also a kind of confessional. But here sin is neither forgiven nor condemned, it is simply heard, like the voice of unregenerate nature, innocent of theology, untroubled by the failure of faith, existent and nothing more. "Dogma," Joyce said early in life, "is a most proper thing in a priest but a most improper in a poet." [41] Aware of this, Joyce was not likely to confuse the two in his own

---

[40] Kain and Magalaner, *James Joyce: The Man, the Work, the Reputation*, p. 149.
[41] Stanislaus Joyce and Ellsworth Mason, *The Early Joyce: The Book Reviews, 1902–1903*, p. 18.

work nor, after his faith in dogmatic theology was lost, was it likely that he would try to find or to create a substitute for it in literature. Yeats, had he been a Catholic and an apostate, almost certainly would have made the attempt. But not Joyce. For him the boundaries between art and religion were clearly defined; when faith in an absolute could no longer command his assent, though it never had his denial either, the dogmatically trained Joyce did not continue to seek it where experience had taught him it could never be found—in the shifting and relative values of secular literature. Joyce may then have begun to live for literature, but he continued to live in doubt. It was because of this habitual doubt, plus the intensity of his adolescent temptation to the priesthood, that the shadow of the priest falls constantly across the work of the artist. So it is that in *Ulysses,* and even in *Finnegans Wake,* the shadow-structure is the Catholic Mass in which the priest, performing the specific sacrifice for which he was ordained, celebrates the communion of God and man. But the artist secularizes this function of the priest, and his sacrament is a celebration of the communion of humanity. This is not substitution, it is simultaneity. This is what makes it difficult, if not impossible, to read Joyce's work even as "spiritual autobiography." Who and what the author is and was is everywhere implied or suggested in the multiple disguises of his surrogates and alter egos. But the ghost of the priest Joyce did not become is not present in the text—he is, like Joyce, forever outside the work of creation. And there, of course, he is and must remain unknown. Yet once at least his voice was heard—sufficient proof perhaps of his reality to Joyce—when the author, a candy replica of the first copy of *Ulysses* on a table before him, in solemn mockery, mocking solemnity, intoned: *Hoc est enim corpus meum.*[42]

---

[42] Eugene Jolas, "My Friend James Joyce," in *James Joyce: Two Decades of Criticism,* ed. by Givens, p. 8.

V

The long evening walk through the suburbs of Dublin and the intense painful talk that took place during the course of it, had, according to J. F. Byrne, a basis in fact. "However," Byrne adds, "as usual, he [Joyce] mixes this event with events of other times and places." [43] At one point in the conversation there is the following exchange:

—It is a curious thing, do you know, Cranly said dispassionately, how your mind is supersaturated with the religion in which you say you disbelieve. Did you believe in it when you were at school? I bet you did.

—I did, Stephen answered.

—And were you happier then? Cranly asked softly, happier than you are now, for instance?

—Often happy, Stephen said, and often unhappy. I was someone else then.

—How someone else? What do you mean by that statement?

—I mean, said Stephen, that I was not myself as I am now, as I had to become. [P 283]

What Joyce, too, became at UCD was something different from what he had been at Belvedere. But like Dedalus, like most Irishmen, he never wholly escaped the past. At all his feasts of learning there attended the familiar ghost.

[43] *Silent Years*, p. 84.

4

On Stephen's Green

When a multitude of young men, keen, open-hearted, sympathetic, and observant, as young men are, come together and freely mix with each other, they are sure to learn one from another, even if there be no one to teach them; the conversation of all is a series of lectures to each, and they gain for themselves new ideas and views, fresh matter of thought, and distinct principles for judging and acting, day by day.

JOHN HENRY NEWMAN *Idea of a University* (DISCOURSE VI)

WHEN JAMES JOYCE left Belvedere in June, 1898, to enter University College, his Jesuit education, though far from complete, was in reality at an end. True, he was to spend four more years, starting the following September, in and around the premises on Stephen's Green where the Jesuits, in academic desperation, were attempting to maintain for the Catholics of Ireland an institution of higher learning. But though technically Joyce was again under their supervision, that supervision was so inadequate that the boy did not in fact continue to receive a typically Jesuit education. The supervision was inadequate because the Jesuits, though burdened with the responsibility of a college, at no time possessed an authority commensurate with their responsibility. They had not, for example, an entirely free hand even in the preparation of the curriculum. Under such circumstances, the prescriptions of the *Ratio Studiorum* were inapplicable, and they would have proved ineffective even could any real attempt have been made to apply them. The truth is that the Jesuits, during their quarter of a century on Stephen's Green (1883-1909), were little more than educational caretakers.

To understand this state of affairs, to appreciate the atmosphere —so different from that around Clongowes or Belvedere—in which Joyce moved during his years at the University, it is necessary to go back a little in time and to trace briefly the history of higher education in Ireland. That history, like the history of the country itself, was a nightmare—part of the general historical nightmare from which Dedalus in *Ulysses* was trying to awake.

For centuries the educational center of Ireland, the only center of higher learning, had been Trinity College, Dublin. This was a venerable institution founded by the first Elizabeth as an intellectual breakwater of Protestantism set against the dark swirling tides of Irish Catholicism. It stood sturdily enough through the dark night of the seventeenth and eighteenth centuries, but toward the close of the nineteenth even Irish Protestants, those at any rate of nationalist sympathies, were beginning to question its usefulness and purpose. Lady Gregory, for example, when asked why she had sent her son to Oxford, replied obliquely: "Oxford, you know, is much nearer Ireland than Trinity College!" A remark interpreted to mean that Trinity was not only a bulwark of Anglo-Irish culture but also an obstacle to the inexhaustible literary supplies in the manners, beliefs, and turns of speech of the surrounding native Irish.[1] Yeats was even more emphatic in his assertion that the Theosophical Society had in a few years done more for Irish literature than Trinity College in its three centuries.[2] Joyce's own feeling about Trinity may be fairly reflected in the attitude adopted by Stephen Dedalus. On his morning walk across Dublin Stephen comes upon "the grey

---

[1] Eglinton, *Irish Literary Portraits*, p. 6.   [2] *Ibid.*, p. 44.

block of Trinity on his left, set heavily in the city's ignorance like a dull stone set in a cumbrous ring." The sight "pulled his mind downward" so that as he continued on his way towards Stephen's Green he strove "this way and that to free his feet from the fetters of the reformed conscience" (P 209).

It was this reformed conscience more than anything else that would have made Trinity inimical to Joyce and to generations of Irish Catholics before him. For Trinity was essentially a Protestant preserve to which, from the date of its foundation until as late as 1871, Roman Catholics had small welcome. In this policy of exclusion Trinity had, of course, simply conformed to the pattern established earlier at Oxford and Cambridge, and at first glance there would seem to be no difference between the Irish and the English universities. Actually, however, the difference was enormous. Trinity was a Protestant university established in the capital city of a predominantly Catholic country; as such it was more than a symbol of racial domination, it was also the central bastion of religious intolerance. On either count it was bound to be regarded askance by Irish nationalists, Catholic or Protestant.

When in 1871 religious restrictions were lifted, a few Catholic students—the very few who could obtain the necessary permission from their bishops—began to attend Trinity. But their numbers were never large. It was anyhow rather late in the day to effect this kind of reform, a reform which was far from being complete even then. Long before 1871 there had existed the need for a different kind of university, wholly Irish in character and Catholic in atmosphere, where, if ever they were to produce educated leaders from among themselves, the native Irish might educate their sons in the traditions of their own faith and race. By the middle of the nineteenth century this need was real, but against Ireland's greater needs at the time it was not yet pressing. For these were the years of the famine and, with the dawn of a

new nationalist spirit, of deepening political unrest. Relief and reform were the really pressing needs, bread and politics were more
urgent than books. A people must be fed and free, their lands
reclaimed from pestilence and their rights recognized by government, before they could be expected to show much interest in the
graces or luxuries of learning.

The University Question, as it came to be called, was first
posed at this time. Robert Peel, then British prime minister,
thought to divert the Irish from what seemed to his government
an unreasonable preoccupation with Home Rule—a subject
which Peel firmly refused even to consider—by offering them
instead the sop of higher education. The plan was to found a
Queen's University to be located in Dublin and tightly controlled
by Dublin Castle. Affiliated with it were to be a number of provincial colleges which would prepare students for university examinations in Dublin. Unlike Trinity, for which Oxford and
Cambridge provided the pattern, Peel's institution was modeled
on the recently established (1836) University of London. Briefly,
what this meant was that in practice Queen's University was to be
an examining not a teaching institution; that in principle it was
to be essentially utilitarian, and that in function and atmosphere
it was to be wholly and unalterably secular. As such it was of
course clearly unsuited and unacceptable to the people for whom
it had been designed. And when, through their bishops, the people repudiated Peel's Greek gift, it was only to be expected that
the British government should see in the repudiation another
example of Irish intransigence and ingratitude.

The Irish hierarchy, however, having on grounds of conscience
condemned these "godless colleges," now felt morally obliged
to provide their people with an adequate substitute for them. The
substitute they founded was the Catholic University of Ireland, a
noble and unfortunate experiment which has since been described

as "an institution of hope, founded on faith, on the basis of charity." [3] It was all of that and, unfortunately, little more. Its hopes centered chiefly on John Henry Newman, who in November, 1851, was invited over as rector, and on June 3, 1854, was solemnly installed. Its faith was that of the Irish bishops who opposed Peel, and its charity was the good will and contributions of the Irish people. But despite the theological virtues attendant at its birth, Catholic University was from the beginning marked for failure. It was unendowed, underequipped, and ill-housed (at No. 86 Stephen's Green). It might, however, have surmounted even these disadvantages if at any time it had been empowered by the government to confer legally recognized degrees. This power was never granted, and so long as the government refused a charter, students from Catholic University were never able to qualify legally for civil or professional careers. The University was, then, in effect defeating its own purpose, and, in a practical sense, wasting the students' time. That, as result, the number of students was always small—never more than forty —is less surprising than that there should have been any students in attendance at all. Why Catholic University did not flourish is more understandable than that it survived as long as it did.

It survived as such until 1879. In that year an act of Parliament established the Royal University of Ireland. Catholic University, now in loose affiliation with Colleges in Cork, Galway, and Belfast, was incorporated into the Royal and was henceforth known as University College. But this arrangement, too, was far from satisfactory, for the Royal, like its predecessor, was not in fact a university at all. It was a cumbersome examining machine whose principal function was to award degrees to candidates from any of the colleges affiliated with it, or indeed to anybody bold enough to present himself for examination, whether he had at-

[3] *A Page of Irish History*, compiled by Fathers of the Society of Jesus, p. 18.

tended one of the colleges or not. An educational makeshift, it was morosely described by its first Jesuit rector, Father William Delany, as "at least better than nothing." [4]

The Jesuits first came to Stephen's Green in 1883, and within a year of their arrival registration rose from less than thirty to more than one hundred and sixty students.[5] This was an encouraging development, due in part perhaps to the Jesuits' reputation as educators. But the real explanation was that students could now enroll in University College and, upon completion of the necessary requirements, receive from the Royal University a degree that was legally recognized. Unlike Catholic University, University College was at last in a position where, whatever its defects, it could at least offer its students an education of some practical value. And the Irish, being a less impractical people than is sometimes supposed, were quick to take advantage of the opportunity.

The opportunity, however, was less than ideal, and the Jesuits themselves had no illusions about the academic character of the education available. Its defects had been built into the charter of the Royal University under which their college operated. Commenting on the difficulties inherent in this arrangement, the official Jesuit historian writes: "The course for degrees and for all examinations [at the Royal University] were laid down so as to apply to five [*sic*] University Colleges, all different, to the Seminaries, at least three Women's Colleges, and to a large number of extern students of both sexes, including many who were undergoing courses in Training Colleges both Catholic and Protestant." [6] This catch-all of sects, sexes, schools, seminaries, and colleges was indeed an educational nightmare. Only Jesuits perhaps

---

[4] Tierney, ed., *Struggle with Fortune*, p. 4.
[5] *Ibid.*, p. 27. Only three years previously, 1879–80, before Catholic University was incorporated as University College into the Old Royal, "there were about a half-a-dozen students for its ten professors." *A Page of Irish History*, p. 49.
[6] *A Page of Irish History*, p. 180.

would have the courage, or the presumption, to attempt to introduce an appearance of order, an attempt never more than partially successful. What, for example, was one to do with a curriculum in which no distinction was made between major and minor subjects? in which a student specializing, as Joyce did, in modern languages, received as much credit toward his degree from courses in physics and biology as those in French and Italian? Or how was one to administer examinations when, in order to insure fairness, it was considered necessary to ask all students the same questions? "Considering not merely the terms of its charter," the Jesuit historian continues, "but also the constitution of its governing body, the wonder is, not that the system was defective, but that it was not infinitely worse than it actually proved to be." [7] The appraisal is as accurate as it is candid.

I

Long after his last lecture on Stephen's Green, Joyce whose appetite for any odd news of Dublin was always insatiable, followed in whatever Irish papers were at hand the results of the examinations at his old university. "With a cynical curiosity," a friend adds, "satirical about those who got all the prizes." [8] His cynicism is understandable when one remembers the conditions of academic life at the old Royal. For even as an undergraduate Joyce, whose admiration for Newman was immense, was aware that the establishment on Stephen's Green was less than a shadow of that great man's idea of a university. He knew that, like its predecessor, Catholic University, it had not in reality been born of Newman's noble dream of a great center of learning, but that it had been troubled into existence by the wearying conflict between Ireland's two intransigent masters, the imperial British state and the Roman Catholic and Apostolic Church. Even had

[7] *Ibid.*   [8] Colum, *Life and the Dream,* p. 392.

he wished it he could not, once he entered University College, have escaped the awareness that against the person of the priest at his right hand was set now the shadow of the policeman at his left.[9]

Newman's original idea had been of a university which would combine the best features of the tutorial system he had known at Oxford with an added emphasis on formal teaching and lecturing. This idea was never fully to materialize, and by Joyce's time there were few if any traces of it still remaining in the educational structure of University College. Joyce himself did have the advantage of a private tutor during his last year when he studied Italian under the direction of Charles Ghezzi, S.J., on loan in Dublin from the Venetian province of the Society.[10] But this instance seems to have been the exception rather than the rule, and if Father Ghezzi at all resembled his namesake in the *Portrait* or his prototype in *Stephen Hero,* the experience could not have left Joyce with a very favorable impression of the tutorial system. It was not, in any case, sufficient to convince him that he was attending a university that embodied in action the fine ideas of his much admired Newman.

Indeed, the only real link still binding Joyce's university to Newman's was the medical school on Cecilia Street. (But this, too, had meanwhile developed into an all but autonomous and separate institution.[11]) On Stephen's Green the last connection with the past was a handful of former faculty members who were newly appointed to Fellowships at the Royal University. Among

[9] Gorman (*James Joyce,* p. 135) reproduces one of Joyce's earliest (1904) entries in his notebook: "spiritual and temporal power / Priests and police in Ireland." For the use Joyce made of priests and policemen in his work, see Magalaner's essay on *Dubliners* in *James Joyce, The Man, The Work, The Reputation,* pp. 53–101.

[10] *Catalogus S.J.,* 1902.

[11] "The Catholic University School of Medicine (1855–1909)," in *Struggle with Fortune,* pp. 61–79.

these the oldest and, in many ways, the saddest figure was Thomas
Arnold, Matthew's brother, who had followed Newman to Ireland in 1856 and, on the latter's withdrawal to the Oratory, had
followed him back home again in 1862. Returning to Dublin
twenty years later, he was still lecturing in English literature when
Joyce entered University College in the autumn of 1898.

According to Stanislaus Joyce, Arnold on at least one occasion
took favorable notice of young Joyce's talents, finding much to
praise in an essay the young man wrote attacking *Macbeth*.[12]
It is doubtful, however, that Joyce was at any time much impressed by Professor Arnold. The man was a relic of the past, a
reminder of the practical failure of an ideal, and of the futility of
a present in which that ideal was beyond all realization. Just so,
perhaps, Joyce thought of Arnold as he sat at his lectures, marking on the gray face the disappointment of an exhausted intellectual, detecting in the hesitant and unfamiliar speech of the
English convert a veiled note of defeat. What young Joyce may
not have known was that behind this tired old man was a youth
so full of life and gaiety, so compact of passion, that the poet
Clough, hardly bothering with disguises, could transform him
in *The Bothie* into the poetic, passionate, and improbable hero,
Philip Hewson.[13] Nor could the student Joyce have guessed that
Thomas Arnold's life—his early academic success, his fear of
paralysis at Oxford, his apostasy (from Anglo-Catholicism), his
wanderings abroad, and finally the long years of exile spent in
Dublin—had anticipated the general pattern, though the pattern
was often inverted, of much of the life he was himself to experience. As it was to be with Joyce, literature was Arnold's love early
and late, learning his preoccupation, and religion the ghost that

[12] Stanislaus Joyce, "James Joyce: A Memoir," *The Hudson Review*, II (Winter, 1950), 488. See also *My Brother's Keeper*, p. 100.
[13] He is identified as such in *A Page of Irish History*, p. 90.

was to follow him to his grave. The old Englishman, looking up from a lecture on Shakespeare and finding himself surrounded by a sea of bored young faces, congenitally Catholic and unconscionably Irish, might have been forgiven the thought, which at the end was Joyce's own thought: "My people were not their kind out beyond there so far as I can" (FW 627). For the Englishman in exile, especially if his place of exile is Ireland, is a far lonelier figure than the loneliest of Irishmen.

But to Joyce and his contemporaries, Professor Arnold was less a figure of compassion than an object of indifference. They all knew he was the brother of a distinguished English poet and the last surviving son of the famous Dr. Arnold of Rugby. They had heard, too, of his reputation as a learned authority upon the beginnings of English literature. But their knowledge of his family and acknowledgment of his reputation did little to relieve the tedium of his lectures. From the exterior which he presented to his students he appeared "very shy, slow of speech on account of a slight impediment, far from bright in conversation, rather, to tell the whole truth, a dull-seeming person." [14] A colleague, in an unsuccessful attempt to soften truth with charity, has said of Arnold's teaching that "He prepared his lectures on Shakespeare carefully but they were wanting in power and originality." [15] Similarly, the official historian of University College, after a brief nod in the direction of Arnold's "learning and gentleness," sums up the man with the blunt avowal: "it must be allowed that he did not count for much in the *entourage* of St. Stephen's Green." [16]

It is easy to suppose, then, that in attending Arnold's lectures Joyce was as bored as any of his fellows. He may have been even more deeply disappointed. His passion for literature had been

[14] *Ibid.*, p. 89.   [15] *Ibid.*, p. 118.

[16] *Ibid.*, p. 89. For a somewhat kindlier estimate of Arnold at University College, see in this same volume (p. 241) the "Recollections of Rev. Professor P. M. MacSweeney."

growing all during his last year at Belvedere, and at the end of that year had grown so intense that he felt that it must be satisfied at all costs—even at the cost of a vocation. Once that decision had been made, he looked forward eagerly, and with all the excitement of adolescence, to the free indulgence of his passion at the university. Instead he encountered Professor Arnold. Disappointment might have been more tolerable if, in want of an inspiring teacher, the course in English literature had offered Joyce material that was itself intellectually challenging and enough of such material to engage his interest throughout the academic year. But neither was this the case. The deficiencies of the curriculum were as disheartening as the ineptitude of the teacher.

To qualify for a degree, Joyce had simply to pass satisfactorily four sets of annual examinations. These were "Matriculation, First University, or First Arts, as it was usually called, Second University, and B.A., and the standard was 30% for pass, 60% for second class honours, 70% for first class honours." [17] These standards, in terms of percentages, are hardly impressive. They are even less impressive when one examines the kind and quantity of work to which they were applied. Joyce, for example, in his Matriculation examination in English in 1899, offered for pass, in addition to "grammar" and an essay, Scott's *Ivanhoe,* Book 1 of *Paradise Lost,* and "Lycidas." [18] That was all. That was also absurd, for Joyce at Belvedere had already studied "Lycidas" in preparation for his Intermediate examinations, had probably gone on to read the rest of Milton's poetry, and may at least have been tempted to read *Ivanhoe,* since that novel had once caused a minor furor at his old school when recommended by one of the Jesuit masters.[19]

[17] Tierney, ed., *Struggle with Fortune,* p. 53.

[18] Calendar for the year 1900, Royal University of Ireland. Joyce's name appears in the calendar for the first time this year as one of those who passed the matriculation examination in the summer of 1899.

[19] Byrne, *Silent Years,* pp. 21–23.

Had Joyce elected to try for honors in his Matriculation examination, he would also have offered selected essays and satires of Dryden, *Richard II,* and *The Tempest.*[20] But Joyce never took honors in English at University College, nor is there any evidence that he ever tried for them. It is not hard to see why.

He did, however, this year win second class honors in Latin.[21] For pass he was required to offer Book xiv of Ovid's *Metamorphoses,* along with Cicero's *De Senectute* and *De Amicitia.* For honors he offered, in addition, Book xxi of Livy, Sallust's *Jugurtha,* the *Ars Poetica,* and selected odes and satires of Horace.[22] This material offered for examination in Latin seems a more respectable test of a university student's knowledge than that prescribed in English. Even so, for a student like Joyce, who the year before at Belvedere had been translating Horace into accurate and graceful English verse, the program could not be considered much of a challenge. That it was any challenge at all may be indicated by the fact that this was the only occasion during the whole of his university career that Joyce interested himself in scholastic honors of any sort.

Besides English and Latin, students at the end of their first year had also to take examinations in mathematics, natural philosophy, and one modern language. Of the latter it is not clear whether Joyce elected French or Italian, the two languages he had begun to study at Belvedere. But it is more than probable that he was examined in Italian, the language of Dante, whom he already considered an artist superior to Shakespeare.[23] If so, he may now

[20] Calendar for the year 1900, Royal University of Ireland.

[21] *Ibid.:* "Second Class Honors in Latin—James A. Joyce."

[22] *Ibid.* The pass examination also included Latin grammar, "easy" sentence translation (i.e., from English into Latin), and Roman history (390–27 B.C.). A more detailed knowledge of Roman history (133–65 B.C.) was required for honors. The specific assignments in Horace were *Odes,* Books i (xiii, xix, xxiii, xxv, xxxiii) and iv (i), and *Satires,* Book ii (omitting vii).

[23] Stanislaus Joyce, "James Joyce: A Memoir," *The Hudson Review,* II, 488.

for the first time have become acquainted with Tasso's *Gerusa-lemme Liberata,* the first three cantos of which, along with Goldoni's *Il Burbero Benefico,* comprised the matter for examination in Italian.[24] As for mathematics and natural philosophy, not only were the subjects of no interest to Joyce, but the matter for examination in these subjects, like much of that in Latin and English, was merely a repetition of what he had already studied at Belvedere. Algebra, for example, and geometry (the first three books of Euclid) comprised the matter of mathematics; the elementary principles of mechanics, hydrostatics, and pneumatics that of natural philosophy.[25] Joyce, it is safe to assume, did not bother seriously with any of these.

This curriculum of his first year was a fair sample of what Joyce might expect from his courses during the remainder of his time at University College.[26] Its deficiencies were apparent. The Jesuits, mournfully aware of them but without a free hand in the conduct of the university, had simply to endure for as long as they could. Education was to them a means not an end, and though University College was a sad excuse for a university, it was still "better than nothing." For "nothing" was, at that time and in that place, the only other alternative. Yet with the sorry means at their disposal, the Jesuits were often uneasy about how

[24] Calendar for the year 1900, Royal University of Ireland. Grammar and translation were matter for examination in both Italian and French. The French works read were Souvestre's *Au Coin du Feu,* and Coppée's *Récits.*

[25] Compare the requirements with those given in the *Rules and Programme* of the IEBI, 1898, pp. 59–60. The year he graduated from Belvedere, Joyce was responsible for the first *six* books of Euclid; as a University student he had only half as much work to do in the same subject, and that half he had already completed before coming to University College.

[26] For example, in Joyce's second year, 1899–1900, all that was required for a pass in Latin was the *Aeneid,* Book VI, and Livy, Book XXXIV; in his third year, 1900–1901, for a pass in English, Sidney's *Defence of Poesie, The Merchant of Venice,* and *Paradise Lost,* Books I–II. That this last was in part a repetition of the English requirement in Joyce's first year seems not to have mattered—another indication of the inconsequence of the curriculum at the old Royal.

well they were attaining their end. Believing that the human will is harnessed firmly to the intellect, they had grave misgivings about the intellectual basis of the faith their students professed. Most of these students were Catholic by birth and upbringing, but they were not what the Jesuits would consider intellectual or even, in any true sense of the word, educated Catholics. Father Henry Browne, S.J., who taught Joyce Latin at UCD, afterwards expressed these misgivings in his recollections of student life. He was writing not of the "one or two" students who lost their faith— "men of talent but not of influence . . . intellectual cranks," as he calls them—but of those "finer spirits among our Catholic students."

They had neither been trained [Father Browne wrote] nor even encouraged to think of their religion as something that could be questioned. Its mystery they grasped vaguely, but they knew little of the inherent structure, of the logical fibre, of the dogmatic triumph of Catholicity—still less of its hard won struggles in the past, saving only so far as they had affected the history of their own country.

The causes of this defect in the Catholic mentality of young Irishmen of forty or fifty years ago were historical. . . . What we wish to insist upon here is that their religious training was defective on the intellectual side; that they had not been in a position to think out its philosophical basis.[27]

From Father Browne's recollections it is clear that University College, incapable from the beginning of providing its undergraduates with an adequate education in secular subjects, was equally incapable of providing a solid intellectual foundation for the traditional Catholicism of most of its students. Part of the explanation of this is that courses in religion received no official recognition, and therefore no academic credit, under the charter of the Royal University. The Jesuits, however, did conduct such a course during Joyce's time and attempted to attract students to

[27] *A Page of Irish History*, p. 414.

it by awarding medals and money prizes for excellence in the sessional written examination.[28] The attempt seems to have met with small success. The student's reaction to the course and the examination has been recorded, lightly but no doubt accurately, in one issue of the college magazine, *St. Stephen's*.

The Religion exam was an extraordinary revelation. The amount of heresy sent in for the corruption of the Reverend examiner was something abnormal. This, however, is not due to any growing spirit of agnosticism, but merely to the phenomenon of each man answering upwards of twenty names every week at Tuesday's lectures. . . .[29]

The particular ruse is of course an ancient one, and there is no reason to believe that its practice was confined to unaccredited courses in religion at UCD. The same sort of thing is reported in the *Portrait* (p. 222) when the roll is called at the beginning of the physics lecture. But even if the evidence of the *Portrait,* not always a reliable guide in such matters, is dismissed, there is still reason to suppose that University College students, at least the brighter ones among them, were quite as casual as Dedalus in attendance at lectures. For if, like Joyce, they were uninterested in honors, they could still pass their yearly examinations without any real show of effort. This is especially true when, as was often the case at UCD, the matter of these examinations was the same or very similar to that in which they had been examined in their secondary schools. Indeed, one cannot escape the impression that, for a student as talented as Joyce, the curriculum at University College was intellectually contemptible, and that Joyce must have known before the end of his first year that if he was to be educated at all, he must set about educating himself. This he proceeded to do.

Unfortunately, however, the autodidact, which is what Joyce became and remained, labors under certain disadvantages. Often it does not matter that the education he has given himself is far

[28] *Ibid.,* p. 417.   [29] *St. Stephen's,* I (June, 1903), 269.

superior to what he might have received through more formal university processes. Joyce learned that it did not matter some few years after leaving Dublin, when casting about for means to support his family in Trieste, he applied for a teaching position in the Italian school system. His application was rejected on grounds of the "inadequacy of his Dublin degree," an action which Herbert Gorman rightly characterizes as deserving "a very high place indeed in the annals of Comic Opera Culture." [30] Certainly Joyce, superbly self-educated, was more than qualified for the position, but that is not the point. The point is that he did not have the necessary academic qualifications. Officialdom, even academic officialdom, seldom recognizes talent, much less genius, at first sight, and there can be little doubt that the officials who presumably had only Joyce's academic record to go on, made the correct, however absurd, decision.

Joyce, remembering this experience, and remembering too, the futility of the final years of his "formal" education on Stephen's Green, may perhaps be forgiven the cynical curiosity with which years later he scanned the examination results of his old university.

II

It is usual to assume that Joyce's preoccupation with scholastic philosophy was a consequence, fortunate or otherwise, of his more or less formal and systematic training in philosophy by the Jesuits at University College. That assumption will now bear some reexamination.

Stephen Dedalus, while still a student of the Jesuits, called the esthetic theory he was there formulating "applied Aquinas," and he admitted to his friend Lynch that "so far as this side of esthetic philosophy extends Aquinas will carry me all along the line"

[30] *James Joyce*, p. 208. Italo Svevo ("James Joyce: A Lecture delivered in Milan in 1927," pp. 11–12) says that Joyce "sat for an examination to compete for a *professorship* in English." Italics mine.

(P 245), an opinion expressed earlier in conversation with the dean of studies (P 218). Lynch's rejoinder at one point to Stephen's hair-splitting dialectic, "That has the true scholastic stink" (P 251), has been echoing through Joyce criticism ever since. A similar note is sounded in the opening episode of *Ulysses* and is made to resound throughout the whole work. Buck Mulligan, one of that "brood of mockers" whom Stephen loathes, scores "the jejune jesuit," and taunts him with "the cursed jesuit strain . . . injected the wrong way" (U 10). That, says Mulligan, whose function is to understand nothing, is the real explanation of why Stephen would not kneel down to pray at his mother's deathbed. A moment later he urges his companion to "chuck Loyola," and when Haines asks Stephen for his ideas on Hamlet, Mulligan shouts in pain: "No, no . . . I'm not equal to Thomas Aquinas and the fifty-five reasons he has made to prop it up" (U 19). Jesuitism and scholasticism, Loyola and Aquinas, are all one to Buck Mulligan for whom "it's all a mockery and beastly" (U 10).

But Dedalus is only a *persona,* one who shares in the nature of the person of his creator but does not mirror perfectly the personality of that creator. What Dedalus mirrors, and that only imperfectly, is the cerebral, self-conscious, and self-defeating aspects of the Joyce original. He is the object of irony, not the manipulator of ironies. His thought is a brilliant patchwork of pain, not an organized pattern of creative and comic joy. He accepts defeat at the hands of the usurper, Mulligan (U 24), while Joyce, speaking in his own person, inflicts defeat on all the Mulligans of this world:

> Those souls that hate the strength that mine has
> Steeled in the school of old Aquinas.[31]

[31] "The Holy Office," in *The Portable James Joyce,* ed. by Levin, p. 659.

The lines lend strength to the assumption that, even granted Dedalus at UCD and after is not Joyce, Joyce himself would identify "the school of old Aquinas" with the philosophical discipline to which he was now exposed during his last four years with the Jesuits. The phrase need not of course be interpreted so narrowly, for certainly Joyce continued to attend the "school" after he had left the university. The Paris and Pola notebooks, with their commentaries like those of any medieval schoolman on the texts of Aristotle and Aquinas, are sufficient evidence of this.[32] But it would seem natural to assume that so persistent an interest in scholastic thought and method began with his courses in philosophy under Jesuit guidance at University College.

The assumption is natural, but unfortunately it is not borne out by the facts. In a definitive study of Joyce and Aquinas, William Noon, S.J., states categorically: "No regular course in scholastic philosophy was offered at all in the old University College during the period of Joyce's attendance . . . very much contrary to what one might at first have expected." [33] Noon then goes on to say that Joyce was "scholastically oriented" by "indirect contact with Aquinas's ideas through catechisms, sermons, conversations on politics and economics, interpretations of novels, poems, and so on." [34] His conclusion is that Joyce's exposure to Thomism was far from systematic, that the influence of Thomism was in the atmosphere rather than in the curriculum.

This general conclusion appears correct, but it would be more readily acceptable if Noon could explain the apparent contradiction of it that appears in the Jesuits' own story of University College, *A Page of Irish History*. When one reads that in 1901

[32] Gorman, *James Joyce*, pp. 95–99, 133–35.

[33] *Joyce and Aquinas*, p. 3. See also Morse, "Aquinas and Joyce," *The James Joyce Review*, I (February, 1957), pp. 19–30.

[34] *Ibid.*, p. 14.

Father Darlington replaced Father Thomas Finlay as Professor of Metaphysics,[35] and that William Magennis held first a studentship, and during Joyce's time, a fellowship in what was called Mental and Moral Philosophy,[36] one would like to know what these courses were if one or the other of them was not a "regular course in scholastic philosophy." Neither the authors of *A Page of Irish History* nor Father Noon, who was assisted in his work by Jesuits of the Irish Province, can provide a clear and satisfactory explanation. The former work does indicate the difficulty involved in designing a program in philosophy suitable to the needs of "students belonging to various schools of thought," and indicates also how the problem was eventually resolved: "A very sensible solution was finally arrived at, namely the adoption of alternative courses, one of which was based more strictly on scholastic lines." [37]

"More strictly," a Jesuit might hasten to point out, here means a good deal less than "strictly." For certainly had there been a vital and energizing course in Catholic philosophy taught at University College, Father Browne would not later have had occasion to lament that the students' "religious training was defective on the intellectual side; that they had not been in a position to think out its philosophical basis." Noon's conclusion, then, is not far wide of the mark, though the truth of the matter is less clear-cut than the formulation of that conclusion would make it appear. But readers of Father Noon are on more certain ground than those who have read in Mr. Gorman that the university men of Joyce's youth "lisped Latin in their cradles and devoured Aristotle as later generations of young men devoured Mr. Edgar Wallace." [38]

When, however, Father Noon claims that Joyce's only contact

---

[35] *A Page of Irish History*, p. 215.   [36] *Ibid.*, p. 219.
[37] *Ibid.*   [38] *James Joyce*, p. 99.

with Thomism was indirect—through catechisms, sermons and the like—he is on much less certain ground. Joyce's catechetical days were over by the time he entered the university, and during his years there he does not appear to have been the kind of student whose intellectual enthusiasms might be readily aroused by Jesuit sermons. Doubtless he had many and long conversations, of the kind reproduced in the *Portrait,* on philosophy and art and on the philosophy of art. "The talk of these young men," John Eglinton writes, "their ribald wit and restless manner of life, their interest in everything new in literature and philosophy (in this respect they far surpassed the students of Trinity College) are all reproduced in Joyce's writings." [39] This is all true enough, but even Dedalus's imperfect grasp of Aquinas's thought presupposes a more than casual or conversational acquaintance with Thomism on Joyce's part. Moreover, it was not a new but an old philosophy that attracted Joyce, as it attracted Dedalus, and its attraction was not that of an intellectual fad but of a coherent structure of thought—"the most coherent effort" Joyce later came to feel that had yet been made "to achieve spiritual and material stability." [40] If Joyce as a student had no formal or systematic training in philosophy—and there is now no evidence that he attended any of the lectures (unaccredited in the curriculum at UCD) given by Fathers Finlay and Darlington or by William Magennis—still his introduction to scholastic thought was sufficiently intimate to enable him afterwards to consider Aristotle and Aquinas with a certain scholarly familiarity. Fortunately, there is evidence to show that Joyce could and did receive such an introduction to Thomism during his last year at University College.

On Wednesday evening, November 27, 1901, Joyce was present

[39] *Irish Literary Portraits,* p. 133.
[40] Stanislaus Joyce, "James Joyce: A Memoir," *The Hudson Review,* II, 511.

in the old physics laboratory on Stephen's Green when the first inaugural meeting of the Academy of St. Thomas Aquinas was opened by the rector of the University, the very Reverend William Delany, S.J.[41] Joyce was one of only a handful of undergraduates who attended. Most of those present were either members of the teaching staff of the college or were otherwise academically connected. The presence of Fathers Darlington and Finlay, incoming and outgoing professors of metaphysics, was only to be expected, as was that of William Magennis, a fellow in philosophy. But present also were Father Ghezzi, tutor in Italian, Fathers Browne and O'Neill of the faculties of classics and English, and from Trinity College the brothers Geoffrey and Dudley White. Mr. Geoffrey White was on hand to read a paper entitled "A Note on the Philosophy of Supposition."

The general tenor of Mr. White's lecture and the general trend of the discussion that followed, has been preserved in the minutes of the meeting. Since it is definitely known that Joyce attended this meeting, certain extracts from these minutes may be given here as suggestive of the philosophic "atmosphere" that sur-

---

[41] The material used on this and the following pages is taken from a manuscript notebook (now in the library of the National University, Dublin) which describes itself as "The Academy of St. Thomas Aquinas: Addresses of Members and Minutes of Meetings." The peculiarity of Joyce's entry in this register is worth noting: as first given, his name and address—"James Joyce, 32 Glengarrif Parade N.C.R.?"—are crossed out (as is that of C. J. Joyce, M.A., directly above his), and a new address—"60 Sandy Serpentine Avenue, Sandymount"—is written in at the top of the page. This Sandymount address is also crossed out, but an obvious attempt has been made to delete the deletions and the word *stet,* is written to the right. Because of these peculiarities Father William Noon, who had no opportunity to examine this manuscript personally, may have been led to believe by his Irish correspondent, Fergal McGrath, S.J., that Joyce did not belong to the Academy of St. Thomas Aquinas. But the evidence of the manuscript seems to indicate otherwise. Not only Joyce but his friend J. F. Byrne were included in the membership of the academy, and the minutes for the meeting of November 27, 1901, include Joyce's name (though not Byrne's) among the dozen laymen who attended the inaugural session. This, it seems, is sufficient evidence for the point of view advanced here.

rounded him at University College—or, more properly, of that specifically Thomistic atmosphere in which Joyce chose to move while at the university.

After defining conception [the minutes begin] and its relation to truth, the lecturer illustrated his general argument by the action of the mind of the player at draughts: Before moving his piece on the board he makes a variety of suppositions. These hypotheses underly his game, and upon the correctness of his final choice, depends success.

Mr. White then discussed *supposition* necessary to the attainment of the practical good, giving us the science of ethics. Its use in the search of truth, in natural science [*sic*]. He contended that supposition or hypothesis was necessary at every stage of induction, then in the conception of Beautiful as an end in itself. From the fine arts Mr. White put music and architecture apart.

.   .   .   .   .   .

Mr. Magennis said [that] the principles of St. Thomas Aquinas are the true principles of reason in every department. There can be no changing what is unchangeable. St. Thomas' philosophy needs no reconstruction or readaptation, but we should attend to the form of its delivery; we should speak and write not in an unknown tongue but in language understandable. Whilst so many systems are attracting attention for their style, and so many books are written to support other systems, Catholic principles are unstudied by these writers and the general public because untranslated into modern jargon.

The Rev. T. A. Finlay . . . criticized one of the definitions in the preface of the address, viz., that the mind can know something which it recognizes to be untrue and to which therefore no reality of any kind corresponds. The Reverend Speaker could not understand this.

Mr. Vessey Hagen, M.S., maintained that modern science, so far from making Philosophy futile, gave it greater value and scope. He criticized what the lecturer had said with reference to music; thought has an inner and an outer side, and in its inner side music finds an end in itself.

Mr. Coyne too agreed with Mr. Magennis as to the distinction between the principles of St. Thomas and the best expression in modern times. What he would emphasize was the necessity of urging the immutability of those principles as of prime importance, so that attention to modern style might not weaken the true issues.[42]

There is no point in attempting to relate these extracts to Joyce's text. Joyce never saw these minutes, and he may have remembered in detail little or nothing of what was done or said at this or any other meeting of the academy. But if these minutes are accepted as indicative and representative of the kinds of discussions that Joyce attended, their general significance is clear. They show that Joyce had specific opportunity to come in contact with the best-trained minds at University College as members of its faculty discussed, with constant reference to the "unchanging and unchangeable" first principles of St. Thomas Aquinas, the role and function of scholastic philosophy in the intellectual life of contemporary society. At least three, and probably more, of these faculty members were specialists in the field, and they may be expected to have quoted frequently and to have referred even more frequently to specific texts in St. Thomas in their contributions to the discussion which followed each lecture. It would have been natural for Joyce, with his instinct for scholarship, to take note of these references, and to have followed them up with private reading and study. This is especially true when, as at the inaugural meeting of the academy, the lecturer touched upon "the conception of the Beautiful as an end in itself," and the discussion turned at times upon considerations of "modern style" and "an inner and an outer side" of thought. These were precisely the kinds of problem that then engaged Joyce's mind and continued to engage it, as his notebooks show, for some time after he left the university. If, as an undergraduate, Joyce did not take

---

[42] This is the Coyne whose name appears in Joyce's Pola notebook (Gorman, *James Joyce,* p. 136): "Coyne: Beauty is a white light. Joyce: made up of seven colours." The note immediately following this reads: "Coyne and religious landscape."

part in these discussions himself, he had ample opportunity after they were over to buttonhole any of the speakers and press them for further information (or, possibly, to impress them with information of his own). For, according to *A Page of Irish History,* when a meeting "had been turned out of the College on account of the lateness of the hour, the discussions were continued on the college steps and even in the streets." At times they were even started up again the next day. "During the day sometimes," the account continues, "the metaphysicians were observed still hammering out their arguments, in the College corridors, and giving the Philistines an opportunity to jeer." [43]

This sort of thing provides an interesting sidelight on that passage in the *Portrait* in which Stephen Dedalus discusses with the dean of studies St. Thomas's definition of the beautiful. The dean of studies was Father Darlington, but Father Darlington was also professor of metaphysics, though no hint of this is given in the *Portrait.* One may wonder whether the exchange between Dedalus and the dean was not patterned after a similar discussion between Darlington and Joyce the day following one of the meetings of the Academy of St. Thomas Aquinas. [44]

The larger significance of Joyce's membership in this academy is something else. Disgusted with a curriculum that was more suited to the mentality of a schoolboy than to that of a university man, indifferent therefore to the formal processes of education which the defeated Jesuits would put him through, and realizing that his intellectual salvation depended now largely upon himself alone, he interested himself only in those aspects of university life which he felt would advance his own self-education. From about the middle of his first year, Joyce's participation in

[43] *A Page of Irish History,* p. 351.
[44] According to Byrne (*Silent Years,* pp. 33–37), it was he, not Joyce, who was in the Physics Theatre the morning Darlington entered to light a fire.

the life of University College was for the most part limited to those activities which lay outside the curriculum with which the Jesuits and their less gifted students struggled in vain. The Academy of St. Thomas Aquinas was one of these activities, but it was not the only one.

III

The official historian of University College has described the decade 1894–1904 as a "period of triumphant success." [45] However relative that success, the general claim is not exaggerated. The University Question still awaited an answer, the curriculum remained as sorry a thing as ever, and among the faculty there suddenly appeared no new and inspiring personality. The machinery of the university was still the same, and so for the most part were the machinists, Jesuit and layman, who kept it running. But toward the close of the century there did appear on Stephen's Green Newman's "multitude of young men, keen, open-hearted, sympathetic, and observant, as young men are, come together . . . to learn one from another even if there be no one to teach them." [46] Dismal as he may have found the ways of "formal" education at University College, Joyce was fortunate in the young men who were his contemporaries. For among them was a group of alert undergraduates who, like himself, were intellectually alive and who, no more than he, could be content with the dull and lifeless ways marked out for them by academic routine. They applied their energies of mind to other things than study, espe-

---

[45] *A Page of Irish History,* p. 327. See also Tierney, ed., *Struggle with Fortune,* p. 105, where reference is made to "the golden age of the later 1890's." The author adds wryly: "Today, it seems, one's mere presence in The College in the days of Joyce has become a major source of dollar income. But the glamour of having been a young man at the same time as the artist is not solely dependent on that."

[46] "Knowledge Viewed in Relation to Learning," Discourse vi, in *Idea of a University,* p. 146.

cially to the undergraduate societies and academies which seem to have been the true center of intellectual vitality at University College. It is not too much to say that it was in the company of such young men, at the meeting of these various societies, especially the Literary and Historical Society, that Joyce, in so far as he participated at all, actually shared in the intellectual life of the university. But it is important to note that, though his presence among them was felt and his "weird sort of talent" was recognized, he was not considered the most gifted, most original, or most promising of the group.

Tom Kettle, a year ahead of Joyce, enjoyed—and to many minds still enjoys—the reputation of having the clearest and most capable intelligence of his generation. He and Joyce had probably met socially, before the latter entered University College, at the home of their fellow undergraduates Richard and Eugene Sheehy. It was there that Kettle was to meet his future wife, Mary Sheehy, the young lady who, as we have seen, knew and admired young Joyce. Tom Kettle, as auditor for the year 1898–99, may have been the person who proposed Joyce for membership in the Literary and Historical Society which was then beginning to flourish anew on Stephen's Green. He seems, in any event, to have befriended the younger man from the start, for Joyce's first appearance at a meeting of the L & H—the first meeting, that is, of which there is record of his attendance—the two men successfully defended the negative side of a debate on the resolution "that in the last decade of the nineteenth century English literature reached a very low ebb." [47] Despite the banality of the subject, it would seem that from this time on, possibly with Kettle's encouragement, Joyce took an active interest in the affairs of the society.

Another undergraduate has described Tom Kettle as "a genial

[47] Minutes of the Literary and Historical Society, Saturday, January 28, 1899.

cynic, a pleasant pessimist, an earnest trifler . . . a fellow of infinite jest and infinite sadness." [48] The description is accurate
enough, but also general enough to apply to any number of his
Irish contemporaries—to Joyce himself, for example, in whose
work humor is handmaid to sorrow, and whose laughter "palliates
the sense of doom that is the heritage of the Irish Catholic." [49]
The Kettle family itself was of ancient Norse stock settled in
Ireland long before the battle of Clontarf, in comparison with
whom the Joyces, of Norman extraction, were practically par-
venus. [50] "We came out of the sea along the Black Beach," Tom
Kettle told Gogarty, "we won all before us. We won it with our
battle-axes. We hold it still. We have been in the neighborhood
ever since." [51] It was the Kettle of infinite jest who spoke thus
to Gogarty, though the jest may have been in earnest. For the
Irish may at times laugh most readily at what they believe in
most deeply, as they can believe most deeply in what is beyond
the shadow of a proof. One wonders whether Joyce as a young
man had ever heard Tom Kettle's boast and whether it was still
in mind when his later dream drew another Norse invader across
the sea to Howth Hill and environs.

Tom Kettle had come to the university from the fashionable
College of Clongowes Wood, and before taking his degree was
to spend a year abroad studying philosophy and history at Inns-
bruck. His scholastic accomplishments were taken for granted, his
special gifts as an orator were acknowledged by a medal from

---

[48] William Dawson (UCD 1900) in his introduction to the posthumous edition
of Kettle's *Poems and Parodies*.

[49] Nolan, "An Editorial Note," *Envoy*, V (April, 1951), 11.

[50] Andrew Kettle, Tom's father, a successful Leinster farmer, was at one time
a famous Irish Land Leaguer, a man whose earnestness in the nationalist cause
had once prompted Parnell to pun that the name of Kettle was a household
word in Ireland. See Chesterton, *Irish Impressions*, p. 59.

[51] Gogarty, *It Isn't This Time of Year At All!*, p. 20.

the L & H,[52] and he was already something of a linguist, speaking French and German fluently, and Gaelic too, but with less fluency than enthusiasm. Young Joyce was not so mean of mind that he would have envied Kettle his natural gifts and the admiration and popularity that these gifts brought him. But Joyce may have been human enough to envy Kettle his background— the successful if not distinguished father, the comfortable rather than wealthy home, the gentlemanly education, the leisure to travel abroad, and as a result of all this the manner of decent refinement, the honest self-assurance and poise which provided Kettle, as it provided Oliver St. John Gogarty, with an entree to polite and cultivated society. Lady Gregory pronounced that society's judgment upon Joyce when, according to Gogarty, she expressed the view that the young man was not quite "out of the top drawer." [53] But no one, not even "Gregory of the Golden Mouth," [54] as he later tagged her, was more sensible of his status than Joyce himself. At college his acquaintance with Tom Kettle who, in terms of material and social advantages, had all that he himself as a child had once a right to expect, could only have deepened his awareness of himself now as *declassé*. Kettle, the old Clongownian, was a constant reminder of the hopes that had been discarded, albeit unknowingly, when he was forced to leave Clongowes Wood in the fall of 1891. There was some reason, then, for envy. Kettle might be the noblest fellow on Stephen's Green, but Joyce, like archduke turned doorman, could not bring himself to any real familiarity. Instead he affected a formality which, however naturally he may have inclined to it by temperament, seemed strangely out of place in a skinny young man of seventeen who did not wash regularly and who went about town in

---

[52] Minutes of the Literary and Historical Society, November 14, 1900.

[53] Gogarty, *Mourning Became Mrs. Spendlove*, p. 50.

[54] "Gas from a Burner," in *The Portable James Joyce*, ed. by Levin, p. 661.

tennis shoes and oddly shaped hats. It was all of course quite absurd. It was not Kettle who was a snob—the same cannot be said of Oliver Gogarty [55]—it was Joyce who was a displaced snob.

Kettle is conspicuously absent from that gallery of ironic miniatures in which the artist Joyce later included most of the prominent, and some less prominent, members of the college community. He is absent of course because there is really no place for him in the *Portrait,* and there is no place for him for much the same reason that there is no place for Joyce himself. For James Joyce—as distinct from Stephen Dedalus—and Tom Kettle, despite the difference in their backgrounds and the divergence of their subsequent careers, shared a common point of view on most of the important problems that confronted thoughtful young Irishmen at the beginning of the century. Kettle, the economist and politician, might be expected to express those views differently from Joyce, the poet and man of letters, but behind this difference of manner was a striking similarity, and often an identity, of thought and sentiment.

Dublin, "the center of paralysis" to Joyce,[56] was to Kettle the focal point of contemporary Irish degradation. "Dublin," he wrote, "focuses with lamentable truth the arrested development of the nation as a whole. . . . While human beings continue to be born into a sub-human existence, from which only the strongest and the luckiest can hope to escape, our civilization is, so far forth, a contradiction in terms." [57] It is this contradiction and sub-

---

[55] Gogarty might gladly have admitted this, but even did he not, the snob in him shows through in his cruel and witty dismissal of Joyce's protective pretenses: "He had the formal and diffident manners of a lay brother in one of the lower orders of the Church." *It Isn't This Time of Year at All!,* p. 73.

[56] Letter to Grant Richards, May 5, 1906, in Gorman, *James Joyce,* p. 150.

[57] "Labour and Civilization," in *The Day's Burden and Miscellaneous Essays,* pp. 121, 125. All of Kettle's essays hereafter cited are from this same volume.

human existence from which Joyce extracted "the special odour of corruption" which, he hoped, floated over *Dubliners*.[58] He had, too, the strength and luck to escape, though he remained always "an Irish emigrant the wrong way out" (FW 190). To Joyce specifically Kettle might have directed the advice he murmured to himself each time he left Ireland: "Do not cry out against *la patrie*. Your native land after all will give you the two most exquisite pleasures of your life, that of leaving her and that of coming back." [59] Joyce would doubtless have agreed, though in the end he was denied, or denied himself, the second of these pleasures. That also requires strength, the kind of strength Tom Kettle had in mind when he wrote of Irish exiles such as Joyce: "All his courage is a courage of adieus." [60]

In exile Joyce, never ceasing to be Irish ("O Ireland my first and only love" [61]—a bitter and angry but true avowal, as avowals of love so often are), became as truly European an artist as Dante or Dostoyevsky, Goethe or Flaubert. That he should have become so was implicit in the embryo artist at University College who in "The Day of the Rabblement" heaped youthful scorn upon a literary movement that was too timidly national, too dangerously parochial. His heart was Dublin, but Dublin was all Ireland, and Ireland was set like a great misted glass in the western sea to reflect back not a city but a civilization, not an isolated country but a vast, varied and unified culture. The Great O'Neill's failure in the sixteenth century was redeemed by Joyce in the twentieth—Ireland became again a part of Europe. Thomas Kettle thought as Joyce thought but, like the O'Neill, he was a politician and a soldier, not an artist. His hopes for Ireland were parliamentary not poetic, and his defense of Europe was on the

[58] Letter to Grant Richards, October 15, 1905, in Gorman, *James Joyce*, p. 146.
[59] "On Saying Good-Bye," p. 101.   [60] *Ibid.*, p. 103.
[61] "Gas from a Burner," in *The Portable James Joyce*, ed. by Levin, p. 660.

deadly banks of the Somme, not by the deeply imagined waters of the Liffey. "My only counsel to Ireland," he wrote in October, 1910, "is, in order to become deeply Irish, she must become European." [62] Like Joyce, Kettle followed his own counsel, and paid in death what Joyce continued to pay in exile for his belief. When the first war broke out he resigned his seat in Parliament, where he had sat for East Tyrone, and took a commission in the British army. He was killed at Ginchy in September, 1916. He did not die as an English officer, but as a European who happened also to be an Irishman. There is no paradox here. In Stephen's Green today there is a bust in memory of Kettle, and inscribed on the stone beneath is a fragment of verse which he wrote for his daughter a few days before he was killed.

> Know that we fools, now with the foolish dead,
> Died not for flag, nor King, nor Emperor,
> But for a dream, born in a herdsman's shed
> And for the secret Scripture of the poor.[63]

Kettle and Joyce shared the same dream, however differently it turned out for each of them. They shared still more, but it would require a separate study to do full justice to their communion of spirit. Read Kettle's essays (he had time to write all too few) and, whether he is writing on economics, politics, literature, or philosophy, you encounter everywhere a mind that is its own master, interested apparently in all things, contemptuous of none. It is a mind that would have inevitably interested and attracted Joyce, so like it is in many ways to his own. Even in that in which they seemed farthest apart, the matter of religion (Kettle

---

[62] "Apology," p. xii.

[63] "To My Daughter Betty, the Gift of God," in *Poems and Parodies*, p. 8. The verses quoted above are the concluding lines of a sonnet which, like most of Kettle's verse, is more sincere than successful.

remained always a devout Catholic), the difference is more apparent than real.

It is indeed part of the mission of the Church [Kettle wrote] to safeguard those ethical truths which lie at the basis of all society; but when it comes to a question of the technical processes of society, economic and political, every man must effect his own synthesis of principle and technique, and he must be free to follow the light of his own conscience and his own experience.[64]

Substitute "literary and artistic" for "economic and political," and Joyce himself could have signed his name to this passage. Joyce's Irish Catholic sense of doom lay just as heavily on Tom Kettle. He was acquainted with Chesterton, who in turn admired him greatly, but the Englishman's bumptious optimism irritated him as it must certainly have irritated Joyce. "Who," Kettle once asked, "can forgive Mr. Chesterton his awful jolliness? Show him a corpse just fished out of the Thames, or the murderer of it, or an international financier, or any other hideous object, and he is off at once to dictate an article for the *Daily News,* explaining how awfully jolly the whole thing is." [65] Mr. Belloc with his "knock-about anarchism, which he mistakes for political health," comes in for the same kind of treatment, the same kindly scorn.[66]

Kettle had as little use for simplistic Catholicism as had Joyce himself. Philosophically, he would probably have described himself as a Catholic pessimist, for "a pessimism," he wrote, "stabbed and gashed with the radiance of epigrams, as a thunder-cloud is stabbed by lightning, is a type of spiritual life far from contemptible." [67] This was, he believed, the "indispensable propaedeutic to any valorous religion." [68] But though he disdained the simple-

[64] "Labour: War or Peace?," p. 174.
[65] "A Man Troubled about Everything," p. 196.   [66] *Ibid.*
[67] "Anatole France," a review of *L'Ile des Pingouins* and *Les Contes de Jacques Tournebroche,* p. 86.   [68] *Ibid.*

minded optimism of a too hearty Christianity, the imposing simplicity of revealed truth which, as St. Augustine confessed, might satisfy the mind of a child while challenging still the critical and contemplative minds of scholars, this truth colored the whole of Kettle's thought. The destiny of a man, darkly veiled in moral evil—"a problem too hard to understand, too heavy to endure" —stirred Kettle to vague protest, but his protestation was not a rebellious yawp of denial. "For my part," he confessed, "I can only fall back on the serpent and the apple, and an obscure something which, as my Penny Catechism says, 'darkened our understanding, weakened our will, and left in us a strong inclination to evil!' " [69] Joyce can quote the same Penny text word for word (U 209), and the "obscure something" which troubled Kettle becomes in Joyce the central obscurity, full of dark suggestion and hilarious implication, of Finnegan's fall and *Finnegans Wake*.

After they left University College, Joyce and Kettle seem to have seen little of one another. In a year or two Kettle accepted a professorship in political economy at his alma mater (Joyce had also been offered an "assistant professorship" in modern languages, which he refused).[70] In September, 1905, Kettle founded and, with the assistance of former university men, edited the *Nationist,* a paper strongly political in tone (he was then chairman of the United Irish League) but which boldly protested its interest *de omni re scibili*.[71] The paper continued to appear until March, 1906, in which year Kettle was first elected to Parliament. But he continued to write—verse, reviews, criticism, economic and political essays, belles-lettres—all of which, his verse excepted, showed a sane, witty, original, and lively intelligence. His essay on "A New Way of Misinterpreting Hamlet" is interesting for

[69] "Reveries of Assize," pp. 60–61.
[70] Stanislaus Joyce, "James Joyce: A Memoir," *The Hudson Review*, II, p. 490. See also, p. 224 below.
[71] *A Page of Irish History*, p. 489.

its perceptions as well as its paradox and to compare with the famous theory advanced by Stephen Dedalus in *Ulysses*.

The last connection between Joyce and Kettle is the latter's review of *Chamber Music* in the June 1, 1907, issue of the *Freeman's Journal:* "Those who remember University College life of five years back," the review began, "will have many memories of Mr. Joyce. Willful, fastidious, a lover of elfish paradoxes, he was to the men of his time the very voice and embodiment of the literary spirit. His work, never very voluminous, had from the first a rare and exquisite accent. . . . It is clear, delicate, distinguished playing, of the same kindred with harps, with woodbirds, and with Paul Verlaine. . . ." [72] Kettle's review, along with that of Arthur Symons in the *Nation,* set the pattern, as William York Tindall has pointed out,[73] for most of the subsequent criticism of *Chamber Music*—a pattern, it may be said, which Professor Tindall, in his definitive edition of the poems, rearranges with all the skill, but none of the preconceptions, of a Freudian exegete. James Joyce in Trieste could only have been pleased by his fellow alumnus's cordial reception of his first book, a reception which also helps to correct the impression that from the beginning the response to Joyce in Ireland was uniformly unfavorable.

At University College the two young men, in default of a sound formal education, seem to have followed Newman's advice and to have learned from one another. The circumstances on Stephen's Green surely conduced to such informal education, and the likeness of their two minds indicates a similar intellectual orientation, the differences in the later development of their talents notwithstanding. But though Tom Kettle may have been the most important influence on Joyce among his college com-

[72] This review is reproduced by William York Tindall in the introduction to his edition of *Chamber Music*, pp. 19–20.

[73] *Ibid.*, p. 20.

panions (it would be typical of Joyce to omit mention of him in the *Portrait* and *Ulysses* because he *was* important), he was not the only young man at the university who brushed minds with Joyce.

There was, for example, Frank Skeffington. Contemporaries who thought Kettle more generally gifted than Joyce were convinced that Skeffington was even more eccentric. Indeed, by comparison, Joyce, despite his "weird" talent, may have seemed a rank conformist. There was first the matter of appearance. Frank Skeffington affected a beard such as Joyce, frail and fuzzy-cheeked, could never have equaled, and he trimmed it after the fashion of Tsar Nicholas of Russia, whose photograph in the *Portrait* Stephen Dedalus identifies as "the face of a besotted Christ" (P 227). There was a Christlike quality about Skeffington, too, not to be denied by the loose Norfolk tweeds that hung limply over his angular frame. But it was the oppressive altruism, the militant pacifism, the outspoken feminism of Skeffington which was most suggestive of a Christ. He was a man who to live must live always for a cause. "He was a radical and democrat," a contemporary said of him, "blending the English tradition of John Stuart Mill and W. T. Stead with the Irish and international outlook of Michael Davitt. . . . He loved argument and had a set opinion on every point of human behavior. At an age when students are usually content to hold many opinions in loose solution, his were all armed *cap à pie* and ready for battle. His every opinion was a principle for which he was ready to die." [74]

It is not hard to see in this description the figure of MacCann, Skeffington's surrogate in the *Portrait*. MacCann is the only character in the novel who can hold his own against Stephen's mordant wit. When the latter refuses to sign the Tsar's peace petition, the zealot MacCann accuses him of reactionism.

[74] Curran, "A Broadcast Talk from Radio Éireann, May 2, 1954," reprinted (pp. 221–30) in *Struggle with Fortune,* ed. by Tierney, pp. 226–27.

Do you think you impress me—Stephen asked—when you flourish
your wooden sword?—
    —Metaphors—said MacCann bluntly.—Come to the facts.
    Stephen blushed and turned aside. MacCann stood his ground and
said with hostile humour:
    —Minor poets, I suppose, are above such trivial questions as the
question of universal peace.—   [P 231]

Dedalus thereupon moves away angrily, almost sulkily, saying
as he goes, "If you must have a Jesus, let us have a legitimate
Jesus," a remark that leaves MacCann undisturbed. For he is not
really a hostile person, he is utterly without malice, and he bears
Stephen no grudge or ill-feeling. "Dedalus," he remarks to the
young aesthete, "I believe you're a good fellow but you have yet
to learn the dignity of altruism and the responsibility of the human individual" (P 232).
    It is possible that Skeffington's opinion of Joyce as an under-
graduate was much the same. For the bearded, knickerbockered
idealist could have seen little in his friend of the disinterested
rebel, which is what he himself was. Joyce's internationalism was
cultural, but Skeffington's, like Kettle's, was primarily social and
political. Still the seeds of revolt stirred in both young men, both
demanded independence of mind and freedom of action in the
provinces they were then staking out for themselves, and each
may have cultivated in the other that specific seed of revolt which
in each was to have so different a flowering. It is altogether natural, then, that on one occasion, confronted by college censorship,
they should have combined forces and circumvented the censor
by publishing independently in a two-penny pamphlet essays pro-
scribed by the college authorities.
    There was much of the bourgeois in Joyce, temporarily con-
cealed behind a front of youthful arrogance; there was none at all
in Skeffington. He remained a rebel, an outsider, a nonconformist
to the end. But he was more naive than Joyce in thinking that by

remaining in Dublin he could raise its existence from a sub-human to a more human, even to a superhuman level. His utopianism was incurable. Like Kettle and Joyce, he also was offered a post at University College after he had been graduated, and strangely enough he accepted and served for a while as bursar. But he soon enough found himself in conflict with University authorities over the subject of coeducation. He resigned in protest, and shortly after married Hannah Sheehy, of the ubiquitous Sheehy sept, from which time on he perpetuated his protest in behalf of women by answering only to the name of F. Sheehy-Skeffington. By marriage he was now brother-in-law to Tom Kettle, and he worked with him for a while on the *Nationist*. But not quite satisfied—it was not in Skeffington ever to be satisfied—with Kettle's prescription for the ills of Ireland, he founded his own paper, the *National Democrat,* which lasted no more than a few months.[75] A year later (1907) he was at work on a political biography of his idol, Michael Davitt, and it is typical of the man that he should have written and published it over the protests of Davitt's widow who had made it quite clear that she herself was preparing the "official" biography of her husband.

This was the only full-length work by Skeffington to be published during his lifetime.[76] But he continued to write pamphlets and throwaways, and his staccato Ulster accent continued to crackle on Dublin street corners preaching pacifism and "votes for the bitches," as his feminism is epitomized in the *Portrait* (P 228). When the first war broke out his opinions soon had him in trouble with the British civil and military authority in Dublin. His opposition to conscription landed him in jail, where he

[75] *A Page of Irish History,* p. 493.

[76] *Michael Davitt.* For a bibliography of Skeffington's other published writings, eight items in all, see O'Hegarty's *Bibliographies of 1916 and the Irish Revolution,* pp. 5–7.

promptly went on a hunger strike that won him release in a week's time.[77] But his end in the dark days ahead could almost have been foretold; the Christ in him required martyrdom, and the Don Quixote sought it in the most fantastical way. The Easter Uprising was not a day old when F. Sheehy-Skeffington went out calmly into the streets of Dublin in the innocent belief that he could talk *both* the rebels and the military into laying down their arms. The British of course arrested him. There was no trial. While his wife's brother, Lieutenant Eugene Sheehy, was leading a company of British troops into Dublin to put down the insurrection, another British officer, a psychopath named Colthurst, murdered Skeffington with a bullet in the back at the Portobello Barracks. He died certainly as he had lived.

A few years after this murder, Sean O'Casey, former secretary of the Irish Citizen Army, in his history of that organization (O'Casey's first published work), singled Sheehy-Skeffington out from all those who had fallen during Easter Week for special remembrance:

Unwept, except by a few, unhonoured and unsung—for no National Society or Club has gratefully deigned to be called by his name—yet the ideas of Sheehy-Skeffington, like the tiny mustard seed today, will possibly grow into a tree that will afford shade and rest to many souls overheated with the stress and toil of barren politics. He was the living antithesis of the Easter Insurrection: a spirit of peace enveloped in the flame and rage and hatred of the contending elements, absolutely free from all its terrifying madness; and yet he was the purified soul of revolt against not only one nation's injustice

[77] His *Speech from the Dock* in June, 1915, was published as a pamphlet a year after his death by the Skeffington Memorial Committee, then operating out of New York. Printed with this speech is a letter from George Bernard Shaw, who was interested in Skeffington's trial and imprisonment but did not openly intervene. He did not, he told Mrs. Skeffington, because the British alarmists at the time considered him pro-German ". . . and if they knew that I sympathized with your husband they would declare that nothing but his imprisonment for life could save England. I can fight stupidity; but nobody can fight cowardice."

to another, but he was also the soul of revolt against man's inhumanity to man. And in this blazing pyre of national differences his beautiful nature, as far as this world is concerned, was consumed, leaving behind a hallowed and inspiring memory of the perfect love that casteth out fear, against which there can be no law.

In Sheehy-Skeffington, and not in Connolly, fell the first martyr to Irish Socialism, for he linked Ireland not only with the little nations struggling for self-expression, but with the world's Humanity struggling for a higher life.[78]

All that Skeffington later became, or failed to become, was foreshadowed in the bewhiskered undergraduate at University College. Temperamentally he had more in common with Joyce than with Kettle. He seems indeed to have had even more in common with Stephen Dedalus, though his kind of idealism and naïveté were not at all artistic and were a good deal more altruistic. Once at a meeting of the Literary and Historical Society the rector, Father Delany, remarking Skeffington's knickerbockers, suggested that on such occasions he should wear the evening attire proper to a gentleman. "I'll come as I am or not at all," was the crisp answer,[79] an answer that reminds one of Stephen's equally crisp, self-contained rejoinder to his friend Davin: "I shall express myself as I am" (P 237). The same crankery and self-containment also made an apostate of Skeffington, and in this too he resembles Joyce (and Dedalus) more than he does Kettle. The latter had too balanced a mind, too poised a spirit, to push reform to the barricades of rebellion; in this he was an Erasmus to Joyce's Luther, and to Skeffington's Savonarola. Still Kettle and Joyce were more evenly matched, the intellectual strength of one against the artistic cunning of the other. Skeffington, like Dedalus, was a "character," aflame with fiery naïveté. If one wonders, then, why as MacCann he does not figure more prominently in the *Portrait,*

[78] O'Casey [P. O. Cathasaigh], *The Story of the Irish Citizen Army,* pp. 63–64.
[79] Curran, "A Broadcast Talk," p. 227.

the answer must be that for Joyce's purposes two "Lord Byrons" were one too many. Stephen, as a pseudo-Christ, could only have suffered by comparison with a more legitimate type of Jesus.

Among Joyce's acquaintances at the university, Kettle and Skeffington represented the more serious-minded element, enthusiastic, intellectually alert, the energizing leaven which gave the college its essential character during this "golden age." The group also included Hugh Kennedy, afterwards Chief Justice of Ireland, who in *Stephen Hero* shares with Frank Skeffington the identity of McCann.[80] Kennedy was extremely active in the extracurricular life of the college; but, a less colorful character than Skeffington (and a less original mind than Kettle or Joyce), he has no part—nor part of a part—in the final version of the novel. Arthur Clery, later a professor of law at the university, was another auditor of the L & H during Joyce's time. He, too, is missing from the *Portrait*. So are the Sheehy brothers, Richard and Eugene, Constantine Curran (another professor in later years), John Marcus O'Sullivan (later Minister of Education), Robert Kinahan (auditor in Joyce's last year), as well as older acquaintances of Joyce from earlier years—the "sons of Thunder," Cecil and James, from Clongowes, and William Fallon and Albert Connolly from Belvedere.[81] He knew them all, but he was intimate with none.

[80] McCann is there identified as auditor of the L & H and as the first editor of the college magazine, *St. Stephen's,* both of which offices Kennedy did indeed fill, neither of which, during Joyce's time, ever devolved upon Skeffington. But this auditor-editor McCann is also described in the first draft of the novel (p. 31) as a "blunt, brisk figure, wearing a cavalier beard and shooting suit," whose originality the students rewarded with the sobriquet "Knickerbockers." Further, the brief exchange between McCann and Stephen (p. 150) is a reproduction of one of Joyce's earliest epiphanies, in which he and Skeffington are the speakers. See Silverman's edition of Joyce's *Epiphanies,* p. 4.

[81] All of these names may be found in "The College Register," *A Page of Irish History,* pp. 589 ff. Felix Hackett, an editor of *St. Stephen's,* is mentioned in the *Portrait* (P 233); Moynihan (P 223, 26, 27, 30) may be an approximation of

But these were the men with whom Joyce mixed daily, the students with whom he shared such intellectual companionship as was possible on Stephen's Green. His nights he probably spent in other company, less intellectual, more bohemian, among the medicals from Cecilia Street. There Oliver St. John Gogarty began his training in 1897, but shortly thereafter transferred to the medical school at Trinity College. Doubtless he knew Joyce as an undergraduate, but it was not until after Joyce had taken his degree that the two seem to have had any close relationship.[82] Their life together in the Martello Tower is well known—Gogarty has told and retold the story many times, Joyce but once and with devastating effect in the first chapter of *Ulysses*. Two other medical students, friends of Gogarty, are to be included in this second, seamier group of undergraduates. John Elwood—"called the Citizen to ridicule his advanced views"[83]—was almost certainly the prototype of Temple in the *Portrait*. Temple is there presented as a radical and a socialist, a loose-mouthed fellow fond of Jean-Jacques Rousseau, not at all fond of Jesus, who believed in nothing and admired only "the mind of man independent of all religions" (P 232). He is one of Stephen's hangers-on—hateful to Cranly, Stephen's self-appointed guardian, and obnoxious to the rest of his fellows—who persists despite threats, curses, and ridicule in proclaiming loudly and wickedly his admiration of the artist: "He's the only man I see in this institution that has an individual mind" (P 235). John Elwood apparently had similar views, and his opinion of Joyce was just as exalted. "He's terrific,"

James Murnaghan, a member of the L & H; Dixon and O'Keefe, two other supernumeraries in the novel, may be James Dixon and Joseph O'Keefe.

[82] Joyce once urged Gogarty "to compete for the Gold medal for English verse in the Royal." Gogarty did so, and won. However, in order to be eligible, he had to have passed his First Arts examination, which means that he would have completed two years of study at the Royal, during only one of which he and Joyce were fellow undergraduates. See *It Isn't This Time of Year At All!*, p. 33.

[83] *Ibid.*

he told Gogarty, "a great artist!" "Artist," Gogarty hastens to add, "in Dublin stands for a practical joker or a playboy; someone who prefers diversion to discipline." [84] No one will deny this, but neither will anyone claim that Joyce's diversions as a young man are incompatible with his discipline as a mature artist.

Elwood is supposed to have praised Joyce as an artist (or "artist") after the latter had accused him of inscribing his name in lead pencil on the backside of the Venus of Cnidus. In the *Portrait* it is the Venus of Praxiteles whose backside is in question, and the perpetrator of the crime is not Temple, but Lynch (P 240), alias Vincent Cosgrave. If Gogarty's account of Cosgrave is believed, Lynch bears a good likeness to the original. "He was cynical and amusing," Gogarty reports, "pensive at times, and cynical with himself. He caused jealousy by walking out with Nora Barnacle. . . ." [85] Lynch's principle function in the novel is to provide Stephen with an audience for his aesthetic theory. He reveals himself in brief flashes of dialogue as an intelligent, witty, at times impatient listener, who doesn't care a fig really about anything ("Damn you and damn everything," P 243) and whose chief interests are himself and women (P 244, 293). He reveals himself in another way to Stephen: "his face resembled a devil's mask" (P 248). If Cosgrave, with a like weakness for women, did have designs on Nora Barnacle, this may explain the "devil's mask" fastened to his surrogate in the *Portrait*. In the end Vincent Cosgrave did go to the devil. But he went first to London, where, after squandering a small inheritance, he threw himself off one of the bridges over the Thames.

Joyce was hardly more intimate with this group of undergraduates than with their more sober-minded contemporaries on Stephen's Green. In a way the two groups complemented one another, and when Joyce was weary of discussion with one he

[84] *Ibid.*   [85] *Ibid.*, p. 70.

could always find diversion with the other. But it was no more than diversion. He may have been what Gogarty called "a medical student's pal," [86] but he did not find among these carousers —any more than he found among the Kettle-Skeffington-Kennedy group—one student whom he would have acknowledged as an intimate friend. His reticence was insuperable, and he found it difficult to approach others; his "seedy hauteur" was insufferable, and made it equally difficult for others to approach him. Nevertheless he did have two close friends among the undergraduates with whom he may have shared the trouble and truth of himself. With the rest he shared only his ideas or his idiocies.

The first of these was George Clancy, the Davin of the *Portrait*. The story that Davin there tells Dedalus about his midnight adventure in the west of Ireland (P 211–13), is, according to Byrne, almost exactly as Joyce had it from Clancy himself.[87] It is a tale characteristic of the man, filled with a simple, open-eyed wonder, and shadowed by a mystery that lifts like country mists from the land and settles over the mind in drifts of unpremeditated poetry. On the surface, Clancy and Joyce seem to have had nothing in common. At the University and later Clancy's interests were simple: Irish sports, the Gaelic revival, and the freedom of Ireland, interests which certainly did not preoccupy Joyce. Nor were the two alike in temperament. There was nothing "cunning" about Clancy, and his country man's gift for vituperation, in an excited mixture of Gaelic and English, was in hard, happy contrast to Joyce's silences or the metallic bite of his Dublin wit. Doubtless Joyce was drawn to Clancy by the warmth and sincerity that won the man a host of friends in Ireland, but even beyond this the basic bond of friendship between the two men, otherwise so different, seems to have been the conscious identity of race.

[86] *As I Was Going Down Sackville Street*, p. 284.
[87] *Silent Years*, pp. 54–55.

With Clancy, Joyce could afford to drop the mask behind which pride and intelligence protected him from the essentially alien world of the Protestant ascendancy, and from that more familiar but hardly less alien world of the Irish Catholic bourgeoisie. With Clancy, Joyce could be himself, and whatever else that self may have been or may have become, it remained ineluctably Irish.

The same truth may lie at the root of Joyce's friendship with J. F. Byrne, the son of a Wicklow farmer. The story of their friendship at UCD has been told in some detail by Mr. Byrne, and is so generally known that it is not necessary to review it again here.[88] It is enough to know that Byrne and Clancy were the only two men whose friendship Joyce courted at University College. They may have contributed less to his informal education as an undergraduate than men like Kettle and Skeffington, but they doubtless contributed a good deal more to whatever consolation that difficult young man was able to derive from human companionship. But that is another story which requires a different telling.

[88] *Ibid.*

5 ⚹

St. Stephen's and the L & H

Trailing clouds of glory, the old gods are departing from us:—"dusk begins to veil their train, and he who listens may hear their footsteps leaving the world."—Those only who knew the College in the old days, and the habitable place it is now, can properly estimate the burden of gratitude that should accompany these master-builders of societies.   EDITORIAL, *St. Stephen's,* NOVEMBER, 1904

IT SHOULD now be clear that Joyce's friends and companions—intimate, intellectual, or casually ribald—constituted something more around Stephen's Green than "a milieu of kneebenders." [1] That description of them is no more than an echo of Daedalus's disgust with "a dayschool full of terrorized boys, banded together in a complicity of diffidence" (SH 208). But the Daedalus of *Stephen Hero* is an even less reliable spokesman for James Joyce than the Dedalus of the *Portrait,* and it would be folly to accept his sophomoric rhetoric and rage against the world as the considered opinion, composed in recollection, of Joyce himself. "Opinions," Dylan Thomas once remarked, "are bloody awful"—they are the stuff of argument, not of art. Joyce as artist had no opinions. But his feelings about University College, while he himself was an undergraduate, are not altogether inscrutable. If they cannot be clearly defined, they can at least be generally indicated by showing to what extent Joyce took part in the intel-

---

[1] Gorman, *James Joyce,* p. 57.

lectual life of the university. For no man, least of all a man like Joyce, is likely to devote much time or interest to what he considers contemptible. A final survey, then, of Joyce's university career will show how, in default of a satisfactory curriculum, the Jesuits supplied the young man with other, less formal means of educating himself in the company of his fellows.

Like any young man newly arrived at college, Joyce during his first term on Stephen's Green observed rather than participated in the life around him. Many of his fellow students were old acquaintances from Clongowes and Belvedere, and among the latter especially he would have no trouble in assuming the role —won by his scholastic achievements on Great Denmark Street —of quiet and acknowledged superiority. But there were a great many other students from the four corners of Dublin and from beyond Dublin who did not know him even by reputation, and these young men might understandably mistake his diffidence for disdain, his shyness for aloofness. These are not qualities that recommend a boy, no matter how talented, to his fellows. In their company Joyce, still a frail sixteen-year-old, was probably grateful for the friendship of the rugged, taciturn John Francis Byrne, who quickly constituted himself his protector.[2] The habits of study formed at Belvedere were not easily broken, and for this first term at least Joyce seems to have taken his work seriously —seriously enough, at any rate, to win second class honors in Latin in his matriculation examination. But by term's end he must have realized the futility of the curriculum: intellectual stimulation had to be sought elsewhere at University College.

He found this stimulation first in the Literary and Historical

---

[2] Byrne, *Silent Years,* p. 40: "When Joyce entered University College in 1898 it was only natural for him to cleave to me. . . . I was unusually strong, much stronger than anyone would have thought from my appearance, whereas Joyce was thin, light and weak. Due to this, my attitude toward him became, and to a great degree remained, protective."

Society. This undergraduate group could claim honorable, though not unbroken, descent from that Historical, Literary, and Aesthetical Society established by Newman during his second year (1855-56) as rector of Catholic University.[3] More or less complete records, however, exist only for the period of the Jesuits' tenure at University College. In the eighties the society had known the presence of Gerard Manly Hopkins and Thomas Arnold, and from that time on it was to hear the voice of almost every man prominently associated with the history of modern Ireland —O'Leary, Yeats, AE, Larkin, De Valera, and others. The year before Joyce's arrival on Stephen's Green the society had been newly activated, for it was in that year that Father William Delany, more aware than his predecessor, William Carberry, of the interests and needs of the undergraduates, returned as rector to University College. In the Fall of 1897 Delany himself assumed the presidency of the L & H, and Frank Skeffington was elected auditor.[4] The next five or six years, which include the whole of Joyce's term at the university, were to prove the most lively and productive of the society's existence.

Tom Kettle had succeeded Skeffington as auditor when Joyce made his first public appearance in L & H debate. That was in late January, 1899. The results of this debate—on the state of English literature in the nineties—have already been given. Kettle and Joyce, since acknowledged by a contemporary as "the two men of genius in my period,"[5] had no trouble convincing the

---

[3] *Centenary History of the Literary and Historical Society: 1855–1955,* ed. by Meenan, p. xviii.

[4] In *A Page of Irish History,* p. 338, it is reported that Skeffington's opponent in this election was James A. Joyce. A more puzzling error, if error it is, is the *Centenary History* report, p. 327, that in 1900–1901 Hugh Kennedy was elected auditor by "fifteen votes to nine for James Joyce." In the L & H minutes available to me I found no record of this contest between Joyce and Kennedy.

[5] Curran, "Memories of University College," in *Struggle with Fortune,* ed. by Tierney, p. 227.

audience that English literature in their time was not, as their (now nameless) opponents sought to prove, in any sad or shocking state of decline. One wonders what Father Darlington, who occupied the chair on the occasion, thought of the young men's defense of Yeats and Wilde, Johnson, Moore, Morris and the rest of the writers whose names possibly cropped up during the course of the debate. There is of course no record of what he thought as, unfortunately, there is no record of Joyce's arguments. But it was an occasion which might have provided Darlington and Joyce further opportunities to discuss literature and art as their surrogates in the *Portrait* discussed them around the fireplace in the Physics Theatre. It is, perhaps, significant that before his seventeenth birthday Joyce is found publicly on the side of the "modern" artist. Of more immediate significance at the time is the effect of this first success on Joyce himself. Encouraged by it, and possibly urged on by his colleague Tom Kettle, he now took a lively and active interest in the affairs of the L & H.

A month later, on February 18, he was elected one of a committee of eight which, under the auditor, governed the Society.[6] General meetings of the Society were held each month, but committee meetings were of more frequent occurrence, sometimes biweekly, and Joyce, according to the L & H minutes, was in general attendance at both. At a committee meeting on March 21, 1899, he and Louis Walsh were nominated for the office of treasurer. Walsh was elected by a vote of five to two. One may guess that Joyce abstained from voting and that of the two votes cast for him, one was that of his opponent, and the other probably that of Tom Kettle. It was of little importance, and Joyce seems to

[6] Minutes of the Literary and Historical Society, March 21, 1899. The register containing these minutes is now in the library of the National University of Ireland, Earlsfort Terrace, Dublin. Hereafter, unless otherwise noted, all further reference to meetings of the L & H will be based on the dates and data provided by these minutes.

have taken this minor defeat (which some may read as a test of popularity) with good grace, for immediately after the election on this date he joined Frank Skeffington in volunteering to read a paper before the society sometime during the year.

His offer was not immediately accepted. A few weeks later he had a slight falling out with some members of the committee, though not on business directly connected with the society. On May 8, 1899, the Irish Literary Theatre held its premiere performance of Yeats's *The Countess Cathleen* at the Antient Concert Rooms. The interruption of the performance by a hostile audience caused a general stir in Dublin, and a particular flurry of indignation at University College, and more particularly within the governing committee of the L & H. For the ringleaders of the reaction were two members of the committee, Walsh and Skeffington, joined by more ardent Gaelic Leaguers among the students such as Joyce's friend George Clancy. The hubbub, the sudden display of theological zeal, the anguished cry of outraged Celticism, annoyed and revolted Joyce. The following morning, on arriving at the University, he found Frank Skeffington in the lobby of the college surrounded by a ring of zealots and armed with a militant manifesto against the un-Irish, anti-Catholic play. Joyce, of course, refused to sign. He and Skeffington crossed swords. George Clancy shook his head sadly—"Are you Irish at all?" (P 236). The teapot tempest went on for days and weeks, but Joyce continued to hold aloof from the multitude of student patriots.[7]

The event may be dismissed as another example of the historic bigotry and disagreement which for centuries has bedeviled Ireland. But it is a mistake to dismiss it quite so casually. The de-

---

[7] This protest was published in the *Freeman's Journal* on May 10, 1899. For the list of signatories to it—and for a somewhat cooler appraisal of what actually occurred in the Antient Concert Rooms on the preceding evening—see the *Centenary History*, pp. 57–58.

bate and disagreement were a good thing, as Yeats and perhaps
Joyce, too, knew. "These attacks are welcome," Yeats wrote to
the press a few days later, "for there is no discussion so fruitful
as the discussion of intellectual things, and no discussion so
needed in Ireland." [8] This was, then, part of Joyce's education,
an event that compelled him to define his own thought more
clearly and, incapable of adopting the position of those around
him, to search out a new position for himself. He was not a
special partisan of Mr. Yeats, as he would make quite clear in
"The Day of the Rabblement," but neither would he now take
part with those who objected to Yeats for the wrong reasons. The
immediate result of all this debate and disagreement was that for
the remainder of the college year—little more than a month remained—Joyce stayed away from meetings of the L & H.

During the following summer, in the long vacation between
the end of one academic year and the beginning of the next, the
passions aroused in May had time to cool, and when Joyce returned to college in the fall of 1899 to begin his First Arts course,
he was again active in the affairs of the society. Arthur Clery was
now auditor and presided at a meeting of the committee on October 9, when Joyce seconded Hugh Kennedy's motion for the
admission of new members. At the conclusion of this meeting
Joyce again offered to read a paper before the society (his previous offer of March 21 had not yet been acted on), and Clery and
the committee accepted with thanks. Two weeks later the committee drew up a provisional list of subjects for the coming year.
Joyce's paper on "Drama and Life" was scheduled for the first
general meeting of the society in the new year.

Joyce kept himself busy during the intervening months. At this
time he probably found Father Darlington's lectures in English

[8] Letter to the Editor, *Morning Leader*, May 13, 1899. Reprinted in *The Letters
of W. B. Yeats*, ed. by Wade, pp. 319–20.

less of a trial than Professor Arnold's had been during the previous year. For Darlington, despite his treatment in the *Portrait* and *Stephen Hero,* is remembered by all of Joyce's contemporaries, without exception, as a man of deep and kindly understanding, and as a devoted if not distinguished teacher. What may have particularly engaged Joyce's attention in Darlington's class was the strong Aristotelian undercurrent in his literary appreciations, and more especially the originality of his approach to *Hamlet* through Aquinas and Aristotle, an approach welcome to students "bored with the solemnities of Dowden and Bradley." [9] But as a preparation for his paper, Joyce began now to read widely in contemporary drama and especially in the work of his early idol, Ibsen. Certainly he planned to impress his audience at the L & H with his views "on drama and life," and his natural desire to excel may have been sharpened by the success of Arthur Clery's address to the society at the general meeting of November 13. Clery then read a paper on "Irish Genius in English Prose," and this was so enthusiastically received that afterwards one of the distinguished visitors of the evening—the Reverend Dr. Hickey, professor of philosophy at Maynooth and vice president of the Gaelic League—moved "that the address be printed and distributed at the expense of the society." The resolution was carried unanimously. Joyce, the competitive instincts of his Belvedere days still alive in him, may have found in Clery's success a stimulus to a still greater success of his own.

Since Joyce's talk was to serve later as the basis of one of the central episodes in *Stephen Hero,* it is of some interest to compare here the bare official record of this meeting with the account given in Joyce's manuscript. The minutes of the Literary and Historical Society read as follows:

[9] Curran, "A Broadcast Talk from Radio Éireann, May 2, 1954," reprinted in *Struggle with Fortune,* ed. by Tierney, p. 226.

A meeting of the Society was held on Saturday, January 20, 1900, Mr. Magennis, M.A., F.R.U.I., in the chair. Mr. James Joyce read a paper on "Drama and Life." A vote of thanks to Mr. Joyce, proposed by Mr. Dowling and seconded by Mr. Kennedy, was supported in vigorous speeches by Messrs. Kettle, Coyne, M.A., Clery and Rev. Father Darlington, S.J., M.A. Mr. Magennis, after an able summing up, declared the vote of thanks carried unanimously. Mr. Joyce replied.

In the manuscript, Stephen, in keeping with his "position of notable-extraordinary," does not, as Joyce did, volunteer but "was *respectfully invited* to read a paper before the Literary and Historical Society." [10] The date was fixed for the end of March and the title of the paper was announced as "Drama and Life" (SH 31). Later when trouble develops over possible censorship, Stephen, interviewing the rector, Father Dillon (William Delany, S.J.), refers to the organization as "the Debating Society" (SH 77). This, like the date of the paper, is only a minor inaccuracy. A major distortion, however, is the fact of censorship. A censor, Father Henry Browne, S.J. (not Father Delany), did prevent Joyce's essay on "The Rabblement" from appearing in the college magazine, but there does not appear to have been any censorial interference with his paper before the L & H. Joyce here combines the two events for purposes of his own. His general method is suggested at the opening of the manuscript account of this meeting (SH 86–91). Stephen, reflecting on his recent interview with the rector, "in default of another's service, began to annotate the incident copiously, expanding every suggestive phase of the interview." Just so Joyce. With some of his minor details he is quite precise: at a committee meeting on November 25, for example, he had agreed with his fellow members that there should be "at each debate a pair of white candles for the convenience of the gentleman occupying the chair"; in

---

[10] *Stephen Hero*, p. 31. Italics mine.

the manuscript Stephen is caught "shading his face from the light of the candles on the Chairman's table." The day (Saturday), the setting (the Physics Theatre), and the subject of the essay are all reported accurately. But Joyce also introduces, by addition or distortion, other details so emotionally charged that Stephen, the "notable-extraordinary," remains always a "hero" impervious to the opinions or criticisms of a lesser breed of men. The minutes of the meeting, for example, indicate only vigorous support of Joyce's paper, but in the manuscript "Stephen was subjected to the fires of six or seven hostile speakers."

The last speech from the floor—"the climax of aggressiveness"—is worth noting, not because it is any more reliable than the others, but because in it there may be a clue to a more exact dating of the *Hero* manuscript. The main argument of this speaker ("But a man that was of all countries was of no country—you must first have a nation before you have art") was actually the subject of a debate ("Cosmopolitanism—the Legitimate Goal of Political Evolution?") between Queens College, Belfast, and University College, Dublin, on May 14, 1906.[11] These debates were regularly reported in the press, and it is well known that Joyce in exile had an insatiable appetite for Irish newspapers, for the most trivial news of events in Dublin. Again, the Belfast debaters, like the L & H speaker, defended the nationalist position, and the latter is reported by Joyce to have declared himself "in ringing Northern accents"—the accent, that is, of a Belfast man. All this may be no more than coincidence, but if it is more than that, Joyce could not have written this portion of his manuscript before the end of May or the beginning of June, 1906, a somewhat later date of composition than has been generally agreed upon.[12]

[11] *A Page of Irish History*, p. 348.

[12] Theodore Spencer, in his introduction (p. 6) to the first edition of *Stephen Hero* (1944), which is unchanged in the Slocum-Cahoon edition of 1955, allows

The final discrepancy between the L & H minutes and *Stephen Hero* is the statement in the latter that "Stephen contented himself with acknowledging the vote of thanks." The minutes say only that "Mr. Joyce replied." But others present that evening, reminiscing on the event many years later, recall Joyce as replying at considerable length and with great effectiveness.[13] And this certainly is what might be expected of an interested and talented undergraduate like Joyce, actively engaged in the affairs of the society. It is not what one would expect from the solipsistic Dedalus.

This comparison of the event with its retelling is one example of how Joyce worked factual material into matter for literature. Important to remember, however, is that *Stephen Hero* is only *matter,* rough and unfinished, which in the *Portrait* was given *form*. It is interesting chiefly as a link, missing in most works of art, between the experience of life and the reality of literature. The present example is, moreover, waste matter. It has been discarded wholly from the final version.

Whatever acclaim Joyce may have won locally by his paper on "Drama and Life" was overshadowed a few months later by

---

that the manuscript may represent "the work of the years 1901 to 1906." He argues to this last date on the basis of Joyce's letter to Grant Richards (reprinted in Gorman, *James Joyce,* p. 148) on March 13, 1906, in which Joyce informed the publisher that he had already written "twenty-five chapters, about half the book." If my surmise above is correct, Joyce was still writing, or revising, the manuscript as late as June, 1906, some three months after the date supposed by Spencer.

[13] Eugene Sheehy, in conversation with me, August, 1954. See also *A James Joyce Yearbook,* ed. by Maria Jolas. The latter reproduces a stenographic report by an unidentified interviewer in which Joyce's father recalls: "There was a debate and Kennedy if you please took exception to something Jim said. The cool, calm and calculating Jim putting his hand on the table took a note of what Kennedy said. At last Jim stood and my God he spoke for half an hour and he left Kennedy in a condition that he was not fit to be washed." Something like this may well have happened, but, as we shall see, it is more likely that it happened after Joyce's paper on Mangan, February 1, 1902.

the appearance in the *Fortnightly Review* (April, 1900) of an article entitled "Ibsen's New Drama" and signed James A. Joyce.[14] Around Stephen's Green only Kettle and one or two others may have appreciated the essay as an intelligent contribution to Ibsen criticism, but even those students who knew nothing of Ibsen began now to look on Joyce with a new kind of respect. Perhaps none of the Jesuits knew much about Ibsen either, but they doubtless felt a sense of pride in their student's accomplishment, and one would suppose that Father Darlington took occasion to congratulate the young man who sat that year in his class on English literature. As for Joyce himself, anyone who has had the youthful pleasure of seeing his words in print for the first time, can imagine the extent of his personal satisfaction. J. F. Byrne, at whose side in the National Library Joyce had been preparing both paper and essay, says that as a result of his appearance in the *Fortnightly Review* "Joyce's relationship with his few associates became impaired by either their jealousy or sycophancy." [15] Whatever may be the truth of this, it did not affect Joyce's participation in the activities of the L & H nor, apparently, his association with members of that society. He continued to attend meetings regularly through the spring, and on May 14, when Hugh Kennedy was named auditor, Joyce was again elected to the committee of eight. There is nothing in this to indicate that, as far as his university acquaintances were concerned, Joyce reacted other than normally to his first literary success. When a year later (March, 1901) he wrote to Ibsen in Christiana, he made explicit mention of his efforts on the master's behalf among his

[14] According to Curran ("A Broadcast Talk," p. 228), Joyce's paper before the L & H was "an assault on the romantic theatre and a vindication of Ibsen, but unfortunately nothing of it survives." Possibly, however, the paper was a remote preparation for the essay which appeared three months later.

[15] *Silent Years*, p. 63.

fellow students at University College—"defiant" but certainly not isolated efforts.[16]

Byrne further says that it was about this time that Joyce "was forced . . . to rely more than ever on me for companionship." [17] It is probably true that the two of them now began to see more of one another, but the evidence, though slight, indicates that it was Joyce who began to interest Byrne in college activities which until then the older student had had no part in. When, for example, the two men returned to Stephen's Green in the autumn of 1900, Byrne, who had not bothered to join the L & H, was admitted as a member at a meeting on November 16. More than likely, Joyce, as a member of the committee, proposed his name for membership.

The two friends continued to attend meetings throughout most of that year. In November, Hugh Kennedy spoke on "The Irish University Question," an incendiary subject for most undergraduates, but one which left Joyce profoundly indifferent. Nor could he have worked up much enthusiasm for William Dawson's talk on "Ireland and Imperialism," delivered on January 26, 1901. Politics simply did not interest him. A month later, however, the resolution "that the modern novel exercises an evil effect on society" was introduced for open, general debate at a meeting of the society, and Joyce, if present, must have enjoyed the spectacle of Arthur Clery, then college orator, arguing *solus contra mundum* in lonely support of the vague, unpopular, and slightly foolish proposition. Joyce himself did not take part in the debate. Indeed, at most of these meetings he seems to have been a silent, possibly amused, spectator. He continued active, however, in the L & H committee. The last public debate in which he took part

---

[16] *Letters of James Joyce*, ed. by Gilbert, pp. 51–52.
[17] *Silent Years*, p. 63.

was at a general meeting of the society on March 9, 1901. The resolution read "that the influence of Irish women is not an essential factor in the Anglicisation of Ireland." The motion, supported by Joyce, was carried.

After March, the minutes of the Literary and Historical Society for 1901 contain no further mention of Joyce. He drops out of sight until the following February when, wanting an audience, he reappears before the society to read his essay on James Clarence Mangan. But his return then would appear to be solely for the sake of an audience, for he was not afterwards to resume membership in the society. It would be easy to read into Joyce's defection at this time a Dedalean contempt for the puerilities of his associates, but such is not quite the case. It is true that many of the topics presented for discussion or debate were trivial, and others, though timely and vital to local patriots and national zealots like Kennedy and Clery, were entirely outside Joyce's immediate interests. Moreover, besides being dull, the meetings had apparently begun to degenerate into frivolous rowdyism.[18] Many of the rowdies came from outside the society, often from outside the college, and there seems to have been no effective way of controlling these disruptive elements. Once serious discussion was precluded, more serious students were discouraged, and Joyce was not alone in his discouragement. At a meeting on June 1, 1901, he did not stand for reelection to the committee. Defections from the society were general, and there was nothing singular about Joyce suddenly dissociating himself from the group.

I

But Joyce did not at this time go into Dedalean isolation. There were other university activities to claim his attention, and he began to interest himself now in these. At the end of this same

[18] See *A Page of Irish History*, p. 345.

month, March, 1901, the Library Committee of the university, under the chairmanship of W. P. Coyne, formed a discussion group which shortly after became known as the Library Conference. This organization was also in part an offshoot of the university sodality, in which Coyne was again the leading spirit, and as such it was "originally intended merely to promote the use of the books by Sodalists." [19] Joyce's friend J. F. Byrne seems to have taken an early interest in the new organization.

Readers of Mr. Byrne's autobiography, led to believe that the boy was an acknowledged skeptic at ten years of age and a self-confessed atheist at fifteen,[20] may be surprised to discover that he was, according to the register of attendance, a practising member of the University College sodality between December, 1899, and February, 1904.[21] The inconsistency, for so it must appear to the ordinary mind, is not perhaps entirely inconsistent to the mind of an Irishman. However that may be, Byrne as a sodalist would naturally gravitate toward the Library Conference which was mothered forth by the sodality. Joyce almost certainly did not attend sodality meetings at the university,[22] but as a friend of

[19] *Ibid.*, p. 434.   [20] *Silent Years*, pp. 12, 13.

[21] Register of Attendance, University College Sodality, now in the library of the National University of Ireland, Earlsfort Terrace, Dublin. Each sodalist signed his own name in this register. On December 9, 1899, appears the signature: "John Francis Byrne"; thereafter it appears simply as "J. F. Byrne." It appears for the last time under the date of February 13, 1904. In *Stephen Hero* Cranly is identified "as a member of the Sodality" (p. 107), and later there is attributed to him the virtue supposedly characteristic of all true sodalists: "Cranly's chastity was famous . . ." (p. 200).

[22] In the sodality register for November 10, 1900, there appears, in what is doubtless the writer's own hand, the entry "J. F. Byrne," and directly beneath, in a similar hand—it is almost certainly not Joyce's—is scribbled "Jas Joyce." The latter signature is difficult to read, but is still legible. It is probably no more than an example of undergraduate japery: other sodalists have signed the register by transliterating their names into Greek, and one uninspired piece of tomfoolery reads "his mark XX G. O'Brien." This sort of thing may indicate the approximate level of intelligence, perhaps of devotion, among some sodalists at UCD. Young Joyce may at times have overplayed his part as "artist," but he would not willingly have played the fool.

Byrne's he began tagging along to Library Conferences and taking part in the discussions which followed the reading of prepared papers. On Sunday, June 16, for example, he and Byrne both contributed to the discussion that followed a paper on "My New Curate" read by Arthur Clery.[23]

But of more interest to Joyce than the Library Conferences were the preparations, begun in the spring of 1901, for the publication of a new college magazine. Daedalus in *Stephen Hero* is characteristically contemptuous of the whole enterprise. When the editor, McCann, suggests that Stephen contribute something, there is the following exchange:

—Of course there is a censor? said Stephen.
—Well, said McCann, the person who originated the idea of the paper in the first instance was Father Cummins—
—The director of your sodality—
—Yes. He originated the idea so you see he acts as a kind of sponsor to us—
—He is Censor then?—
—He has discretionary powers but he is not at all narrow-minded. You needn't be afraid of him—
—I see. And tell me, will I be paid?—
—I thought you were an idealist, said McCann—
—Good luck to the paper, said Stephen waving his hand in adieu.
[SH 161]

McCann, elsewhere identified in *Stephen Hero* with Frank Skeffington, is here Hugh Kennedy, who was in fact the first editor of *St. Stephen's*. Other members of the staff were Felix Hackett, John O'Sullivan, James Murnaghan, and Arthur Clery —all associates of Joyce in the now failing Literary and Historical Society. Father Cummins was Henry Browne, S.J., professor of Latin and Greek and director of the University Sodality, who,

---

[23] *A Page of Irish History*, p. 440. The appendix to Chapter XI of this volume (pp. 439–48) is a transcript of the Minute Book of the Library Conference.

it is true, "had not a little to say to the conduct" of the new magazine.[24] It was probably Father Browne who arranged the details of its publication with Messrs Sealy, Bryers & Walker of Middle Abbey Street, and who persuaded the rector, Father Delany, to underwrite the venture.[25]

Once again, Daedalus's cavalier dismissal of *St. Stephen's* cannot be accepted as an accurate reflection of Joyce's own attitude toward the college magazine. The grounds of this dismissal were censorship and—to be taken less seriously perhaps—the refusal or inability of the editors to pay their contributors. But neither of these reasons prevented Joyce from publishing his paper on Mangan in *St. Stephen's* a few months after he read it before the L & H in February, 1902. It is more natural to expect that Joyce, already absorbed in the art and function of literature, had a genuine interest in the literary plans then afoot on Stephen's Green. He may even at this time have prepared and written his essay on the Irish Literary Theatre with a view to early publication in *St. Stephen's.*

It was this essay apparently that incurred the displeasure of the college censor, and not the paper on "Drama and Life" that Joyce had already read before the Literary and Historical Society. The writer, transposing these events into fiction, was at liberty to rearrange them in whatever way he wished, but it would be a mistake to accept Joyce's fiction as more or less literal fact. A footnote to *A Page of Irish History* (p. 286) gives one version of the facts: "On one occasion the Censor of *St. Stephen's* rejected a youthful essay of his, partly because of its tendencies—but also on the ground that it was too flimsy for publication!" This last charge, if actually made by Father Browne, must have struck Joyce, as it now strikes any impartial reader, as a piece of censorial silliness. "The Day of the Rabblement" is a bold, tightly argued

[24] *Ibid.,* p. 586.   [25] *Ibid.,* p. 275.

indictment of the contemporary Irish Theatre, at times flexing its muscled rhetoric too openly, but at the same time exhibiting a knowledge of literature which would do credit to a far more mature critic than its then nineteen-year-old author. The "tendencies" of the essay, however, were another matter.

Joyce's criticism is more than a frontal attack on the Irish Literary Theatre, it is a flank attack on the pride of the Irish themselves. "A nation," Joyce wrote, "which never advanced so far as a miracle play affords no literary model to the artist, and he must look abroad." [26] Whatever the merit of this claim (though it will be remembered that Joyce, once abroad, never ceased to look back to Ireland, if not for a "model," always for the material for his own work), it was not likely to be received calmly by Gaelic Leaguers whose influence was already strong in University College.[27] Nor was it politic of Joyce to make the claim without qualifying it with the usual historical apologies for the present dismal state of Irish art and letters.[28] Still less politic was his reference to the Irish as "the most belated race in Europe." Neither Father Browne nor any of the other Jesuits on Stephen's Green appear to have been ardent Gaelic Leaguers, but to allow an essay of such tendencies to appear in *St. Stephen's,* still no more than a literary experiment, was to invite unnecessary trouble, involv-

[26] Text from Gorman, *James Joyce,* p. 72.

[27] Ironically, it was not until after Joyce had entered University College that the influence of the Gaelic League began to make itself felt, and this largely through the enthusiasm and organizing skill of Joyce's friend George Clancy. See *A Page of Irish History,* pp. 477 ff., 496–501.

[28] As, for example, Tom Kettle "apologized" a few years later in his introduction (p. vii) to Paul-Dubois's *Contemporary Ireland:* "A civilisation shaken by Norman invasion before it had quite ripened; swept by Anglo-Norman invasion before it had quite recovered; a people plunged in unimaginable chaos of races, religions, ideas, appetites, and provincialisms; bronzed in the mortar without emerging as a consolidated whole; tenacious of the nationalist idea, but unable to bring it to triumph; riven and pillaged by invasion without being conquered —how could such a people find leisure to grow up, or such a civilisation realise its full potentialities of development and discipline?"

ing perhaps the early collapse of the magazine itself. In a few years time, Father William Delany, a generally popular rector, was to stir up a storm of opposition—and bitter personal attacks upon himself—by his refusal to make the study of Gaelic compulsory at University College.[29] It was not enough that he had always encouraged the voluntary study of Gaelic; it was insufferable to the Gaelic Leaguers that he did not enforce its study as more essential to the nation than English literature or the classics. Those same forces that were later to embarrass Father Delany were already active and influential in Joyce's time on Stephen's Green. Joyce and the Jesuits, indeed, seem to have had quite similar views on this subject, though they shared them neither publicly nor privately. The Jesuits had the gift of compromise, the shield of maturity; Joyce had the gift of integrity, the sword of youth. Meanwhile, however, the sword was to be kept hidden behind the shield: Joyce's essay was rejected by *St. Stephen's*.

Joyce of course found a way of circumventing the censor. During the summer of 1901 he and Frank Skeffington, another victim of college censorship who felt as strongly about the position of Irish women as Joyce did about Irish art, joined forces and finances to publish the rejected essays in a two-penny pamphlet. This pamphlet, eight pages of text in an ice-cream-pink wrapper, appeared in mid-October.[30] The next issue of *St. Stephen's* (December, 1901) found the joint enterprise a matter for amusement. Chanel (alias Arthur Clery) included the following item in his column, "Parvula Blandula":

Talking of pamphlets, we publish the following extract from a State Paper, *Aet. Eliz.*, furnished to us by Mr. P. W. Kent, of the Record Office:—"And we also call to your Lordship's notice that there beeth

[29] *A Page of Irish History*, pp. 494 ff.
[30] Mr. Gerrard afterwards recalled that he did the job, "handsetting the type himself, for a fee of 10 guineas which to his surprise was promptly paid on delivery." See the *Centenary History*, p. 62, note.

a certayne unlicensed press, owned by one Gerard, a printer, where-from there doe issue sundrye rioutous and sedytious publications under the names of one Skeffington and one Joyce, whom we believe to be a rebell, and which are most like to ruine the good manners of this our citie; for whereas the lattere, corrupted, as we do verily be-lieve, by the learning of Italie or othere foreigne parts, hath no care for Holye Religion, but is fain to mislead our players, so that they do perform evill workes: the latter doth distracte our young maydes, who doe quit the distaff and would lief invade our schules and have it out with the lads as being their equalls, nor will they cease their fooling till they be whipt, the which we do submit to your graces were mete punishment for they that do mislead them.

Skeffington's eccentricity made him a natural target for under-graduate satire. A lean knight of impossible causes, he tilted with whatever Dublin windmill turned in the wind of popular preju-dice. It did not matter that a few years before he and Joyce had been on opposite sides in the controversy stirred up by *The Countess Cathleen*. Those differences were now forgotten, not in a common cause so much as in common resentment of authority. Until now Joyce had generally avoided attracting attention to him-self. If he was thought eccentric, it was only because of his com-plete indifference to questions which excited the general body of students. At times this indifference—one manifestation of his in-ner integrity—lent him what one of his contemporaries has called "a false appearance of arrogance," [31] but his arrogance was never so conspicuous as Skeffington's spectacular idealism and excita-bility. Now, however, their loose journalistic alliance coupled them together in student opinion, and both could be tarred with the same brush. Joyce was now as much a "character" as Skeffing-ton, an impression never to be wholly eradicated from the minds of his fellow Dubliners.

With self-conscious humor, *St. Stephen's* laughed at the two of

[31] Curran, "A Broadcast Talk," p. 228.

them. Neither of them would be likely to take offense at the awkward satire. But the self-conscious morality of an editorial in the same issue may well have irritated Joyce, delivered as it was from the upper reaches of platitude. Possibly the work of the editor, Hugh Kennedy, the piece rattled along to the orthodox echo of Father Browne's sermons before the University Sodality.

The second of the essays is entitled "The Day of the Rabblement," by James A. Joyce. The opening sentence describes his attitude toward the subject which he treats, the Irish Literary Theatre. He begins thus: "No man, said the Nolan, can be a lover of the true and good unless he abhors the multitude." In deference to the multitude, or, as Mr. Joyce prefers to say, the rabblement, of which "the Irish Literary Theatre must now be considered the property," the directors have refrained from presenting Ibsen, Tolstoy, Hauptmann, Sudermann, Bjornson, and Giacosa, "where even Countess Cathleen is pronounced vicious and damnable." Now, as we understand the Literary Theatre, its object as to educate a vulgarized public, in a word, to rescue the Irish rabblement from the influences which, from the point of view of the artist, were working havoc. But this rabblement clung to a standard of morality—the tradition of the Catholic Church, the ethical teaching of Christendom. For a spiritual life based thereon it had sacrificed material prosperity and well-being, and it now showed itself willing, in the same interest, to forego all that art might add to the surroundings of life. So it was when this rabblement protested against "Countess Cathleen," our fellow students approved and supported the protest. Mr. Joyce alone, to our knowledge, stood aloof. If Mr. Joyce thinks that the artist must stand apart from the multitude, and means that he must also sever himself from the moral and religious teachings which have, under Divine guidance, moulded its spiritual character, we join issue with him, and we prophesy but ill-success for any school which offers an Irish public art based on such a principle.

The prophecy, so far as the Irish public is concerned, turned out to be accurate. Significantly, it is based on the same general grounds as the criticism directed at Daedalus's paper on "Drama and Life" before the Literary and Historical Society. On that occasion a young man named Magee had found Daedalus's essay "hostile to the spirit of religion itself" (SH 88), and Hughes, decrying "foreign filth" and "obscure authors," had cried out that "Ireland would be on her guard against the insidious theory that art can be separated from religion" (SH 89). The editorial affects the same rhetorical eloquence as the critics in *Stephen Hero,* and is no less emphatic on the matter of moral principles. Joyce would hardly have need to consult it in writing these few pages of his manuscript, but it might readily have served as a rough model of that mindless reactionism which he is there ridiculing.

It was no comfort to Joyce later in life to realize that *St. Stephen's* prophecies were fulfilled by the course of Irish history. But at the time he paid small heed to them. He held still to his own theories and principles, ignoring the moral champions of the rabblement, knowing it was idle to argue with zealots who fell back behind prepared positions—the ramparts of Catholic Ireland towering over the ditches of Irish Ireland—when an intellectual challenge was thrown down before them. It was not on their grounds he chose to fight; he would pick his own.

But though he might ignore them, he was no longer to be ignored. He had indeed become, like his editorial accomplice, Frank Skeffington, a "character." His ideas, which no one pretended to understand, were less interesting now than his personality. This they treated kindly, for it was "weird" the way the Irish are, exceptional, independent, individual; and in this he was more nearly like what these young Irishmen thought they were and expected other Irishmen to be. The paradox is almost a national characteristic: if you are different enough, you will be just like everybody else. *"That dreadful Mr. Joyce,"* Chanel wrote in the same issue (December, 1901) of *St. Stephen's,* "is quite a respectable person in private life." A respectable comment, in which one may perhaps read the distance Joyce had already moved from mere respectability. Another writer picks him out for special mention among the audience present at one of the college debates.

A disturber [the item reads] who answered the orator's question, "Why are there no anarchists in Ireland?" "Because there is no king," certainly scored a point. Moreover, we all felt individualism had received a severe blow at the hands of collectivism, when an interrupter was expelled. We would certainly like to have heard more from the rearguard socialists, whilst *dreamy Jimmy* and J. F. Byrne, standing on a window sill, looked as if they could say things unutterable.[32]

Commenting on one of the speakers of the evening, the same writer compliments him by a comparison with Joyce: "a style that reminds one of our own Joyce at his best." The praise is, however, qualified: "he has a broadness of sympathy that the latter [Joyce] has yet to acquire."

Joyce, still refusing to be drawn into general debate or discussion of his theories—"he preferred," a contemporary reports, "to talk with one friend at a time" [33]—apparently took all this gentle mockery and mild criticism with good grace. He remained a favorite figure of fun with the *St. Stephen's* clique, and in the next issue of the magazine (February, 1902) he and J. F. Byrne were parodied in the figures of the Mad Hatter and the White Bishop. The parody, written by Hugh Kennedy's brother, John, is an amusing piece of nonsense worth reproducing in full.

Alice at a Debate

"There's to be a debate in the Physics Theatre," said the Red Queen to Alice, "so let's go now, for I have to take the chair."

"If you do, what will they sit on?" asked Alice, as the Red Queen dragged her upstairs.

"Oh! the old members sit on the new, and the Chairman sits on them in turn."

Before Alice could say another word, she found herself in a large

---

[32] Italics in original.   [33] Curran, "A Broadcast Talk," p. 228.

room. The Red Queen had sat down between the March Hare and the Dormouse at a table with a candlestick and writing materials on it.

Alice went to the gallery and sat down. She saw her old friend, the Hatter, sitting far back in a corner, raving but thinking beautiful thoughts, produced evidently by the remarks of the White Bishop (of the Cistercian Order), who sat near him.

"Who is the old woman over there eating feathers, and whispering jokes to Tweedledum and Tweedledee?" asked Alice.

"Hush!" said the Red Queen, "that's not an old woman, that's Chanel, ST. STEPHEN's Chanel."

"Anything to St. George's Channel?" asked Alice, remembering her geography.

"Silence! child, you are a West Briton! Your questions have taken hours, so we'll have to leave out the minutes."

"I beg your pardon, but—" began Alice.

"It is not respectable to beg," said the Red Queen, "we always take what we want, and often more; proceed with the questions."

"Have you any rules in this society, Mr. Secretary?" asked Alice.

"Rules," said the March Hare, "of course not; this is not a University!"

"But what's the debate on?" asked Alice.

"The Irish Revival, of course," said the March Hare. "What else *could it be on*? But you are allowed to discuss any subject you wish."

"I call upon the Hatter to open the debate," said the Red Queen.

The Hatter, as usual, was dreaming beautiful dreams; but a sharp prod of a needle awoke him. He stood, and commenced.

Alice, being only human, could not understand, but supposed it was all right, although there was much mention of Ibsen, Hauptmann, Bjornson, and Giacosa.

Everyone said it was divine, but no one seemed quite to know what it meant.

Alice's friend, the Flamingo (who is a CLARKE in the Choral Union) was asked to sing something.

"How funny!" said Alice, "do you sing at debates?"

"You can sing, roar, or recite Davis here, if you like," said the March Hare.

"Impossible and undesirable," roared Alice.

There was a noise. A rafter fell from the ceiling and caught her by the arm.

"Kindly leave the room," it roared.

"What an amusing debate! I suppose nothing is impossible or undesirable there!" thought Alice, when she found herself again on Stephen's Green.

The White Bishop was aptly named. Byrne was a serious student of chess, a game which Joyce considered a mere waste of time, and he spent long hours at the Dame Street D.B.C.—while Joyce sat by in impatient silence—immobile over a chess board across from John Howard Parnell, the dead chief's brother.[34] But the sobriquet was equally appropriate for other reasons. The Jesuit historian of these years at University College refers to him as "our most ascetic student, the so-called White Bishop, J. Francis Byrne." [35] Whatever may have been his private belief or lack of belief, Byrne's outward appearance was that of a somewhat seedy ecclesiastic, and it is as such that Joyce presents him in the *Portrait.* Cranly is quite plainly cast in the part of a lay confessor not only to Dedalus (P 292) but to others as well (P 266). Even his voice betrays him: "its energy an echo of the sacred eloquence of Dublin given back flatly by a Wicklow pulpit" (P 228). The asceticism of Byrne lent itself naturally to Cranly's symbolic role as John the Baptist, precursor to Stephen's pseudo-messiah. His seediness is a sort of symbolic joke: he is an eater of figs and spends an unconscionable amount of time dislodging fig seeds from his teeth on the point of a rude toothpick (P 270). In Byrne, the White Bishop, Joyce found much of the material for his sketch of Cranly already at hand.

It is not hard to see why the *St. Stephen's* satirist presented

[34] *Silent Years*, p. 53. See also *Ulysses*, p. 245: "John Howard Parnell translated a white bishop quietly and his gray claw went up against his forehead whereat it rested."

[35] *A Page of Irish History*, p. 398.

Joyce as "the Hatter." He was considered a little "mad" and madness, among these undergraduates, was more an endearing than a dangerous quality. This does not mean of course that the students now took Joyce to their hearts, or that Joyce allowed himself to be seduced from his almost virginal reticence. His relationship with most of them remained what it had been, distantly polite and cordially indifferent. If they, in turn, were not always stuffily polite, they were never from this time on entirely indifferent. Their mockery, which by no means precluded admiration, was a simple form of flattery. As with Joyce and Father Henry at Belvedere, so with his fellows and Joyce at the University: *on se moque de ce qu'on aime.*

The skit in *St. Stephen's* is interesting for still another reason. It contains the first published criticism of Joyce's thought and style: "Everyone said it was divine, but no one seemed to know quite what it meant." The sentence may serve as a commentary on many of the Joyce commentators, those who, following the example of Dr. Johnson, but without the great doctor's thunderous honesty, would rather praise than read the man.

II

The nickname "the Hatter"—he was otherwise known as "Jimmy" around the university—stuck with Joyce. On Saturday evening, February 1, 1902, he read his last paper before the Literary and Historical Society. The subject was James Clarence Mangan; its style was intricate and ornate, rhythms and images interweaving there "like soft luminous scarves," as the young man said of Mangan's style, and his words, again like Mangan's, "ring like brilliant mail." [36] The essay is often more interesting

---

[36] Photostats of Joyce's text in Hutchins, *James Joyce's Dublin*, pp. 57–59. A reprint of Joyce's essay recently appeared in *The James Joyce Review*, I (February, 1957), 39–46.

as a reflection of the writer's own experience and as a revelation of his own mind than as a valuation of its ostensible subject. Speaking of Mangan's childhood and his unfortunate relations with his father, "a human boa-constrictor," Joyce writes of "how keenly a sensitive boy suffers from contact with a gross nature." And of Mangan's youth he says: "His manner is such that no one can say if it be pride or humility that looks out of that vague face, which seems to live only because of those light shining eyes and of the fair silken hair above it, of which he is a little vain. This purely defensive reserve is not without dangers for him, and in the end it is only his excesses that save him from indifference." Finally, in a passage whose tone was of a kind to charm and puzzle his audience, he gently criticizes and all but justifies Mangan's "narrow and hysterical nationality," but through the criticism emerges Joyce's own vision of Ireland:

In the final view the figure which he worships is seen to be an abject queen upon whom, because of the bloody crimes that she has done and those as bloody that were done to her, madness is come and death is coming, but who will not believe that she is near to die and remembers only the rumour of voices challenging her sacred gardens and her fair, tall flowers that have become the food of boars. . . . when this feeble-bodied figure departs dusk begins to veil the train of the gods, and he who listens may hear their footsteps leaving the world.

The minutes of the Literary and Historical Society on this meeting are brief, almost abrupt: "Mr. Joyce read an able paper on 'Mangan' at the conclusion of which the vote of thanks was proposed by Mr. Kennedy and seconded by Mr. T. Kettle. It was supported by Messers Walshe, Murnaghan, and Cleary." The press notices that appeared the following Monday (February 3, 1902) in the *Freeman's Journal* and the *Irish Daily Independent and Nation,* were almost identical and somewhat more generous. The *Independent* gave the following account:

A meeting of the . . . society was held on Saturday evening in the Physics Theatre of the College, Mr. W. Magennis, F.R.U.I., being in the chair. Mr. James Joyce read an extremely brilliant paper on "Mangan," and was deservedly applauded at the conclusion of what was generally agreed to have been the best paper ever read before the Society. Mr. J. Kennedy, who proposed the vote of thanks to Mr. Joyce, was very good. He was followed by Messers Kettle, Walshe, Murnaghan, Cleary, and Rev. G. O'Neill, S.J., F.R.U.I., the former being welcomed back after a long absence. The chairman then made a remarkably able summing up speech, and a vote of thanks for his presiding concluded the proceedings.

Not until a month later, in the March, 1902, issue of *St. Stephen's,* were a few more intimate details of this meeting brought to light.

The "hatter's" paper [*St. Stephen's* reported] proved highly interesting. Everyone went home feeling that he knew a great deal more about Mangan's purposes and aims than he had known when he entered the theatre. The most entertaining part of the evening was the boy orator's rentreé. Filled (doubtless by reason of his golden spoils even in the past) with a confidence and daring that the poor ordinary member could never attain to, he made a bold frontal attack on Mr. Joyce and the Nolan. The rabblement, whom the mention of Giacosa and Paracelsus customarily appals, rallied with timid courage to the side of the new-found champion. The idealistic cat was belled, and ignorance had a *field-day* for the nonce.

Here is evidence of a general attack on Joyce such as, according to *Stephen Hero,* supposedly followed the reading of his paper on "Drama and Life." The references to the Nolan, Giacosa, and the rabblement, make clear the general grounds of the attack— the cosmopolitanism that Joyce had advanced in his October pamphlet. Joyce's image of Ireland as a dying queen, his allusion to "narrow and hysterical nationality," were enough to stir up again the smoldering resentments of the previous October and to spark anew the fiery nationalism of hotblooded patriots. The leader of the attack (Mr. Hughes in *Stephen Hero*) was possibly Hugh Kennedy, whose first name may be read as a clue to Hughes's identity. The latter's "ringing Northern accents" (SH 89) also fit the *St. Stephen's* reference, in a subsequent paragraph, to "the Philistinism of young Ulster." [37]

Yet, notwithstanding the Philistinism of young Ulster, Mr. Joyce certainly read a paper which displayed exceptional qualities both of thought and style. If Mr Magennis alone could understand what was meant by the "retreating footsteps of the gods," and even he did not seem to be a thick and thin supporter of the doctrine that death is the highest form of life; still, apart from the mists that overhung the writer's closing remarks, the *exposé* and appreciation of Mangan's life and writings was almost perfect. In parts the paper itself reached to no mean height of eloquence.

More important than the identification of Hughes with Hugh Kennedy is the one of the *St. Stephen's* criticism. The "attack" on Joyce is not taken too seriously; it is rather an occasion for "entertainment," and the attackers are bluntly identified with the party of ignorance and philistinism. Joyce, the "hatter," is still a source of undergraduate humor, but Joyce the essayist is treated with all fairness, even with generous praise and admiration. He may not have been fully understood—who among the audience could have been expected to read into his words the personal note that seems apparent to later critics? [38]—but whatever the lack of understanding, it did not amount to rejection of Joyce. Most of the audience that evening were impressed by the "hatter's" performance, and his essay on Mangan was not only to appear shortly in the pages of *St. Stephen's* (May, 1902), it was to be remem-

---

[37] The *Centenary History*, p. 65, identifies the speaker as Louis J. Walsh from Maghera, County Derry. The point is debatable, but hardly worth debating. Joyce, whose sketch of McCann is a partial composite of Skeffington and Kennedy, probably used both Kennedy *and* Walsh for his sketch of Hughes.

[38] For Joyce's literary-biographical borrowing from Mangan, see Magalaner and Kain, *Joyce: The Man, The Work, The Reputation*, p. 28 ff.

bered and spoken of admiringly even after Joyce had graduated from University College.

For his part, Joyce reacted like "Jimmy" Joyce, not like Stephen Dedalus. The day after he read his paper, his twentieth birthday, he was back at the college sitting around a conference table with many of the same young men who had "attacked" him the night before. He was there to hear Byrne read a paper on Thomas à Kempis which was " 'good'—but not too 'good' for a Cistercian." Joyce took part in the discussion which followed, "and the discussion was as lively and pleasant as anyone could wish." [39] This was a new role for Byrne who, when not acting as confidant to Joyce, spent most of his time organizing walking trips and handball tournaments or officiating over a chessboard. Joyce's presence on this occasion may have been no more than an act of friendship, for the Library Conferences, held under the auspices of the University Sodality, were hardly his cup of tea.

From this time on there is no clear record of Joyce's activities at the university. The Literary and Historical Society, which had begun to falter a year before, seems now to have failed completely. A week after Joyce's paper, on Saturday, February 8, Kennedy, Clery, and Murnaghan resigned from the society in a body. It is tempting, but it would be rash, to see in this group resignation any causal connection with the events of the Saturday before. The minutes which record these defections make no mention at all of Joyce, and his name does not appear in the records again. The Minute Book itself reflects the disintegration of the society; the script degenerates into a careless scrawl, and the entries become progressively perfunctory. A short time later Frank Skeffington too resigned, after demanding back his subscription money which, he claimed, as part of the society's fund had been

[39] "Library Conference and Sodality Notes," *St. Stephen's* (March, 1902), pp. 101–2.

illegally disposed of for purposes unnamed. A guess is that the alleged misappropriation was in behalf of the Gaelic League.[40] Skeffington's resignation was accepted, and his subscription refunded. An attempt may have been made at this time to dissolve the society within the college with the intention of reforming it outside—a schism that did come about in a few years' time [41]— but this is uncertain. All that is certain is that in the spring of 1902, soon after Joyce's "extremely brilliant" paper on Mangan, the L & H swiftly deteriorated and ceased, for the time being, to be of any consequence in the life of University College. Joyce himself apparently did not bother to resign, but one may be sure he kept himself aloof from the squabbles, whatever they were, that were undermining the society. Indifferent even to more important issues, he did not find it difficult to ignore minor divisions among undergraduate Irishmen.

His reputation, however, both as a character and as a serious student of literature, was undiminished. As the college year drew to a close, Hugh Kennedy was preparing to yield his position as editor of *St. Stephen's* to his assistant Felix Hackett. The event was commemorated by Chanel in the June, 1902, number of the magazine.

It is an open secret [Chanel began] that a recent contributor to this journal is preparing a prose poem, entitled "Dirge on a departing Grea [*sic*] Editor." We understand that the following touching passage occurs at the end of the second volume:—"There is a dusk about the feet of *Hugius,* tho' there be still a gleam of his eyes veiled by the gathering darkness, yet growing dimmer and dimmer ever, as he departs in the trail of the gods. His will be the elaborate life no longer. Tho', as Plotinus was fain to utter, absence is the highest form of presence in the chair of the editor, there is a joyless emptiness of him

[40] Minutes of the Literary and Historical Society for April 23, 1902.

[41] This was in 1906. For an account of the events that led the undergraduates to open defiance of Jesuit authority, see *A Page of Irish History,* pp. 542 ff.

that is departing. 'My twilight, my moonlight, begone not! begone not!' *Du bist gegangen!!* Yet tho' there be of thee now but as a gleam of the sun setting, the shadow of a fitless reflection, the earthly adumbration of the deified, in the spirit thou shallst not wholly be absent. For the *esoteric* he still is. They shall scatter purple flowers, and mingle tears dourfully, both youths and maids. Vain task of petty mind! Hugius, the golden youth, the azure one, lives yet. Felix—child of fortunate name—shall be his earthly shape, his wordly incarnation."

The reference to "a recent contributor" (Joyce's essay on Mangan appeared in the preceding issue of *St. Stephen's,* May, 1902) is clear, but Joyce of course did not write this parody of himself. It is pretty much nonsense, even grammatically—uninspired nonsense of a kind that too often bedevils undergraduate attempts at humor. It is worth noting only as an example of an attitude toward Joyce that persisted to the end of his time at University College. But perhaps one may also read into it a rivalry between Kennedy and Joyce, the only remaining trace of which is the latter's invidious sketch of Hughes in *Stephen Hero.* The awkward satire flatters Joyce with mimicry and mocks Kennedy by flattery, and of the two Joyce clearly has the better part of it. Though his manner, literary and personal, remained a source of amusement, it continued also to hold the serious respect not only of his contemporaries but of students who came after him. A year later, in June, 1903, another writer in *St. Stephen's* announced: "We do not propose to increase the library of Manganese. But may we suggest that Mr. Joyce's essay, published in this magazine exactly twelve months ago, is now due for re-reading? we have looked it up, and find that it wears uncommonly well. . . ." And more than a year after this (November, 1904), an editorial, nostalgically recalling "the good old days," again echoes Joyce's essay on Mangan and implies the debt of gratitude owed by the college to Joyce and his contemporaries.

III

On Friday, October 31, 1902, Joyce was one of two hundred and fourteen young men and women who received degrees from the Royal University of Ireland. He was one of nine graduates in Modern Literature. The day of the "Conferring" at any other university, in any other city, might have passed uneventfully in the usual dull round of interminable commencement exercises. But this was the Royal University, and this was the city of Dublin. The day provided the graduates and undergraduates alike with a splendid opportunity of demonstrating their grievances publicly.

Those grievances were real enough. Most of the students were as aware as Joyce himself of the inequities of the university system as it was then constituted and of the deficiencies of the education to which they were exposed. But, unlike Joyce, most of them had also a political-religious axe to grind, and the University Question provided them an excellent whetstone. The chancellor of the university, Lord Meath, was a stout conservative and an unyielding imperialist, whose appearance on the dais at the conferring of degrees was a sign to the patriots to loosen their traditional axes.[42] When Meath began his address, a group of students began to chant patriotic ballads, and the voice of the imperialist was drowned out by resounding choruses of "A Nation Once Again." At this moment, Sir James Meredith ("one of the supreme officials of the Masonic body in Ireland"), who represented the Protestant element in the University Senate,[43] came to the chancellor's assistance by summoning the Dublin Metropolitan Police. Confusion was controlled and the ceremony hastily concluded, but unfortunately to the strains of "God Save the King." The anthem was hissed heartily, and the students poured out of the hall in a state of rollicking excitement that under the

[42] *A Page of Irish History*, p. 538.   [43] *Ibid.*, p. 144.

circumstances might easily have foamed into riot. Joyce, caught up apparently in the enthusiasm bubbling around him, is reported to have made himself the center of one group of excited students and was about to harangue them when the police moved in again. "Sunny Jim"—the students' ironic sobriquet for Sir James Meredith—was roundly booed, Jimmy Joyce leaped on a passing car and made good his escape. That, in any event, is one version of his final departure from University College—a comic, symbolic escape from the authority of the policemen and the priests who had stood guard over his youth.[44]

Stanislaus Joyce has written that, soon after he received his degree, Joyce "was offered a post as assistant professor at the University College of Stephen's Green—an offer which he turned down in order not to be dependent on the Jesuits. It was his second rejection of their blandishments." [45] Whatever the truth of this, it may be said at once that there was nothing singular or unusual about the Jesuits' offer. They made similar offers to a number of Joyce's contemporaries—to Kettle and Skeffington, for example, and to his friend George Clancy, who later accepted a position as teacher of modern languages at Clongowes Wood.[46] There is surely nothing exceptional in such invitations to promising graduates by their alma mater. To describe the offer as jesuitical "blandishments" is mere invidiousness. But it is doubtless true that on graduating Joyce desired to be henceforth free and independent of the Jesuits, and the reason for this is plain.

During his four years on Stephen's Green he had lost the faith

[44] See Hutchins, *James Joyce's Dublin*, pp. 69–70, for an account of the conferring patched together out of random comment in *St. Stephen's* (December, 1902).

[45] "James Joyce: A Memoir," *The Hudson Review*, II, 4 (Winter, 1950), 490. In *My Brother's Keeper*, p. 187, Stanislaus says only that James "was offered a few evening classes for French at University College," and later adds, p. 189, that he thought James "had been foolish" to refuse the Jesuits' offer.

[46] *A Page of Irish History*, p. 479.

of his boyhood. Why he lost it is a question to which there can be no simple answer. Part of the answer, however, must surely lie in Father Browne's confession that religious training at University College "was defective on the intellectual side," that the students "had not been in a position to think out its philosophical basis." Joyce, whose will was as firmly harnessed to his intellect as that of any Jesuit, could never have brought himself "to do the right deed for the wrong reason"—or, what is worse, for no reason at all. But it must not be thought that he "rejected" the faith as he had once rejected a vocation to the Jesuit order. The one was a decisive act, clean-cut, definite, and irrevocable. Loss of faith is a slow, wearing-out process, the gradual unraveling of the garment of belief into the strings and threads of skepticism. One can never be sure just when faith is lost, one is sure only that it has been lost. So it was with Joyce at University College: religion, as dogmatic belief, simply ceased to interest him, while the stuff of religion, the raveled threads and strings of belief, still remained to be reworked as he wished. So, years later when a lady asked Joyce if he had found a substitute (that is, a sectarian substitute) for Catholicism, he answered significantly: "Madam, I have lost my faith, I have not lost my mind." [47] But by November, 1902, it is clear that a literary conscience had already superseded a religious conscience, that the center of his interest was no longer the Word that was in the beginning but the word that was yet to be. It was this new conscience that guarded his artistic integrity, as he now conceived it, and made it impossible for him to accept the Jesuits' offer.

Such is one explanation of the facts provided by Stanislaus Joyce. But there may be some question as to the reliability of the

[47] This remark is no more than an echo of Stephen's reply to Cranly (P 287) when the latter asked Stephen if he intended to become a Protestant: "I said that I had lost the faith," Stephen answered, "but not that I had lost selfrespect."

facts themselves. Consider, for example, the following letter which James Joyce wrote in November, 1902, to Lady Gregory:

Dear Lady Gregory:

I have broken off my medical studies here and am going to trouble you with a history. I have a degree of B.A. from the Royal University, and I had made plans to study medicine here. But the college authorities are determined I shall not do so, wishing I dare say to prevent me from securing any position of ease from which I might speak out my heart. To be quite frank I am without means to pay my medical fees and they refuse to get me any grinding or tuitions or examining—alleging inability—although they have done and are doing so for men who were stuck in the exams I passed. I want to get a degree in medicine, for then I can build up my work securely. I want to achieve myself —little or great as I may be—for I know that there is no heresy or no philosophy which is so abhorrent to the church as a human being, and accordingly I am going to Paris. I intend to study medicine at the University of Paris supporting myself there by teaching English. I am going alone and friendless . . . into another country, and I am writing to you to know can you help me in any way. . . .[48]

A brave, pitiful letter of a very young man who is sure of nothing but himself, this is also a flat contradiction of Stanislaus's account of what happened in November, 1902. Stanislaus's account, however, may be more than pure invention, for the letter can also be read as an early example of Joyce's "cunning"—the appeal to a lady's sympathies for a young, persecuted, misunderstood artist; the appeal to the ascendancy's prejudice against the Roman Catholicism of the mere Irish; an appeal for help out of the repressive, depressing milieu of the Dublin lower-middle class into

---

[48] *Letters of James Joyce,* ed. by Gilbert, p. 53.

the company of his intellectual and, he would like to think, his social equals. In writing this letter Joyce may well have been guided by his "literary conscience," which allowed him to present a picture of himself in which facts could be subordinated to the ulterior ends of his rhetoric. It has already been suggested that Joyce was a kind of displaced snob, and it is in this snobbism that his fellow Dubliners have found still another explanation of his apostasy: to be a Catholic, of that class, at that time, in that place, was simply not the thing.[49] This is no more than an impression, not a fact or an argument, but an impression in no way weakened by Joyce's letter to Lady Gregory.

The letter bore fruit. Through Lady Gregory's influence Joyce obtained books to review for the literary page of the *Daily Express,* a conservative pro-English newspaper. Yeats, too, helped introducing him to Arthur Symons in London (Joyce in December, 1902, was passing through on his way to Paris), and getting work for him from the *Academy* and the *Speaker*.[50] James Joyce was at this time not quite twenty-one, and the world was beginning to open up for him, though it cannot be said that it was opening very wide. Still it was a world beyond the suffocating purlieus of Dublin. The young man could have had but little sense of regret setting out from Ireland this first time. His heart was in the future, his mind turned not at all upon the past—

---

[49] Montgomery, "Joyeux Quicum Ulysse," *Envoy,* V (April, 1951), 34: "An artist has no message, no mission, and Joyce isn't even a heretic; the *Osservatore Romano* has praised his work. His theological difficulties were really social; he felt it was not the thing to be a Catholic."

[50] *The Letters of W. B. Yeats,* ed. by Wade, p. 386. On December 4, 1902, Yeats wrote to Lady Gregory: "I have had Joyce with me for a day . . . I am trying to get him work on the *Academy* and *Speaker* and I have brought him to Arthur Symons." Joyce's review of *Catilina,* a French translation of an early Ibsen play, appeared in the *Speaker,* March 21, 1903. See *The Early Joyce: The Book Reviews, 1902–1903,* pp. 17–19. Others also offered help to the "friendless" young man, among whom were George Russell, William Archer, and Maud Gonne. See *My Brother's Keeper,* pp. 191–94.

Clongowes Wood, Great Denmark Street, Stephen's Green. There would be time enough to think of them again later, to remember them into literature. For the present they were hopefully forgotten.

IV

The last allusion to Joyce in *St. Stephen's* appeared in an editorial written two years after he had graduated from University College:

The change in the management of the paper synchronizes to a large extent, with a change in the life of the College. Trailing clouds of glory, the old gods are departing from us:—"dusk begins to veil their train, and he who listens may hear their footsteps leaving the world." —Those only who knew the College in the old days, and the habitable place it is now, can properly estimate the burden of gratitude that should accompany these master-builders of societies. . . .

Joyce might have been pleased by this late, passing tribute, the coupling of his words with an allusion to Ibsen, the memory of him, however faint, that lingered on at University College. On Stephen's Green he had educated himself, and his contemporaries had helped—less perhaps by positive contribution to the formation of his thought and principles, than by providing an intellectual whetstone on which he might sharpen those principles. More often, perhaps, they had served merely as embodied examples of the artistic and intellectual perils that threatened the still fragile barque of his integrity. But, in one way or the other, they had served. Joyce also had influenced them, had contributed by participation in their intellectual life to "the period of triumphant success," "the golden age," of University College. They also were in his debt, and the debt was gratefully acknowledged by his successor in the pages of *St. Stephen's*.

Joyce might have been pleased by the tribute, had he had occasion to read it. But at the time the occasion did not offer. The editorial appeared in November, 1904. A month earlier, on October 8, Joyce and Nora Barnacle had set out from Dublin's North Wall to a new life in an old, more tolerant world. In the socially respectable circles of Joyce's acquaintance, secured by their pieties or prejudices to the center of Dublin's middle-class Catholicism, news of the elopement came as a shock which their respectabilities absorbed in silence. It was not something to be spoken of—at least not openly. But it was of course generally known. One wonders whether the writer in *St. Stephen's* (probably C. P. Curran, a friend and admirer of Joyce) intended also in his editorial a general allusion to the elopement otherwise veiled in a discreet silence. "The old gods are departing from us . . . and he who listens may hear their footsteps leaving the world"—were the echoes meant to convey more than the words appeared to mean? It would be pleasant to think that they were.

Appendix

PROSPECTUS

Clongowes Wood College, Clongowes, July 1886

Clongowes Wood College was founded in 1813, in the pleasantest part of Kildare, and stands in the midst of beautiful and well-wooded grounds of 500 acres in extent. It is placed between the Great Southern and Midland Lines of Railway, Sallins, on the Great Southern, being 3½ miles, and Maynooth and Kilcock each 5 miles distant by road. There is frequent and easy communication with Dublin daily. A great number of trains, at suitable hours, run to and from Sallins. The drive from town through the valley of the Liffey, occupying about two hours, is one of the most picturesque in Ireland.

There are extensive and well appointed grounds for Cricket, Tennis, Football and all outdoor games. Bathing is permitted when the season allows, and under certain precautions rowing is permitted to the more grown boys.

To prevent bullying, and for the better formation of character, the pupils are grouped in three divisions, each with its own grounds perfectly distinct. Indoors, too, each division has its own playroom, with billiard tables and requisites for indoor games, and for each division there is a separate readingroom well-stocked with books suitable to the age and tastes of the boys.

All the pupils have the advantage of Military Drill. An experienced physician visits the college twice a week, and there is a large infirmary quite distinct from the rest of the college buildings.

II. The religious training of the boys in Doctrine and Morals forms the main feature of the educational system of the Jesuit Fathers. A course of Religious Instruction, of which a programme is annexed, is obligatory on all—nor can anyone obtain any College Prize, Medal, or Distinction in any subject, who has failed in the prescribed examination in Religious Knowledge.

Good conduct, prompt obedience, and fair industry are expected from every pupil, and the Superiors reserve to themselves the right of removing from the College all who fail to satisfy them on these points.

No boy will be received without satisfactory testimony to character, and when those who have been at another school seek admission to Clongowes, a certificate of good conduct from the Head of the School must accompany the application.

III. The course of education includes Latin and Greek classics, English in all its branches, Modern Languages, Mathematics, Physics, Chemistry, Drawing and Music.

Besides class teaching those who are considered to need it will have the benefit of private tuition.

Pupils are prepared for the Royal University, the Intermediate, the Civil Service, the Army and the Legal, Medical, and Commercial Examinations.

Special attention is paid to English and Mathematics. A silver medal is offered for competition in each of these branches. The collection of instruments for the teaching of Experimental Physics is not surpassed by any private collection in Ireland, and a lecture hall for science, and chemical laboratory, have just been fitted up.

To encourage public speaking the best prize in the college is still the Large Medal for Oratory. This is given for proficiency in the Debating Society, which was founded in 1837, in the presence of Daniel O'Connell, Thomas Francis Meagher, and many other remarkable Irishmen, and which has produced such a long procession of able men who owe a good deal of their present eminence to the power of public speaking acquired there.

Subjects of current interest are discussed and the boys are trained to read carefully for their speeches and become acquainted with the leading questions of the day.

IV. There are two vacations in the year, one of eight weeks in summer, and one of three weeks at Christmas. During those intervals no pupil is allowed to remain at the College, but arrangements are made by the Rector by which those whose parents reside abroad are properly provided for during vacation at the seaside or elsewhere.

Boys not returning punctually on the appointed days after vacation are regarded as withdrawn from the College, and the Rector is at liberty to dispose at once of the places thus left vacant.

Before removing a pupil from the College during the school period, three months' notice will be required; but a fortnight's notice will be sufficient whenever a boy is withdrawn at the Summer vacation; and it is strongly recommended that, as far as possible, boys be removed only at that period.

Boys who are not to remain in College beyond the Winter half, should be withdrawn during the Christmas vacation.

V. Terms—The pension is Forty Guineas a year, payable half-yearly in advance, on the 1st of September and the 1st of February. Two Guineas half-yearly are paid by each pupil for Washing, Repairs of Clothing, and the like. One Guinea yearly for the laboratory expenses by those pupils who attend lectures in Natural Philosophy and Chemistry: and Ten Shillings half-yearly for Library, Games, Theatricals and other amusements.

Boys entering during the half-year or leaving for just cause, pay proportionately for the time they are in college.

Music, Dancing, and Drawing are taught by competent Lay Masters, at the yearly charge of Five, Four, and Three Guineas respectively. Medical attendance is charged only when necessary. Entrance Fee Three Guineas.

VI. The necessary outfit for each pupil comprises at least 3 suits of clothes, flannel cricket shirt, 6 shirts, 8 pairs of stockings, 4 pillow cases, 3 pairs of strong boots, 3 pairs of house shoes, and a dressing case.

Special care is taken of very young boys. They have the benefit of female attendance, and the dietary and studies are modified to suit their tender years. Boys are received from the age of seven.

Communications to be addressed to,

THE RECTOR

P & T Station, Sallins

TWO PLAYS PRESENTED BY THE STUDENTS
OF CLONGOWES WOOD COLLEGE

A. M. D. G.

Clongowes Wood College
Shrovetide, 1890

LDS

Programme

Part I

Song. "Kathleen Mavourneen"	D. Kelly
Song. "Old King Cole"	J. C. Murphy
Song. "Poor Old Joe"	Joseph Kelly
Duet. "On the Blue Wave"	Ignatius Little—D. Kelly

Part II
"Boots at the Swan"
a Farce in one Act by Charles Selby

Mr. Henry Higgins	Walter Esmonde
Frank Frisky	Walter Meldon
Jacob Earwig ("Boots at Swan")	Francis Ronayne
Edgar Moonshine	Patrick Rath
James (Butler)	William Murphy
Thomas (Cook)	Thomas Ross
Peter Pippin (Buttons)	Gerald Gill
Miss Cecilia Moonshine	Cornelius Rafferty

A. M. D. G.

Clongowes Wood College

Easter, 1891

LDS

Programme

"Aladdin and the Wonderful Scamp"

A Burlesque

The Sultan (a monarch in difficulties)	William J. Grant
The Vizier (who, amidst other dirty work, is supposed to have cleaned out the exchequer)	Henry Harrington
Pekoe (the Vizier's hope and his own pride)	Louis M. Magee
Aladdin	James M. Magee
The Slave of the Lamp	James J. Clarke
The Genius of the Ring	Patrick Rath
The Widow Twankay (Aladdin's mother, "who," to quote the 'Arabian Nights,' "was rather old and who even in her youth had not possessed any beauty.")	Geoffrey Gill
Princess Badroulboudour (the Sultan's daughter)	Arthur P. O'Connell

Mandarins [10 names], courtiers, attendants, imps, etc. [Joyce is included among these nineteen supernumeraries].

THE RESULTS OF JAMES JOYCE'S EXAMINATIONS
AT BELVEDERE COLLEGE

Compiled from *Results of Examinations* and *Exhibitions and Prize Lists*, printed for the Intermediate Education Board for Ireland by Browne and Nolan, Dublin [1894–98].

James Joyce's Grade and Year

	Maximum	1893–94 Preparatory	1894–95 Junior	1895–96	1896–97 Middle	1897–98 Senior
Greek	1200			*		
Latin	1200	700	636		642	560
English	1200	455	540		457	650
Commercial English	400					
French	700	400	410		528	345
Commercial French	200					102
German	700					
Commercial German	200					
Italian	500	211	223		342	205
Commercial Italian	200					
Spanish	500					
Commercial Spanish	200					
Celtic	600					
Arithmetic	500	430	250		340 (max. 900)	145
Algebra	600	130	175		230	
Euclid	600	230	175		180	40
Plane Geometry	700					20
Natural Philosophy	500		100		175	10
Chemsitry	500		100			
Drawing	500					
Precis Writing	200			*		
Shorthand	300					
Bookkeeping	200					
Total under Rule 38		2556	2699		2927	2077
Examination Number		1055	3829		6174	6800

* Joyce did not compete in examinations this year.

Exhibitions Won by James Joyce at Belvedere College, 1894–98

Year	Total Number of Exhibitions	Joyce's Order of Merit	Value of Exhibition (in pounds)	Tenable for
1894	132	103	20	1 year
1895	164	164	20	3 years
1896	*			
1897	34	13	30	2 years
1898	**			

* Joyce did not compete.   ** 1897 exhibition retained.

Other Prizes Won by James Joyce at Belvedere

1894   £2 prize in Latin (Composition)
1897   £3 prize in English (Composition)
1898   £4 prize in English (Composition)
       £1 third class prize (in books)

A RECORD OF JAMES JOYCE'S STUDIES IN ENGLISH
AT BELVEDERE COLLEGE

Compiled from *Rules and Programme,* printed for the Intermediate Education Board for Ireland by Browne and Nolan, Dublin 1894–98.

Preparatory Grade, 1894
                    English—Maximum of marks, 1200
150   1. *Select Poetry for Young Students;* edited by T. W. Lister, M.A. (Browne & Nolan). Division I., Nos. 3, 5, 6, 7, 9, 10, 11, 16, 17, 21, 23, 25, 29, 31, 32, 33, 36, 41, 44, 45, 46, 47; Division II., Nos. 51, 52, 55, 56.
150   Lamb; *Adventures of Ulysses;* chaps. I to VII inclusive. Andrew Lang's text (E. Arnold), or John Cooke's text (Browne & Nolan).
200   2. Grammar, including Orthography, Punctuation, and Parsing.
250   3. Composition.
200   4. Geography; the meaning and use of maps; size and shape

of the earth; Geographical terms simply explained and illustrated by special reference to the map of Ireland; general outlines of the great divisions of the globe; outlines of the Physical
and Political Geography of Ireland.

250   5. Outlines of the History of England and Ireland to A.D.
_____   1399.

1200

Junior Grade, 1895
   English—Maximum of marks, 1200

175   1. Scott, *The Lord of the Isles;* Cantos I, II, III.
175   Defoe, *Robinson Crusoe;* edited by W. H. Lambert (Ginn,
Heath, & Co.).
200   2. Grammar; the Preparatory Grade Course, with syntax, more
difficult parsing, and analysis of simple sentences.
200   3. Composition.
200   4. Geography; Distribution of Land and Water and their relative compositions and areas; Mountain chains and systems;
seas and oceans; rivers and lakes.
  Physical and Political Geography of Great Britain and Ireland, and the Outlines of our Colonial Empire.
250   5. Outlines of the History of England and Ireland to A.D.
1399 to 1603. [History of Ireland—Joyce's *Concise History of
Ireland* (for prescribed period.)]
_____
1200

Middle Grade, 1897
   English—Maximum of marks, 1200

1. (a) Milton: *Lycidas; L'Allegro; Il Penseroso.*
(b) Gray: *Elegy Written in a Country Churchyard; The
Bard; Ode on a Distant Prospect of Eton College.*
300   Goldsmith: *Selected Essays,* viz.:—"*The Bee*," Nos. 5, 6, 7,
8; from "*Miscellaneous Essays,*" Nos. 5, 15, 20, 34; from "*Chi-
nese Letters,*" Preface, Nos. 13, 14, 26, 27, 31, 37, 61, 64, 70,
84, 92, 101. (Text of C. F. Younge's, or G. Y. Dixon's Editions.) N.B.—Questions will be asked to test whether the candidates understand the matter of the prescribed textbooks.
125   2. Grammar; the Junior Grade Course, and analysis of complex and compound sentences.

250   3. Composition. N.B.—the Composition Exercise will be judged by General Correctness of Phraseology and intelligence in dealing with the subject, and the marks may be partially or totally cancelled for bad Spelling or Punctuation, or for illegible Handwriting.

150   4. Geography: Ocean Currents—their origin and influence; Tides—their origin and influence; the Atmosphere—its constitution; Winds, Rain; Hail, Snow; the causes affecting climate; Day and Night; the Seasons.

Physical and Political Geography of Europe, and outlines of the remainder of the Eastern Hemisphere. An outline map of one of the countries of Europe will be given to be filled up by inserting the chief ranges of mountains, the chief towns, and the chief rivers.

250   5. The History of England and Ireland from A.D. 1603 to 1714.

125   6. Outlines of English Literature; from Chaucer to Milton, both inclusive.

──────

1200

Senior Grade, 1898
English—Maximum of Marks, 1200

175   1. Shakespeare: *Julius Caesar*. Rugby text.

175   Macaulay: *Essays on Clive and Warren Hastings*. N.B.—Questions will be asked to test whether the candidates understand the matter of the prescribed textbooks.

250   2. Composition. N.B.—The Composition Exercises will be judged by general correctness of Phraseology and Intelligence in dealing with the subject, and the marks may be partially or totally cancelled for bad Spelling or Punctuation, or for illegible Handwriting.

100   3. Grammar, the Middle Grade Course, with Prosody and the elements of English Philology [Morris' Elementary Lessons in Historical English Grammar, chaps. i to v, inclusive].

250   4. (a) The History of England and Ireland, from A.D. 1714 to A.D. 1837.
(b) Joyce's *Concise History of Ireland*, Part I.

125   5. Geography—Distribution of plants and animals; man, as af-

fected by conditions of external nature; distribution of races; latitude, longitude; time, how measured; the earth's position as a planet.

Physical and Political Geography of Canada and the United States; outlines of the remainder of the Western Hemisphere.

125 6. Outlines of English literature from A.D. 1674 to A.D. 1832.

1200

Bibliography

MANUSCRIPT MATERIAL

Clongowes Wood College
  Address Book 1888–1889
  Scrapbooks.
      Three untidy albums dating back to the 1850s and containing, in no particular order or sequence, scraps and gobbets of information about the past of the college: school notices, newspaper items, announcements, programs of plays, debates, athletic events, and so on. The Clongowes Wood College *Prospectus,* 1886, and the play programs appended were found in these scrapbooks.
  Students' Ledger H 1886–1907
Belvedere College, Dublin
  Account Book
  Annals of the Congregation of the Blessed Virgin Mary
  Cash Book
  Prefect of Studies Book
University College, Dublin
  Academy of St. Thomas Aquinas, Addresses of Members and Minutes of Meetings [1901–1907]
  Minute Book of the Literary and Historical Society [1884–]
  Register of Attendance, University College Sodality [1898–1904]
  Register of the Literary and Historical Society [1884–]
University of Buffalo, Buffalo, New York
  The James Joyce Collection, In Memoriam Philip J. Wickser. Lockwood Memorial Library of the University of Buffalo.

PRINTED MATERIAL

"Analecta Cluenensia," *The Clongownian,* 1953, 1954.

Athearn, Robert G. Thomas Francis Meagher: An Irish Revolutionary in America. Boulder, Colorado ("University of Colorado Studies"), University of Colorado Press, 1949.

British Broadcasting Commission. The Third Program, February 13, 17, and March 22, 1950. "Portrait of James Joyce," ed. by W. R. Rodgers, produced by Maurice Brown.

Budgen, Frank. James Joyce and the Making of Ulysses. New York, Harrison Smith and Robert Haas, Inc., 1934.

Byrne, J. F. Silent Years. New York, Farrar, Straus and Young, Inc., 1953.

Carleton, William. Traits and Stories of the Irish Peasantry. London, William Tegg, 1868. 2 vols.

Catalogus Societatis Jesu Provinciae Hiberniae, Dublin, Browne & Nolan [*ad usum privatum*], 1888–1910.

Chesterton, G. K. Irish Impressions. London, W. Collins Sons & Co., Ltd., 1919.

Clongowes Wood College. Prospectus [privately printed]. July, 1886.

Colum, Mary M. Life and the Dream. Garden City, New York, Doubleday & Company, Inc., 1947.

Conmee, John S., S.J. Old Times in the Barony. Dublin, Catholic Truth Society of Ireland, n.d.

Corcoran, T., S.J. The Clongowes Record: 1814–1932. Dublin, Browne & Nolan, n.d.

Cullen, J. A., S.J., ed. The Sodality Manual. Dublin, "Messenger" Office, 1896.

Deharbe, Joseph, S.J. A Full Catechism of the Catholic Religion. Trans. from the German by the Rev. John Fander. New York, The Catholic Publication Society, 1875.

Eglinton, John. Irish Literary Portraits. London, Macmillan & Co., Ltd., 1935.

[Fegan, Henry, S.J.] "Clongowes and Father Conmee," *The Irish Monthly,* XXXVIII (August, 1910), 419–28.

Fitzpatrick, Edward A. St. Ignatius and the Ratio Studiorum. New York, McGraw-Hill Book Company, Inc., 1933.

Gilbert, Stuart. James Joyce's Ulysses. New York, Alfred A. Knopf, 1931. Rev. ed., 1952.

Givens, Seon, ed. James Joyce: Two Decades of Criticism. New York, Vanguard Press, 1948.

Gogarty, Oliver St. John. As I Was Going Down Sackville Street: A Phantasy in Fact. London, Rich and Cowan, Ltd., 1937.

—— Mourning Becomes Mrs. Spendlove and Other Portraits, Grave and Gay. New York, Creative Age Press, 1948.

—— It Isn't This Time of Year at All! London, MacGibbon & Kee, 1954.

Golding, Louis. James Joyce. London, Thornton Butterworth, Ltd., 1933.

[Goodrich, Samuel Griswold] Peter Parley's Tales about Ancient and Modern Greece. Boston, Richardson, Lord, and Holbrook, 1832.

—— Peter Parley's Tales about Ancient Rome. Boston, Carter Hendee & Co., 1833.

Gorman, Herbert. James Joyce. New York, Rinehart, 1939. 2d ed., 1948

Gwynn, Denis. The Life of John Redmond. London, George G. Harrop & Co., 1932.

Hoagland, Kathleen, ed. 1000 Years of Irish Poetry. New York, The Devin-Adair Company, 1947.

Hutchins, Patricia. James Joyce's Dublin. London, Grey Walls Press, 1950.

Hynes, Sam, "The Catholicism of James Joyce," The Commonweal, LV (February 22, 1952), 487–89.

Intermediate Education Board for Ireland. Exhibitions and Prize Lists. Dublin, Browne and Nolan [1894–98].

—— Results of Examinations. Dublin, Browne and Nolan [1894–98].

—— Rules and Programme. Dublin, Browne and Nolan [1894–98].

Jolas, Maria, ed. A James Joyce Yearbook. Paris, Transition Press, 1949.

Joyce, James. Chamber Music. Ed. by William York Tindall. New York, Columbia University Press, 1954.

Joyce, James. Dubliners. New York, Random House ("The Modern Library"), n.d.

———— The Early Joyce: The Book Reviews, 1902–1903. Ed. by Stanislaus Joyce and Ellsworth Mason. Colorado Springs, Colo., The Mamalujo Press, 1955.

———— Epiphanies. Ed. by O. A. Silverman. Buffalo, Lockwood Memorial Library, 1956.

———— Finnegans Wake. New York, The Viking Press, 1939.

———— "James Clarence Mangan," *The James Joyce Review,* I (February, 1957), 31–38. This essay appeared originally in *St. Stephen's* magazine, Dublin, May, 1902.

———— Letters of James Joyce. Ed. by Stuart Gilbert. New York, The Viking Press, 1957.

———— The Portable James Joyce. Ed. by Harry Levin. New York, The Viking Press, 1947.

———— A Portrait of the Artist as a Young Man. New York, The Viking Press, 1916.

———— "Some Unpublished Letters of James Joyce," *Envoy,* V (Special Number, April, 1951), 46–61.

———— Stephen Hero. Ed. by Theodore Spencer. New York, New Directions, 1944. New ed. by John J. Slocum and Herbert Cahoon, New York, New Directions, 1955.

———— Ulysses. New York, Random House, 1946.

Joyce, Stanislaus. "The Background to 'Dubliners,'" *The Listener,* LI (March 25, 1954), 526–27.

———— "James Joyce: A Memoir," *The Hudson Review,* II (Winter, 1950), 485–514.

———— My Brother's Keeper: James Joyce's Early Years. New York, The Viking Press, 1958.

———— Recollections of James Joyce by His Brother. New York, The James Joyce Society, 1950.

Kenner, Hugh. Dublin's Joyce. London, Chatto and Windus, 1955.

Kettle, Thomas M. Poems and Parodies. London, Duckworth & Co., 1916.

———— The Day's Burden and Miscellaneous Essays. Dublin and London, Maunsel and Company, Ltd., 1918.

Kiely, Benedict. Poor Scholar. London, Sheed & Ward, 1947.

Lamb, Charles. The Adventures of Ulysses, in *Mrs. Leicester's School and Other Stories,* ed. by Alfred Ainger. New York, A. C. Armstrong & Son, 1886.

MacManus, Seumus. The Story of the Irish Race. New York, The Devin-Adair Company, 1945.

Magalaner, Marvin, and Richard Kain. Joyce: The Man, the Work, the Reputation. New York University Press, 1956.

Meagher, Thomas Francis. Meagher of the Sword. Ed. by Arthur Griffith. Dublin, M. H. Gill & Son, 1916.

Meenan, James, ed. Centenary History of the Literary and Historical Society of University College Dublin. Tralee, The Kerryman Ltd., n.d. [1957].

Montgomery, Niall, "Joyeux Quicum Ulysse," *Envoy,* V (April, 1951), 31–43.

Newman, John Henry. The Idea of a University. London, Longmans, Green and Co., 1907.

Nolan, Brian, "A Bash in the Tunnel," *Envoy,* V (April, 1951), 5–11.

Noon, William, S.J. Joyce and Aquinas. New Haven, Yale University Press, 1957.

O'Casey, Sean [P. O. Cathasaigh]. The Story of the Irish Citizen Army. Dublin and London, Maunsel & Co., Ltd., 1919.

O'Hegarty, P. S., "A Bibliography of the Books of Terence MacSwiney and F. Sheeby-Skeffington," in Bibliographies of 1916 and the Irish Revolution. Dublin, Alex, Thom & Co., Ltd., 1936.

Paul-Dubois, L. Contemporary Ireland. Dublin, Maunsel and Company, Ltd., 1908.

Pope, Alexander. The Iliad and Odyssey of Homer. Ed. by T. A. Buckley. London, Frederick Warne & Co., n.d.

Royal University of Ireland. Calendar 1899–1903. Dublin, Browne and Nolan.

St. Stephen's, June 1, 1901–November, 1904. Dublin, Sealy, Bryers & Walker. This undergraduate journal was published intermittently between June, 1901, and June, 1906, after which date it lapsed and was never revived.

Scantlebury, C., S.J., "Belvedere House," *Dublin Historical Record,* XIII (An Tóstal, 1953), 128–32.

Schwickerath, Robert, S.J., "Ratio Studiorum," in *The Catholic Encyclopedia,* ed. by Charles G. Heberman and others. New York, The Encyclopedia Press, Inc., 1911. Vol. 12, 11. 654–57.

Sheehy, Eugene. May It Please the Court. Dublin, C. J. Fallon, Ltd., 1951.

Sheehy-Skeffington, F. Michael Davitt. London, T. Fisher Unwin, 1908.

—— Speech from the Dock [pamphlet]. New York, The Skeffington Memorial Committee, 1917.

Society of Jesus, Fathers of the. A Page of Irish History: Story of University College, Dublin, 1883–1909. Dublin and Cork, The Talbot Press Limited, 1930.

—— Thesaurus Spiritualis Societatis Jesu. Brussels, De Brouwer & Co., 1932.

Soupault, Philippe. Souvenirs de James Joyce. Paris, Charlot, 1945.

Stanford, W. B., "The Mysticism That Pleased Him," Envoy, V (Special Number, April, 1951), 62–69.

—— The Ulysses Theme, Oxford, Blackwell, 1954.

Strong, L. A. G. The Sacred River. New York, Pellegrini and Cudahy, 1951.

Svevo, Italo [Ettore Schmitz]. James Joyce: A Lecture delivered in Milan in 1927 by his friend Italo Svevo. Trans. by Stanislaus Joyce. New York, New Directions, 1950.

Tierney, Michael, ed. Struggle with Fortune: A Miscellany for the Centenary of the Catholic University of Ireland, 1854–1954. Dublin, Browne & Nolan, Ltd. n.d.

Tindall, William York. James Joyce: His Way of Interpreting the Modern World. New York, Scribners' ("Twentieth Century Library"), 1950.

Troy, William, "Stephen Dedalus and James Joyce," The Nation, CXXXVIII (February 14, 1934) 187–88.

Ussher, Arnold. Three Great Irishmen: Shaw, Yeats, Joyce. London, Victor Gollancz Ltd., 1952.

Williams, William Carlos. Autobiography. New York, Random House, 1951.

Yeats, W. B. The Autobiography of William Butler Yeats. New York, The Macmillan Co., 1955.

—— The Letters of W. B. Yeats. Ed. by Allan Wade. New York, The Macmillan Co., 1955.

Yeats, W. B., ed. Stories from Carlton. London, Walter Scott, 1886.

Acknowledgments

IN COLLECTING the materials for this book I have incurred many debts of gratitude. In Ireland my special thanks are due to Mrs. Thomas Kettle and to her brother Judge Eugene Sheehy, whose recollections of the past, more reliable than those of most "Joyce people," were fresh and usable; to their nephew and niece, Mr. and Mrs. Kevin Collins; to Benedict Kiely, whose knowledge of Dublin may be second only to Joyce's, and whose knowledge of Joyce may be second to none; to my patient Dublin correspondent Miss Irene ffrench Eagar, and to her American counterpart Miss Joan Jurale. The staff of the National Library of Ireland and those at the libraries of the National University and Trinity College, Dublin, have been equally generous with their assistance. I am more especially indebted to various members of the Irish Province of the Society of Jesus: to Father Roland Burke Savage, who made straight my way to valuable sources of early Joyce material; to Father P. A. Baggott, who opened to me the hospitality of Clongowes Wood; to Father R. P. Roche of Belvedere College, Dublin, who either provided me with or directed me to much of the material that appears in my chapters on Belvedere; and, most especially, to Father Richard Ingram, whose many continued courtesies, exceeding cooperation, I cannot hope adequately to acknowledge.

In this country I am indebted to Mrs. Helen Joyce, the daughter-in-law of James Joyce, whose memory of him in his role as husband, father, and grandfather has often confirmed *mutatis mutandis* my own impression of a much earlier Joyce; to Padraic Colum and the late Mary Colum, who so often shared and as often led our discussions; to Charles D. Abbott and his staff at the library of the University of Buffalo, and to the staffs of the New York Public and Columbia University libraries. It is a special pleasure to acknowledge my debt to Professor William York Tindall, who first suggested and continued to encourage the line of research of which this book is the result. Professors Elliot Dobbie, Richard Chase, and Thomas Flanagan also deserve my thanks, the two former for their helpful criticism of the original manuscript, the latter for his care in reading the final proofs. I am thankful to William Bridgwater and Henry Wiggins for their generous editorial advice, to Miss Vergene Leverenz, who edited the manuscript, and to John Kotselas, who provided the index.

Permission to quote from the published works of James Joyce has graciously been granted by the following publishers: The Viking Press, Inc., for *A Portrait of the Artist as a Young Man* (Viking, 1916) and *Finnegans Wake* (Viking, 1939); New Directions for *Stephen Hero* (New Directions, 1944); and Random House, Inc., for *Ulysses* (Random House, 1934). Passages from Stanislaus Joyce's *My Brother's Keeper* (Viking, 1958) are also quoted with the permission of The Viking Press, Inc.

KEVIN SULLIVAN

New York, New York
June 16, 1958

Index